U0648100

中華譯學館

莫言題

中華譯學倡言倡字與

以中華為根 譯與學并重

弘揚優秀文化 促進中外交流

拓展精神疆域 驅動思維創新

丁酉年冬月許鈞撰 羅衛東書

中華譯學館·中华翻译家代表性译文库

许 钧 郭国良 / 总主编

王 韬 卷

屈文生 万 立 / 编

ZHEJIANG UNIVERSITY PRESS
浙江大学出版社

总　序

考察中华文化发展与演变的历史,我们会清楚地看到翻译所起到的特殊作用。梁启超在谈及佛经翻译时曾有过一段很深刻的论述:"凡一民族之文化,其容纳性愈富者,其增展力愈强,此定理也。我民族对于外来文化之容纳性,惟佛学输入时代最能发挥。故不惟思想界生莫大之变化,即文学界亦然。"①

今年是五四运动一百周年,以梁启超的这一观点去审视五四运动前后的翻译,我们会有更多的发现。五四运动前后,通过翻译这条开放之路,中国的有识之士得以了解域外的新思潮、新观念,使走出封闭的自我有了可能。在中国,无论是在五四运动这一思想运动中,还是自 1978 年改革开放以来,翻译活动都显示出了独特的活力。其最重要的意义之一,就在于通过敞开自身,以他者为明镜,进一步解放自己,认识自己,改造自己,丰富自己,恰如周桂笙所言,经由翻译,取人之长,补己之短,收"相互发明之效"②。如果打开视野,以历史发展的眼光,

① 梁启超.翻译文学与佛典//罗新璋.翻译论集.北京:商务印书馆,1984:63.
② 陈福康.中国译学理论史稿.上海:上海外语教育出版社,1992:162.

从精神深处去探寻五四运动前后的翻译,我们会看到,翻译不是盲目的,而是在自觉地、不断地拓展思想的疆界。根据目前所掌握的资料,我们发现,在 20 世纪初,中国对社会主义思潮有着持续不断的译介,而这种译介活动,对社会主义学说、马克思主义思想在中国的传播及其与中国实践的结合具有重要的意义。在我看来,从社会主义思想的翻译,到马克思主义的译介,再到结合中国的社会和革命实践之后中国共产党的诞生,这是一条思想疆域的拓展之路,更是一条马克思主义与中国革命相结合的创造之路。

开放的精神与创造的力量,构成了我们认识翻译、理解翻译的两个基点。在这个意义上,我们可以说,中国的翻译史,就是一部中外文化交流、互学互鉴的历史,也是一部中外思想不断拓展、不断创新、不断丰富的历史。而在这一历史进程中,一位位伟大的翻译家,不仅仅以他们精心阐释、用心传译的文本为国人打开异域的世界,引入新思想、新观念,更以他们的开放性与先锋性,在中外思想、文化、文学交流史上立下了一个个具有引领价值的精神坐标。

对于翻译之功,我们都知道季羡林先生有过精辟的论述。确实如他所言,中华文化之所以能永葆青春,"翻译之为用大矣哉"。中国历史上的每一次翻译高潮,都会生发社会、文化、思想之变。佛经翻译,深刻影响了国人的精神生活,丰富了中国的语言,也拓宽了中国的文学创作之路,在这方面,鸠摩罗什、玄奘功不可没。西学东渐,开辟了新的思想之路;五四运动前后的翻译,更是在思想、语言、文学、文化各个层面产生了革命性的影响。严复的翻译之于思想、林纾的翻译之于文学的作用无须赘言,而鲁迅作为新文化运动的旗手,其翻译动机、翻译立场、翻译选择和翻译方法,与其文学主张、文化革新思想别无二致,其翻译起着先锋性的作用,引导着广大民众掌握新语言、接受新思想、表达自己的精神诉求。这条道路,是通向民主的道路,也是人民大众借助掌握的新语言创造新文化、新思想的道路。

回望中国的翻译历史,陈望道的《共产党宣言》的翻译,傅雷的文学翻译,朱生豪的莎士比亚戏剧翻译……一位位伟大的翻译家创造了经典,更创造了永恒的精神价值。基于这样的认识,浙江大学中华译学馆为弘扬翻译精神,促进中外文明互学互鉴,郑重推出"中华译学馆·中华翻译家代表性译文库"。以我之见,向伟大的翻译家致敬的最好方式莫过于(重)读他们的经典译文,而弘扬翻译家精神的最好方式也莫过于对其进行研究,通过他们的代表性译文进入其精神世界。鉴于此,"中华译学馆·中华翻译家代表性译文库"有着明确的追求:展现中华翻译家的经典译文,塑造中华翻译家的精神形象,深化翻译之本质的认识。该文库为开放性文库,入选对象系为中外文化交流做出了杰出贡献的翻译家,每位翻译家独立成卷。每卷的内容主要分三大部分:一为学术性导言,梳理翻译家的翻译历程,聚焦其翻译思想、译事特点与翻译贡献,并扼要说明译文遴选的原则;二为代表性译文选编,篇幅较长的摘选其中的部分译文;三为翻译家的译事年表。

需要说明的是,为了更加真实地再现翻译家的翻译历程和语言的发展轨迹,我们选编代表性译文时会尽可能保持其历史风貌,原本译文中有些字词的书写、词语的搭配、语句的表达,也许与今日的要求不尽相同,但保留原貌更有助于读者了解彼时的文化,对于历史文献的存留也有特殊的意义。相信读者朋友能理解我们的用心,乐于读到兼具历史价值与新时代意义的翻译珍本。

许　钧

2019 年夏于浙江大学紫金港校区

目 录

导 言

王韬(Wang T'aou,1828—1897),苏州城外长洲县甫里村(今吴中区用直镇)人,原名利宾,曾名瀚、畹①,字兰卿、紫诠、懒今,雅号蘅华馆主等。1862 年遁去香港后,改名王韬,字仲弢,一字子潜(谐音紫诠),自号天南遯(遁)叟,50 岁后又曰弢园老民。② 王韬九岁尽《十三经》,背诵如流,有神童之誉。

王韬文有奇气,家贫,刻苦自励,在中西交流史上是一位绕不开的重要学者,其学术的起点正是融通中西的翻译事业,是"译而优则著"的杰出代表。1849 年,年方二十二岁的王韬前往上海,进入英国伦敦会传教士麦都思(Walter Henry Medhurst,1796—1857)等人创办的墨海书馆(The London Missionary Society Press)工作。

1862 年"遭难逃粤"一事对王韬的一生影响重大,照其《弢园老民自传》自述,自此"杜门削迹,一意治经"。其名、字、号及作品名里自此常带"逃"音或"遁"意,以自谑,如"韬"、"仲弢"、淞北逸民、甫里逸民、《遯窟谰言》等。王韬一生与文字结缘,纵横文海四十余载,著作、译作达六十余种,涉及经学、政论、历史、科技著作及小说笔记、诗文、尺牍等,数量之多、眼界之宽、涉猎之广,实足可叹。

起初,王韬"名为秉笔,实供指挥"③,对译书可谓一窍不通,但仅四年

---

① 曾化名黄畹上书太平天国,吴语中黄王不分。
② 王韬. 弢园文新编. 李天纲,编校. 上海:中西书局,2012:327.
③ 熊月之. 西学东渐与晚清社会. 上海:上海人民出版社,1994:270.

后,他就参与翻译出版了《圣经·新约》教义部分和整部《圣经·旧约》,还被该项译事的主持者麦都思赞为奇才。王韬的翻译天赋和勤勉程度可见一斑。随后二十余年内,王韬笔耕不辍,积累起领先于同辈的见识,引入了诸多西学知识,为其随后著书立说打下坚实的基础。

一、王韬对翻译的认知

王韬很早就认识到翻译之于改良维新和中西交流的意义,并直指政界、学界对翻译的轻视和对译者的鄙夷心态。他说:

> 中外语言文字,迥然各别。彼处则设有翻译官员,及教中之神父牧师,效华言,识汉字,留心于我国之政治,于我之俗尚风土、山川形势、物产民情,悉皆勒之成书,以教其国中之民。而向时中国之能操泰西言语,能识英人文字者,当轴者辄深恶而痛嫉,中国文士亦鄙之而不屑与交。而其人亦多赤贫无赖,浅见寡识,于泰西之政事得失、制度沿革,毫不关心。即有一二从其游者,类皆役于饥寒,仰其鼻息,鲜有远虑,足备顾问。盖上既轻之,则下亦不知自奋也。因是,于其性情日益隔阂,于其国政、民情终茫然罔有所知,通商十余年来,无能洞悉其情状,深明其技能,袂其所短而师其所长。①

王韬所言不虚。其时充作通事的,用李鸿章的话来说,往往"货利声色之外不知其他"②,如早期"广东通事"和"上海露天通事"③。冯桂芬在咸丰十年(1860)曾提到,通事"仅通洋语者,十之八九;兼识洋字者,十之

---

① 王韬. 弢园文录外编. 上海:上海书店出版社,2002:25.
② 蒋廷黻. 近代中国外交史资料辑要(上). 北京:东方出版社,2014:366.
③ 参见:司佳. 从"通事"到"翻译官"——论近代中外语言接触史上的主、被动角色的转移. 复旦学报(社会科学版),2002(3):46,49.

一二"①。李鸿章在1863年曾谓:"各国在沪均设立翻译官,遇中外大臣会商之事,皆凭外国翻译官传述,亦难保无偏袒捏架情弊",相较之下,"中国能通洋语者仅恃通事,凡关局军营交涉事务,无非雇觅通事往来传话,而其人遂为洋务之大害"。在中外交涉中"假手期间,勾结洋兵,以为分肥之计"。②

当然,这并非全然否认通事对于早期中外往来的贡献,但他们也确实带来或加剧了许多本可避免的中西交涉问题。重要的是,这些通事多不关注国家大事,而钻营于市场之间,自然无心关注不能立刻变现获利的泰西著述,更无法引进亟需之西学。为此,王韬提出培养翻译人才及引进西学之计划:

> 欲知洋务……国家亦当于各口岸设立译馆。凡有士子及候补人员愿肄习英文者,听入馆中,以备他日之用。果其所造精深,则令译西国有用之书。西国于机器、格致、舆图、象纬、枪炮、舟车,皆著有专书,以为专门名家之学。苟识其字,通其理,无不可译……将见不十年间,而其效可睹已。③

此外,他还建议,驻各国使节行辕"宜设译官数员,汇观各处日报,而撷取要略,译以华文,寄呈总理衙门,则泰西迩日之情形,正如犀燃烛照,无所遁形。即遇交涉之事,胸中自具成竹,此所谓通外情于内也"④。

王韬上述有关翻译的论见,写于其佐译工作悉数完成之后。有趣的是,王韬在墨海书馆的翻译事业,实由英人优渥的报酬驱动,用其自己的话说,主要是为解全家衣食之忧,其对译书既不热衷,也不认同,并表露出一种译书"与我无涉"的情绪。其挚友江宁管小异明确以西方《圣经》大悖

---

① 冯桂芬.上海设立同文馆议//"中央研究院"近代史研究所.近代中国对西方及列强认识资料汇编(第一辑第二分册).台北:"中央研究院"近代史研究所,1972:1107.

② 参见:蒋廷黻.近代中国外交史资料辑要(上).北京:东方出版社,2014:365-366.

③ 王韬.弢园文录外编.楚流,书进,风雷,选注.沈阳:辽宁人民出版社,1994:47.

④ 王韬.弢园文录外编.楚流,书进,风雷,选注.沈阳:辽宁人民出版社,1994:85.

儒教,因此绝不愿意与裨治文(Elijah Coleman Bridgman,1801—1861)等传教士合作①,并谓之:

> 吾人既入孔门,既不能希圣希贤,造于绝学,又不能攘斥异端,辅翼名教,而岂可亲执笔墨,作不根之论著,悖理之书,随其流,扬其波哉?②

对于挚友之"贬价屈节"的心灵拷问,王韬的回答虽有些许辩解的味道,但更多是忏悔之意,他答道:

> 教授西馆,已非自守之道,譬如赁春负贩,只为衣食计,但求心之所安,勿向其所操何业。译书者,彼主其意,我徒涂饰词句耳,其悖与否,固与我无涉也。且文士之为彼用者,何尝肯尽其心力,不过信手涂抹,其理之顺逆,词之鄙晦,皆不任咎也。由是观之,虽译之,庸何伤。③

为日后不背被唾骂之名,王韬决意再不译书,并感叹道,如果早有管小异这般挚友帮助其剖析义利,分析利害,他断不会在1849年"失足"到沪,帮助西人译书,以致追悔莫及。

> 当余初至时,曾无一人剖析义利,以决去留,徒以全家衣食为忧。此足一失,后悔莫追。苟能辨其大闲,虽饿死牖下,亦不往矣。④

王韬此番言论有故意夸张之嫌,以免其受到背叛名教、以夷变夏等指责⑤,但如此忏悔,明显与其尚未认同翻译之于引进西学的价值有关。

---

① 王韬对《圣经》的评价也不是很高,他在答周弢甫时曾道:"瀚观西人教中之书,其理诞妄,其说支离,其词鄙晦,直可投于溷厕,而欲以是训我华民,亦不量之甚矣。顾瀚窥其意,必欲务行其说而后止,行之则人心受其害矣。"参见:王韬. 王韬日记. 方行,汤志钧,整理. 北京:中华书局,1987:83.
② 王韬. 王韬日记. 方行,汤志钧,整理. 北京:中华书局,1987:92.
③ 王韬. 王韬日记. 方行,汤志钧,整理. 北京:中华书局,1987:92.
④ 王韬. 王韬日记. 方行,汤志钧,整理. 北京:中华书局,1987:92.
⑤ 段怀清. 王韬与近现代文学转型. 上海:复旦大学出版社,2015:67-68.

根据王韬回忆,他本意在走科举仕途,奈何乡试落第,但未放弃求取功名,于 1856 年和 1859 年相继两次参考,均铩羽而归。① 其随后屡屡为清廷和太平天国出谋献计,也是为了扩大名声、获得襄助。更重要的是,王韬本人始终秉有夷夏观,在墨海书馆工作时,并非完全认同西学东渐的意义,故而对翻译工作也产生出复杂、矛盾的心理。王韬既不适应英国清教徒严谨刻板的工作方式,也不甘心放弃"出则以文章显达,退则以诗赋扬名"的名士传统追求②,译书在他看来不过是谋求生计的手段。

就宗教经典翻译而言,无论如何,所谓"涂饰词句""信手涂抹"的说法,某种程度上确实反映出其佐译《圣经》时深受"笔受"身份的苦涩。经文的翻译基调、策略及选词,皆由麦都思等拟定,王韬几无插手之机会,但他在篇章、词句调教、润色等方面绝非任意涂饰,起着极为重要的作用,最终使得西方译者交口称赞。③ 1854 年,麦都思主译的《圣经》正式出版后,王韬便扩充、重写了麦都思等翻译的《宗主诗章》《清明扫墓论》《野客问难记》等宣教小册子④,可谓首次试水著书立说。

二、王韬的译业演进

有了翻译大部头《圣经》的经历后,王韬逐渐认识到翻译西方著作,灌输新知,沟通中西的重要性,并陆续翻译了《格致新学提纲》《华英通商事略》《重学浅说》和《西国天学源流》等科技史与通商史著作。这些译著采

① 参见:王宏志."卖身事夷"的王韬:当传统文士当上了译者. 复旦学报(社会科学版),2011(2):28.
② 朱维铮. 导言//王韬. 弢园文新编. 李天纲,编校. 上海:中西书局,2012:4.
③ 须注意的是,王韬的译文可能受到早于马礼逊(Robert Morrison)译本问世的马士曼(Joshua Marshman)、拉沙(Joannes Lssar)译本的影响,因为麦都思等代表决定以二人的译本为根据,出版订正版本。参见:马敏. 马希曼、拉沙与早期的《圣经》中译. 历史研究,1998(4):54.
④ 韩南. 作为中国文学之《圣经》:麦都思、王韬与《圣经》委办本. 浙江大学学报(人文社会科学版),2010(1):17.

"西译中述"形式,即先由传教士口译原文,后由王韬等中文助手根据自身理解以通行体例转述。这一中西合作翻译模式,显示出当时中国外语人才和西方汉语人才缺乏的现实,也给译者更大的发挥空间,王韬也因此有机会逐渐从"笔受者"走向"笔著/撰者",并对此间产生的作品殊为自得。

1853—1858 年,王韬分别与艾约瑟(Joseph Edkins,1823—1905)和伟烈亚力(Alexander Wylie,1815—1887)合译《格致新学提纲》和《西国天学源流》《重学浅说》《华英通商事略》等著作,并首先于《中西通书》《六合丛谈》等连载。上述译著中,王韬多为"笔受",但在 1890 年《西学辑存六种》版本中,上述译本则有不同程度的增删,体现出王韬的学术精进。

《格致新学提纲》记载自 1543 年(明嘉靖二十二年)至 1848 年(清道光二十八年)欧洲近三百年来的科技发展史,汇集光学、力学、电学、数学、天文学大事件,介绍了 53 位科学家,并首次引入天王星等译名。总体上,牛顿之后的 41 位科学家及其主要成就,多为首次在中国介绍,可见该提纲对于西方科学传播的重要意义。1871 年,《教会新报》再刊《格致新学提纲》,署名为"北京牧师英国人艾约瑟",与 1853 年版《提纲》并无二致。1890 年,王韬基于《格致新学提纲》,编辑出版《西学原始考》,对前两个版本有大规模增补,尤其是文学、医学、政治等方面。1857—1858 年,《西国天学源流》陆续翻译出版,该书与《格致新学提纲》中关于天文学的部分有相似之处,比较系统地陈述了西方天文学的发展历史及西方宇宙观的演进过程,内容讫于 1846 年发现海王星。

1858 年翻译出版的《重学浅说》是近代中国翻译的第一部关于西方力学的专著,具有开创性意义。原版包括"重学总论"(设有杆、轮轴、滑车、斜面、劈、螺旋等六节)、"总论(重学之理)"等两大部分。当时,王韬将伟烈亚力口译的内容,修饰润色后笔述成文,故只题作"笔受",其内容只有"重学总论"和"总论(重学之理)"这两部分,《西学辑存六种》则新增"重学原始",并题作"英国伟烈亚力原译,长洲王韬紫诠笔著"①。

除认识到自然科学技术的重要性外,王韬认为,英法等国之所以富强与重视发展商业是分不开的,故提出"今日中国欲制西人而自强,亦莫如商务始;欲商务之旺,莫如设立商务局始",希望供当政者借鉴,以免"昧于外情,而失驾驭远人之道"。②

1857年,《华英通商事略》连载出版。《华英通商事略》叙述了不列颠东印度公司(The British East India Company)在华商业贸易发展史,暨早期中英200年通商史,较为全面地记载了华英贸易中的若干大事件。其叙事起于明万历二十四年(1596)而讫止于东印度公司在华垄断贸易结束的清道光十四年(1834)。

《华英通商事略》事实上是一部类似于马士(Hosea Ballou Morse,1855—1934)所著《东印度公司对华贸易编年史(1635—1834年)》(*The Chronicles of the East India Company*, *Trading to China 1635—1834*)的一篇东印度公司在华贸易编年简史文章,而非一部完整意义上的中英通商通史。文内涉及诸如1596年伍德使团访华、1637年明英军事冲突或称明英战争、1689年华英冲突之狄番斯事件、1741年英国人乔治·安森驾驶第一艘战舰"孙吐哓"号抵澳门、1759年洪任辉事件、1781年抹拉利事件、1784年"休斯夫人"号事件、1792—1793年马戛尔尼使华、1800年"天佑"号事件、1807年"海王星"号事件、1808年英国占领澳门事件、1814年阿耀事件后小斯当东广州谈判、1816年阿美士德使团访华、1820年陀巴士事件、1822年广州商馆大火以及1834年东印度公司在华垄断贸易终止等。除以上大事件外,该书亦不乏中英、中葡、英印、英法、英葡关系的重要论述,点出贸易之于国家利益的重要价值和国家利益对于国际关系的决定性作用。王韬希望清政府从东印度公司贸易史中汲取有益经验,大力发展国际贸易,以救亡图存。

---

① 孙巧云. 从《西学辑存六种》看王韬西学"笔述者"身份的转变. 浙江社会科学,2018(11):130-131.

② 王韬. 弢园文新编. 北京:生活·读书·新知三联书店,1998:379.

1860 年左右,上述翻译出版工作尽数完成,王韬似心生厌倦。此后,由于被发现曾计陈太平天国攻取上海,受到清政府通缉,王韬便于 1862 年遁往香港避难,适逢英国传教士、英华书院院长理雅各(James Legge,1815—1897)邀其佐译中国经典,王韬就此开启了另一番事业,终成实质意义上的独立学者,即其自谓笔撰或笔著者。实际上,相较西语著述的汉译,王韬对辅助雅各英译中国经典明显更为乐意,反映出其传播中学的超前意识,也透露出其对儒家学说的坚持。① 他曾十分骄傲地说:"昔在英土,曾译《诗》《书》《春秋左氏传》三经,已付剞劂,彼都人士,今皆通读。宣圣之道,居然自东土而至西方,将来中庸所言,当可应之如操券。"②

1867 年,理雅各由于健康问题回英国休养,并邀王韬前往英国译书,他"登宗悫引风之筏,乘张骞贯月之槎"③,成为近代到欧洲访学治学的第一个口岸知识分子。王韬的此次泰西"汗漫游",纵横数万里,途经数十国,经新加坡、苏门答腊、锡兰,入红海亚丁湾至开罗。自苏伊士运河驶进地中海,抵达意大利,经法国马赛至巴黎。经过英吉利海峡往伦敦,终临理雅各家乡苏格兰杜拉村。④ 此行令王韬眼界大开,使其对欧洲政治制度、社会发展、文化娱乐、军事科技等各方面有了不同程度的了解,对王韬的思想和事业有着深刻的影响。

随着王韬越来越热衷于向中国人写作介绍西方,翻译中的所思所悟使他区别于同时的其他"西化论者"。⑤ 王韬的翻译领域也由技术、商业转到政治、制度,他开始超越墨海书馆时期的译者角色,引西学之长,补中体之短,成为真正意义上的"跨文化中间人"⑥。1870 年,王韬与理雅各返回香港。

---

① 魏欣. 在传统与现代之间:晚清域外游记中的西方女性书写——以王韬《漫游随录》为中心. 湖北大学学报(哲学社会科学版),2020(2):108.

② 王韬. 弢园尺牍续钞(卷五,光绪乙丑以活字版排印):3.

③ 王韬. 漫游随录. 北京:社会科学文献出版社,2007:自序 9.

④ 杨华,徐国君. 王韬对欧洲民俗的体验和认识. 民俗研究,2017(6):28.

⑤ 柯文. 在传统与现代性之间:王韬与晚清改革. 雷颐,罗检秋,译. 南京:江苏人民出版社,2003:48.

⑥ 段怀清. 王韬与近现代文学转型. 上海:复旦大学出版社,2015:72.

　　游历欧洲、眼界大开之后,1870—1871 年,王韬陆续撰写、编译了其生涯的巅峰之作——《法国志略》和《普法战纪》,后者在《香港近事编录》《中外新闻七日报》《香港华字日报》等连载。借此二著,王韬也实现了角色转换,以"学贯中西"的知时务名士形象,重新引起中外各界的关注。曾国藩曾有意罗致他入两江总督幕府,但此事因曾氏次年病逝作罢。①《普法战纪》于 1873 年由中华印务总局出版,1878 年日本陆军文库翻刻出版。1886 年,弢园书局出版该书铅印本。须指出的是,《普法战纪》并非严格意义上的译著,而是根据张宗良(字芝轩)等翻译的资料,何玉群、梅自仙、陈蔼廷等译述的文献,以及各种日报所载资料,"荟萃贯串、次第前后、削伪去冗、甄繁录要",依时间先后汇编而成。②

　　《普法战纪》是记述当代战史的急就章。该书出版后,王韬名声大噪。曾国藩、李鸿章、丁日昌等洋务重臣也对其赞誉有加,屡邀其翻译西书,并促成其扶桑之行。该书也得到中日学者的高度重视,日本学者"喜其叙事之明畅,行文之爽快"③;近代著名爱国诗人林昌彝赞其为"闻所未闻"之作;《万国公报》主笔蔡尔康将之比肩魏源的《海国图志》。④

　　书文内容,部分取自日报、张宗良口译材料,另有少部分从他处收集。除日报之外,所有名城古迹、遗闻轶事,皆来自他书或《法国志略》《日耳曼国史》。因剪裁、排版仅王韬一人,故此书虽不分卷目,但首尾贯串,事件脉络清楚。辑译之文,多源于外文邮电、报刊,故某些人名、地名译音未见准确,但仍不失为上佳之译作。

　　该书史料丰富、文字整饬、叙事生动,详细介绍普法战争的起因、经过、议和及善后,并分析胜败因素,探析不同体制对国家、战局的影响,还包括对战后世界形势的评估,内容宏富、分析精当,堪称近代中国人所编

① 朱维铮.导言//王韬.弢园文新编.上海:中西书局,2012:6.
② 邹振环.最早由中国人编译的欧洲战争史.编辑学刊,1994(4):82.
③ 钟叔河.平安西尾跋//王韬.扶桑游记.陈尚凡,任光亮,点校.长沙:岳麓书社,1985:511.
④ 王韬.瓮牖余谈.北京:朝华出版社,2018:序一、序二.

译的时间最早、信息量最大的欧洲战争史著之一。① 该书还收录有王韬翻译的法国著名的《马赛曲》(原译《麦须儿诗》),此举是近代中国译介外国诗的最早尝试之一,领先于苏曼殊和马君武翻译拜伦等人的诗作数十年,②虽然比威妥玛(Thomas Francis Wade,1818—1895)、董恂合译第一首英诗《人生颂》(*A Psalm of Life*)的 1864 年晚几年。③

　　1871 年《普法战纪》撰成后,王韬几乎完全终止了翻译工作,继而创办《循环日报》发表政论,并出版了一批直接或间接受其译著启发的作品,显示出其二十余年翻译工作的重要功效。1877 年,王韬婉拒理雅各翻译《易经》《礼记》等中国经典的再度邀请,可以说正式终结了其非同寻常的翻译生涯。

三、王韬的译者身份

　　王韬的译者身份是值得商榷的。从现有译著和资料来看,王韬多数时候承担的是润色、加工等校准、佐译工作,真正将外文译成中文的,是其他译者。一般认为,《格致新学提纲》《西国天学源流》《重学浅说》《华英通商事略》等译著是王韬与艾约瑟和伟烈亚力合译的,但实际操作中大多是由以上西人口译,王韬笔受。据郭嵩焘的记述,西人所著书"不甚谙习文理",王韬(苏州王兰卿)和海岩李壬叔承担的主要是"校定者"角色,主要是为西人著作"疏通句法而已"④。

　　西人不可能完全依靠英语水平尚浅的王韬独立译书,更何况王韬完成上述译书工作后,赴牛津大学演讲,往游苏格兰、日本时,都需要旁人

---

① 忻平. 王韬与近代中国的法国史研究. 上海社会科学院学术季刊,1994(1):168.
② 李景元. 王韬和他的翻译事业. 中国翻译,1991(3):53.
③ 钱锺书. 汉译第一首英语诗《人生颂》及有关二三事//钱锺书. 七缀集. 北京:生活·读书·新知三联书店,2002:133-163.
④ 郭嵩焘. 郭嵩焘日记(第一卷咸丰时期). 长沙:湖南人民出版社,1981:33.

(如理雅各)协助翻译。① 故而,他们更多的是依赖王韬"加工润色,使其形式、风格和抑扬顿挫",以便受众接受。② 同时,王韬对此也表示不满。他直接指出,"已删订文字皆系所主裁断,韬虽秉笔,仅观厥成。彼邦人士,拘文牵义。其词诘曲鄙俚,即使尼山复生,亦不能加以笔削"③,以表达其对西人的汉文功力和所坚持翻译原则的不满。

到《普法战纪》一书的编译时,王韬的身份出现重大转折变化。王韬的角色虽然仍为润色,但实际上较佐译西人译书,体现出更大的主体性。该书系张宗良等翻译,王韬整理、加工而成。其《凡例》中记载:"是书之作,实推张君芝轩为滥觞,于时余删订法国图志……张君时为日报主笔,译英文成华文,而散诸日报中。此编窃取殊多,或为之润色,加以藻采。然于本意,不敢多所违异……陈君蔼廷方有华字日报之役,于欧洲列国见闻搜罗。"④数年后,王韬重申:"余著《普法战纪》,芝轩佐译之功居多。"⑤也就是说,某种程度上,《普法战纪》是以王韬为主,译者为辅了。这既不同于其佐译伟烈亚力等西人翻译西学作品,也不同于其佐译理雅各翻译中国经典,其时,他至多扮演"翻译顾问"的角色。⑥ 真正从事《普法战纪》翻译工作的译者并未在历史上留下更多的踪迹,而王韬这一非典型译者,则得到了当时和后世的广泛关注。这似乎表明仅凭翻译,还远不能立足政坛、文坛之中。

事实上,王韬十分鄙视仅恃语言之能,以洋务为终南捷径的投机之人。他说:"能识英国语言文字者,俯视一切,无不自命治国之能员,救时之良相,一若中国事事五足当意者;而附声吠影者流,从而嘘其焰,自惜不

① 王韬. 漫游随录. 陈尚凡,任光亮,点校. 长沙:岳麓书社,1985:135.
② 柯文. 在传统与现代性之间——王韬与晚清改革. 雷颐,罗检秋译,南京:江苏人民出版社,1998:52.
③ 王韬. 弢园尺牍(卷2). 台北:文海出版社,1983:1b-2a.
④ 王韬. 凡例//普法战纪(遁叟手校本). 张宗良,陈蔼廷,译. 波士顿:哈佛大学汉和图书馆藏,1895:凡例2b-3a.
⑤ 王韬. 扶桑游记. 陈尚凡,任光亮,点校. 长沙:岳麓书社,1985:396.
⑥ 丁大刚,宋莉华. 王韬辅助理雅各翻译中国典籍过程考. 国际汉学,2020(1):118.

能置身在洋务中,而得躬逢其盛也。"①

当然,王韬也有发挥"译者主体性"的时候。1849 年,"委办本"《圣经·新约》的汉译在王韬之父王昌桂的协助下已完成三分之二(到《罗马书》部分)。王昌桂亡故后,主持者麦都思选择王韬作为继译者。王韬协助翻译《圣经·新约》的教义部分和整部《圣经·旧约》。麦都思对王韬的评价颇高,称赞他"文风典雅""思想圆通",并尤其提到他在《约伯记》《箴言》翻译中的优美表达,前者还被视为王韬最为成功的翻译之一。② 可见,就《圣经》的深文理汉译而言,王韬并未完全遵从先前的"西人口译、王韬笔受"的翻译模式。

其实,王韬在《圣经》翻译中独当一面的情形是鲜见的,因为当时通行的翻译模式就是口译加笔受。京师同文馆 1862 年建立后,并未吸引天资高、勤学译的一流学生,大多是平庸之辈。京师同文馆开办之初,生源多为八旗子弟,但受制于传统观念,对翻译之事并不热衷,甚至持鄙夷态度,仍希图以科举求取功名。③ 1863 年上海同文馆(1867 年改为广方言馆)成立后,学生资质有所提高。尽管如此,两所翻译机构起初大多招收西人担任教员和译员,原因在于其时西人中已成长起一批高水平英汉译者。因此,在其主导下,西人译者通常向中方合作者口译和解释西文著述,并由后者以传统汉文写就。④

根据傅兰雅(John Fryer,1839—1928)的记载,翻译馆译书承袭明清以来来华耶稣会士的翻译模式,由西人口述,中人笔录。

---

① 王韬. 弢园文录外编. 楚流,书进,风雷,选注. 沈阳:辽宁人民出版社,1994:48.

② 韩南. 作为中国文学之《圣经》:麦都思、王韬与《圣经》委办本. 段怀清,译,浙江大学学报(人文社会科学版),2010(1):20.

③ 季压西,陈伟民. 从"同文三馆"起步. 北京:学苑出版社,2007:37.另见:苏精. 清季同文馆及其师生. 福州:福建教育出版社,2018:30.

④ Lawrence Wang-Chi Wong. "Beyond XIN DA YA 信達雅:Translation Problems," in Michael Lackner, Natascha Vittinghoff, eds., *Mapping Meanings:The Field of New Learning in Late Qing China*. Leiden:Brill,2004:242.

　　至于馆内译书之法,必将所欲译者,西人先熟览胸中,而书理已明,则与华士同译,乃以西书之义,逐句读成华语,华士笔述之;若有难言处,则与华士斟酌何法可明;若华士有不明处,则(由西士)讲明之。译后,华士将初稿改正润色,令合于中国文法。有数要书,临刊时华士与西人核对;而平常书多不必对,皆赖华士改正。因华士详慎郢斫,其讹则少,而文法甚精。既脱稿,则付梓刻版。①

由此可见,较王韬年幼的傅兰雅十分认可"与华士同译"这一翻译模式。然而,这般翻译模式其实直接影响译文质量。马建忠注意到:

　　近今上海制造局、福州船政局与京师译署,虽设有同文书馆,罗致学生,以读诸国语言文字。第始事之意,止求通好,不专译书。即有译成数种,或仅为一事一艺之用,未有将其政令治教之本原条贯,译为成书,使人人得以观其会通者。其律例公法之类,间有摘译,或文辞艰涩,于原书之面目尽失本来,或挂一漏万,割裂复重,未足资为考订之助。②

究其原因,可归结于:

　　今之译者,大抵于外国之语言,或稍涉其藩篱,面其文字之微辞奥旨,与夫各国之所谓古文词者,率茫然而未识其名称;或仅通外国文字言语,而汉文则粗陋鄙俚,未窥门径……又或转请西人之稍通华语者为之口述,而旁听者乃为仿佛摹写其词中所欲达之意,其未能达者,则又参以己意而武断其间。盖通洋文者不达汉文,通汉文者又不达洋文,亦何怪夫所译之书,皆驳杂迁讹,为天下识者所鄙夷而讪笑也!③

---

① 傅兰雅. 江南制造总局翻译西书事略//张静庐. 中国近代出版史料初编. 上海:群联出版社,1953:18. 又见:罗新璋,陈应年. 翻译论集(修订本). 北京:商务印书馆,2009:287.
② 马建忠. 拟设翻译书院议(甲午冬)//马建忠. 适可斋纪言纪行. 台北:文海出版社,1968:213-214.
③ 马建忠. 拟设翻译书院议(甲午冬)//马建忠. 适可斋纪言纪行. 台北:文海出版社,1968:214-215.

可见,当时西人口译、中人笔受的做法是通览中西之译书人才的缺乏所致,而这一模式无法准确传递原著的本来面目。须注意的是,同文馆的译书方式一般是由外国教习独立翻译,或由学生翻译而由教习校定,这一方式至少相较上述翻译模式更为可取,但其译书质量也饱受诟病。① 例如,梁启超批评道:"然彼时笔受者皆馆中新学诸生,未受专门,不能深知其意,故义多暗晦。即如《法国律例》一书,欧洲亦以为善本,而馆译之本,往往不能达意,且常有一字一句之颠倒漏略,至与原文相反者。"②其实,这与教习的汉文水平不高有关:"西文教习,非略知西之华人,即不解华文之西士。西教习则指画示意;或俟翻译口述,强半失真。"③总之,由外国教习独译或校定的译文尚不能还原本意,更何况西人口译、中人笔述的翻译模式。

因此,马建忠呼吁应专设翻译书院造就华语、西语兼备之译才,而培养对象宜是"长于汉文,年近二十而天姿绝人者"④,为的是避免行文臃滞艰涩。即便如此,马建忠仍提出延请长于古文词者,专为润色译文,某种程度上可视作对先前翻译模式的无奈妥协。19 世纪末 20 世纪初,同文馆愈渐重视译者的汉学素养,旨在打造一批汉文通达、洋文精练的翻译人才,也走出一批实务译者,但在译书方面并无太大精进。

四、结　语

综观王韬的政治、学术生涯,可以发现,在墨海书馆时期,谙世未深的他在麦都思等西人的调教下,中西对译的水平虽未臻化境,但为其后来的

---

① 参见:季压西,陈伟民. 从"同文三馆"起步. 北京:学苑出版社,2007:97.
② 梁启超. 变法通议. 何光宇,评注. 北京:华夏出版社,2002:146-147.
③ 李楚材. 帝国主义侵华教育史资料——教会教育. 北京:教育科学出版社,1987:125-126.
④ 马建忠. 拟设翻译书院议(甲午冬)//马建忠. 适可斋纪言纪行. 台北:文海出版社,1968:218.

翻译实践和著书立说打下了重要基础。该时期,王韬主要关注格致之学,艳羡西方的器物之利,认为须师其所长,夺其所恃。1870年以后,远渡重洋归来的他,在视野、思想和志趣上有了全面提升,所关心的不再仅停留于机巧工事,而涉足西方政治、经济、军事、社会、文化及历史、地理等经世致用之学,希冀在天下大变之际引介可用之道,启迪思想,推动变法自强,改良中国。

美国汉学家柯文(Paul A. Cohen)曾说:"王韬的特殊之处在于,对他不适宜简单的归类。"①柯文谈的是王韬在政治家、改革家、学者及儒者多重身份之间的穿梭。王韬如果是一位译者,也只能说是一位非典型译者,他是当时传统翻译模式造就的合译者。王韬是不幸的,在传统仕途上并未得偿所愿;但他也是幸运的,身处传统与现代之间的他,在当时得到了政界、学界的广泛认可或关注,更以领先于同代人的胆识,在中国近代史上留下了自己对千年未有之大变局时代的理解,并不断被挖掘、研究。

作为非典型译者的王韬,其学术进路离不开早期译事的助力,日益开阔的视野,不懈的勤学善思,这都促使出身平平的王韬成长为跨越时代的大人物。虽然,王韬和他的思想终未能变乱世之法,但是他深受西学影响的作品明显将19世纪下半叶的中国同此前的中国区别开来了。

五、编选说明

本卷关心的是作为翻译家的王韬,而不是其报人、政论家、小说家与改革家等身份。本着这样的原则,编者这里收录的,是王韬参与或协助翻译的译作。篇幅所限,本书也非王韬有关译作的穷尽式汇编。本卷收录的王韬参与或协助翻译的译作共计十种。分别点校自《中西通书》《春秋朔闰至日考》《六合丛谈》《弢园著述所存书》《中国经典》(英文)等各时期

---

① 柯文. 在传统与现代性之间——王韬与晚清改革. 雷颐,罗检秋,译. 南京:江苏人民出版社,1998:141.

书目。选用的版本,尽可能是最早的版本,而非王韬晚年在脱离原文和原合作译者后重新增订或修订的版本。本卷的原合译者主要有艾约瑟、伟烈亚力、麦都思、理雅各等汉学家以及张宗良等,他们是王韬的主要合作者。本书所附"王韬译事年表"将王韬重要翻译实践活动按时间顺序排列,亦非穷尽式列举。

为方便读者尽快进入上述作品,点校者在每篇前均增加了"点校者按语"板块,主要介绍译文选择的原因与理据。有的篇章还附了原书按语或王韬晚年在其《弢园著述总目》中对所涉作品的简要介绍。

本卷所援用的原书,大多竖排,未加标点。现一律改为横排,并加上了现代标点符号。

对于原书中的帝王年号纪年,本卷采用如"明嘉靖二十二年(1543)"的形式,注明公历纪年年号。对于原作中涉及的人名、地名、著作名和重要术语,点校者添加了夹注注释,一般以[]或()等形式加以提示。个别原文疑似有误的地方,点校时以[]注出。对于文内括号内夹注系原书就有的,编者或在各篇"点校者按语"栏目中做专门说明,或者以[]或()的形式附"王韬注""原作者注"或"原书注"等字样。

本卷涉及历史学、宗教学、文学、力学、天文学等多个学科,为使点校后的译本更具实用性和使用上的便捷性,编者或制作了译名对照表,或提供了对照原文,方便读者对收录的作品展开进一步研究,但原作中仍有大量各学科用语,点校者无力一一破译。

本卷选用的所有插图,部分来自原作,部分由编者新添加,均注明了出处。

第一编

西学东渐

格致新学提纲(上)
(1853 年)

艾约瑟　口译

王韬　笔受

王韬按语(1889):

　　西士艾约瑟原译,长洲王韬重编,后屡加补辑,多所增入。格致之学,中国肇端乎《大学》,特有其目,亡其篇,后世虽有究其理者,绝少专门名家。近日西人精益求精,几于日新月异而岁不同。盖格致一门,所包者广,如算学、化学、重学、电学、气学、声学、地学、矿学、医学、机器、动植,无乎不具;皆由古人所特创,后乃渐造其微。观此书可以略窥一斑矣。①

编者按语:

　　1853—1858 年,王韬陆续与艾约瑟、伟烈亚力翻译完成《格致新学提纲》《华英通商事略》《西国天学源流》《重学浅说》等四部格致之学著作。《格致新学提纲》首刊《中西通书》,后于 1871 年再版于《教会新报》,该版本与 1871 年《教会新报》刊载版本略有差异;后三部连载于《六合丛谈》。1890 年,王韬将以上四种连同《西学图说》和《东西著述考》修订汇集为《西

---

① 此按语为王韬晚年所加。参见王韬所著的《弢园著述总目》,载于《春秋朔闰至日考》(哈佛大学图书馆珍藏本),光绪己丑(1889)年七月。

学辑存六种》出版,并增添许多原书未有的内容,其中《格致新学提纲》改名为《西学原始考》。

内容上,《格致新学提纲》记载自明嘉靖二十二年(1543)至清道光二十八年(1848),欧洲近 300 年来的科技发展史,汇集光学、力学、电学、数学、天文学大事件,介绍了约 53 位科学家,并引入天王星等诸多新名词(译名)。总体上,书中牛顿之后的 41 位科学家及其主要成就,多为首次在中国介绍。

形式上,1853—1866 年的《中西通书》的英文名是 *Chinese and Western Almanac*,其中 Almanac 就是 yearbook 或 annual,即"年鉴";1852 年,艾约瑟曾编过类似的《华洋和合通书》,即 *Chinese and Foreign Almanac*。从上述英文可以清楚地看出,《格致新学提纲》的实质是历书、年鉴。是故,我们在点校出版时,选择以年谱的形式呈现本文。另外,点校者试图以随文夹注的形式,标注出文内所有科学家的姓名和著作名原文,对于重要科技名词,确属费解的,也一并注出。但由于点校者水平有限,个别之处仍留存疑,另有个别名词或提法,尚未完全厘清其源语。

鉴于此后的版本多有增扩等变化,这里选择点校录入的《格致新学提纲(上)》(1853 年)一文,依照的是 1853 年《中西通书》刊载版本。点校者参考了邓亮、韩琦两位先生据牛津大学图书馆藏 1853 年和 1858 年《中西通书》点校的《格致新学提纲》①。本文对于邓韩点校本的若干笔误有订正。

明嘉靖二十二年(1543),波兰歌白泥(Nicolaus Copernicus,1473—1543,今译哥白尼)著《天象旋转考》(*De revolutionibus orbium coelestium*,英译 *On the Revolutions of the Heavenly Spheres* 或者 *On the*

---

① 邓亮,韩琦. 新学传播的序曲:艾约瑟、王韬翻译《格致新学提纲》的内容、意义及其影响. 自然科学史研究,2012(3):146-148.

Revolutions of the Celestial Spheres,今译《天体运行论》),始言太阳居中不动,五星及地球俱环绕之,故太阳行十二宫,诸星昼夜盘旋,皆系地球运动。西洋诸国宗之。

二十四年(1545),以大利(今译意大利)佳但(Girolamo Cardano,1501—1576,今译吉罗拉莫·卡尔达诺)始造开立方法。

三十九年(1560),玻尔大(Giovanni Battista della Porta,1535—1615,今译吉安巴蒂斯塔·德拉·波尔塔)初作穴室取影之法(今译摄影术)。

隆庆十一年(1577),弟谷(Tycho Brahe,1546—1601,今译第谷·布拉赫)测定客星较远于月,又明月离(即月亮运行到某度次)之道,又言金、水二星附日而行,绕于地球。

万历三年(1575),茅鹿理哥(Francesco Maurolico,1494—1575,今译弗朗西斯科·马若利科)始明人目内观物之理,而造远视、近视眼镜。

十八年(1590),咈兰西(今译法国)肥乙大(François Viète,1540—1603,今译弗朗索瓦·韦达)究明代数学,以西洋二十五字头代数目字,不论已知、未知,俱可推之。又造开三乘方法,著《数学纪要》[*Mathematical Collections*,今译《数学汇编》,但该书的作者一般认为是古希腊数学家帕普斯(Pappus)]。是年(1590),英国奇白德(William Gilbert,1540—1605,今译威廉·吉尔伯特)著《磁石论》(*De Magnete*,一般认为该书出版于1600年)。

十九年(1591),以大利加离略(Galileo Galilei,1564—1642,今译伽利略)著《重学》(拉丁文 *De Motu Antiquiora*,英文 *On Motion*,今译论《论运动》;查得伽利略并无关于重力学即 gravity 的著作),始明一斤重与十斤重下坠,同迟速落地之理。

二十七年(1599),荷兰史德文(Simon Stevin,1548—1620,今译西蒙·斯蒂文)明斜面上力重比较之理,及分力并力之理;知入水愈深,压力愈大。

三十七年(1609),刻白尔(Johannes Kepler,1571—1630,今译约翰内斯·开普勒)著《火星运动》(拉丁文 *Astronomia nova*,英译名 *New Astronomy*,该书讨论火星的椭圆轨道,今译《新天文学》)书,论行星轨道皆为椭圆。又论行星用椭圆面积为平行。

三十八年(1610),以大利伽离略造远镜,初见水星有四附星。

明年(1611),又见金星有晦朔弦望(是指月亮从亏到盈再到亏期间的四种状态和对应的日期),一如太阴(指月亮)。又见土星有两耳;又见太阴之体,有高低凸凹之形。

三十九年(1611),刻白尔改正清蒙气差("清蒙气差"是 atmospheric refraction 的早期译名,即大气折射,是指原本直线前进的光或其它电磁波在穿越大气层时,因为空气密度随着高度变化所产生的偏折),论气水中俱有光差。又因悟人目视物之理,如穴室取影。

四十二年(1614),英国那比尔(John Napier,1550—1617,今译约翰·纳皮尔)造对数(logarithms),用加减代乘除。以二零七一八二八一八为元。

四十三年(1615),伽离略用木星附星掩食(是指遮盖之使发生亏蚀现象),定东西里差("东西里差"即地理经度,即 longitude;"南北里差"乃地理纬度,即 latitude)。

四十五年(1617),荷兰师纳拉(Willebrord Snellius,1580—1626,今译威理博·斯涅尔)测定地上若干里,合天上若干度,依此推之,可知地球周围多少里。

四十六年(1618),刻白尔论行星行于椭圆,周时刻方(即周期的平方)之比,同于行星距太阳十字线立方之比(此乃开普勒第三定律,即绕以太阳为焦点的椭圆轨道运行的所有行星,其公转周期的平方与椭圆轨道半长轴的立方之比是一个常量)。

四十七年(1619),师纳拉造光差算术,凡光出入于空质中,必成光差角,与原角恒有比例。

泰昌元年(1620),英国备根(Francis Bacon,1561—1626,今译弗兰西斯·培根)著《格物穷理新法》(*Novum Organum*,今译《新工具》),实事求是,必考物以合理,不造理以合物。

天启四年(1624),英国巴理知思(Henry Briggs,1561—1630,今译亨利·布里格斯)发明对数之理,始取十为元,以令一对十,二对百。

崇祯四年(1631),佳生地(Pierre Gassendi,1592—1655,今译皮埃尔·伽桑狄)初见水星过日面。

五年(1632),伽离略专论天静地动,坐此(指由此)下狱。强使反其说,乃出之。

十年(1637),咈兰西代加德(René Descartes,1596—1650,今译勒内·笛卡尔)合代数几何,以发明直曲诸线之理。

十二年(1639),英国好洛斯(Jeremiah Horrocks,1618—1641,今译杰雷米亚·霍罗克斯)初见金星过日面。

顺治元年(1644),到里直理(Evangelista Torricelli,1608—1647,今译埃万杰利斯塔·托里拆利)造量风气轻重之器(今译气压计)。

十一年(1654),荷兰国国里该(Otto von Guericke,1602—1686,今译奥托·冯·格里克)初造风气车[今译(活塞式)真空泵],能出器中之风气。

十五年(1655),海更士(Christiaan Huygens,1629—1695,今译克里斯蒂安·惠更斯)发明钟摆之理,始作有摆之钟,又名仪坠子。

十六年(1656),海更士初见附土星两耳,实则一光带,又见一附星,作《土星考》(*De Saturni Luna observatio nova*,英译 *About the new observation of the moon of Saturn-discovery of Titan*)。

康熙二年(1663),英国格勒哥里(James Gregory,1638—1675,今译詹姆斯·格雷戈里)作回光远镜(今译反射望远镜)。

三年(1664),于观天器上作远镜窥筒。是年(1664),奈端(Isaac Newton,1642—1727,今译艾萨克·牛顿)初论微分法。此法及积分法为最深算术。凡借根、天元等法不可推者,用此则可。

五年(1666),奈端(即牛顿)初知天上地下万物皆有相引之理,是以重物向地心下坠,与月环地球之理同。

六年(1667),乞理师(John Wallis,1616—1703,今译约翰·沃利斯)造曲线面积算术。

八年(1669),奈端作分光法,白光入三角玻璃分为七色;再加一三角玻璃,仍合为白光。

九年(1670),拉那(Francesco Lana de Terzi,1631—1687,今译弗朗西斯科·拉纳·德·泰尔)作寒暑表(今译温度计)。

十年(1671),葛西尼(Giovanni Domenico Cassini,1625—1712,今译乔凡尼·多美尼科·卡西尼)初见土星第二附星。是年(1671),初明钟摆近赤道则迟,远赤道则速,如明地力在赤道最大,在两极最小。

十一年(1672),奈端初作回光显微镜。

十五年(1676),大泥勒墨尔(Ole Christensen Rømer,1644—1710,今译奥勒·罗默)初明光动之理。是年(1676),葛西尼推定木星自转九小时三刻十分。

十七年(1678),海更士初知星光自远及近,如海潮迅速射及目中,人始能见其光。

二十三年(1684),葛西尼初见土星又有三颗附星,并前而五。

二十六年(1687),奈端著《格物原本》(*Philosophiæ Naturalis Principia Mathematica*,即 *Mathematical Principles of Natural Philosophy*,常简称作 *Principia*,今译《自然哲学的数学原理》)中言:日月星小环于大之理,所行之路,或椭圆,或单曲线,或双曲线。诸行星及地球、月,俱行椭圆。客星、彗星,俱行单曲线与双曲线。重物向地心下坠,与太阴自东而西行,一理贯通也。

四十三年(1704),奈端著《视学》(*Opticks*,今译《光学》),论回光角与原角(今译反射角与入射角)等。是年(1704),葛西尼始见土星有两光带。

五十七年(1718),咈郎西国主(即法国国王)命天文大臣推算地球经纬里差,始知地体(今译地球)系扁圆。

五十九年(1720),革来(Stephen Gray,1666—1736,今译斯蒂芬·格雷)考正琥珀气(electricity,今译电)之理。好里(Edmond Halley,1656—1742,今译爱德蒙·哈雷)考正月行之理。

雍正五年(1727),英国白拉里(James Bradley,1693—1762,今译詹姆斯·布拉德雷)考正地动、恒星视差之理。

八年(1730),英国海特里(John Hadley,1682—1744,今译约翰·哈德利)造纪限镜仪(即双反射八分仪,一种双反射镜测角仪器),以测太阳高弧。

十三年(1733),西国考正地球扁圆周径。是年(1733),西国创考验万物相引法,悬物空中,近山则线斜。

乾隆二年(1737),咈郎西格来罗(Alexis Claude Clairaut,1713—1765,今译亚历克西斯·克劳德·克莱罗)考明三动物相牵引之理(即三体问题)。

十年(1745),白拉里始知地球南北极有动差,十九年一周。

十二年(1747),米利坚佛兰格林(Benjamin Franklin,1706—1790,今译本杰明·富兰克林)始明琥珀气与电气同。

十三年(1748),欧楼(Leonhard Euler,1707—1783,今译莱昂哈德·欧拉)详考各行星相引微差之理。

二十二(1757),好里预推之彗星见(同"现"),每七十五年一周天,适符其数。道光十五年(1835)又见。是年(1757),道伦德(John Dollond,1706—1761,今译约翰·多伦德)造无晕远镜(今译消色差透镜)。远镜透光,俱有彩晕。惟此镜无。以对晕二式玻璃,合而尽消其晕。

二十六年(1761),欧楼阐明差等数,初造积分法。

二十七年(1762),白拉格(Joseph Black,1728—1799,今译约瑟夫·布拉克)始明阴热气之理。

三十九年(1774),英国始明地质松紧之理,测定同体地水二质,其较多五倍半。

四十年(1775),咈兰西拉白拉瑟(Pierre-Simon Laplace,1749—1827,今译皮埃尔-西蒙·拉普拉斯)阐明海潮之理。

四十六年(1781),英国天文大臣侯失勒(William Herschel,1738—1822,今译威廉·赫歇尔)初见土星之外有一行星,名之曰於哣瘴士(Uranus),译即天王星。

四十七年(1782),侯失勒以远镜测见白气数点,如传说积尸之类,同于天河,亦系无数小星之光。

五十二年(1787),拉白拉瑟讲明太阴轨道之理。

五十三年(1788),拉格浪(Joseph-Louis Lagrange,1736—1813,今译约瑟夫·拉格朗日)用微分法详解动静重学之理。

五十四年(1789),侯失勒名威灵,造极大远镜(即一台大型反射望远镜),测见土星又有两附星,并前而七。

嘉庆四年(1799),拉白拉瑟著《天文重学大成》(*Mécanique céleste*,后逐渐完成 *Traité de mécanique céleste*,英译 *Celestial Mechanics*,今译《天体力学》)。

五年(1800),侯失勒初明太阳所出之气有热气、光气、化物气之别;穴室照影肖像法,用第三气。

六年(1801),以大利亚必亚齐(Giuseppe Piazzi,1746—1826,今译朱塞普·皮亚齐)初见木星火星之间有一小行星,名曰"谷女"(Ceres,即谷神星)。

七年(1802),日耳曼阿尔白士(Heinrich Wilhelm Matthus Olbers,1758—1840,今译海因里希·奥伯斯)测见第二小行星,名曰"武女"(Pallas,即智神星)。

八年(1803),侯失勒测见定位星有双星互相环绕。

九年(1804),日耳曼哈尔定(Karl Ludwig Harding,1765—1834,今译卡尔·路德维希·哈丁)测见第三小行星,名曰"天后"(Juno,即婚神星)。

十二年(1807)阿尔白士测见第四小行星,名曰"火女"(Vesta,即灶神星)。是年(1807),侯失勒测见天王星有六附星。

十九年(1814),西国初明露水之理,空中恒有水气,遇地面冷,必垂而为露;夜中无云,地面热气易向太虚透发,故露下。如云掩地面,热气难透,必不成露。树林遮蔽与云无异。

二十四年(1819),日耳曼尔士德(Hans Christian Ørsted,1777—1851,今译汉斯·克海斯提安·奥斯特)发明磁石与电气异同之理。是年(1819),日耳曼恩格(Johann Franz Encke,1791—1865,今译约翰·弗朗茨·恩克)测定彗星行度约六年余一周天(艾约瑟在1858年《中西通书》更正为三年,并称"前校印书误")。

道光二年(1822),侯失勒(区别于上述威廉·赫歇尔)名约翰(John Herschel,1792—1871,今译约翰·赫歇尔)用大远镜测定位星有单星、双星、三星、四星之别,各互相环绕。

三年(1823),日耳曼弗伦好弗(Joseph von Fraunhofer,1787—1826,今译约瑟夫·冯·夫琅和费)初见日光分为七色,中间有无数黑线,其相去度分俱一定。诸行星之光与日大同小异,因借日之光故也。定位星则各不同,因自生光故也。

四年(1824),日耳曼比乙拉(Wilhelm Von Biela,1782—1856,威廉·冯·比拉)测定第三彗星行度,三年余一周天(今查得应为1826年,比拉计算出轨道及其公转周期6.6年)。

十年(1830),英爱理(George Airy,1801—1892,今译乔治·艾里)发明光学,言日月之光,激动空气,如波浪然,千层万叠,宕漾人目,而后觉有光。

二十年(1840),日耳曼德路威(Otto Wilhelm von Struve,1819—

1905,今译奥托·威廉·冯·斯特鲁维)测得太阳率诸行星,环绕女藏星,一年行三千三百三十五万里。后有梅特勒测得昴宿为太阳及天河内诸星所环绕,星数数千,无异象,因其轨道极大故也。(艾约瑟在 1858 年《中西通书》更正称:"改正癸丑年《格致新学提纲》'太阳率诸行星,环绕女藏星'当改为'太阳率诸行星,今向女藏星相近处而行',非环绕也"。)

二十五年(1845),日耳曼亨该(Karl Ludwig Hencke,1793—1866,今译卡尔·路德维希·亨克)测见第五小行星,名曰"严女"(Astraea,即义神星)。

二十六年(1846),咈兰西力佛理亚(Urbain Le Verrier,1811—1877,今译奥本·勒维耶)用算术推知天王星之外,必更有行星牵动天王星,并推得其度分,其友用远镜细测,果见有海王星与所推度分仅差四分耳。是年(1846),英国阿但史(John Couch Adams,1819—1892,今译约翰·柯西·亚当斯)亦用算术推知海王星所在度分。

二十七年(1847),亨该测见第六小行星名,曰"稚女"(Hebe,即韶神星)。是年(1847),英国欣特(John Russell Hind,1823—1895,今译约翰·罗素·欣德)测见第七小行星,名"花神"(Flora);第八小行星,名"虹神"(Iris)[这两颗小行星编号似乎正好颠倒了]。又有人测见海王星有两附星,亦有一光带,此事尚未有确据。

二十八年(1848),英国格来汉(Andrew Graham,1815—1908,今译安德鲁·格雷厄姆)测见第九小行星,名曰"猎师"(Metis,即颖神星)。

格致新学提纲(下)
(1858年)

艾约瑟　口译

王韬　笔受

王韬按语:

此卷内纪年俱用耶稣年,不改用中国者,因有西月日与中国不合,且查彗星簿有在中国去岁见者,今俱在本年,故不改年号。

编者按语:

本文直接录自《中西通书》,江苏松江上海墨海书馆(The London Missionary Society Press)1858年版相关部分。点校者亦参考了邓亮、韩琦两位先生的论文,参见邓亮、韩琦:《新学传播的序曲:艾约瑟、王韬翻译〈格致新学提纲〉的内容、意义及其影响》,《自然科学史研究》2012年第3期,第148—149页。本文对于邓韩点校本的若干笔误有订正。

耶稣后一千六百五十六年,海更士用千里镜初见近参宿处一大星云——即癸丑年所定"星气",今改名。

后一千七百八十六年,侯失勒(即威廉·赫歇尔)造星云表,内载一千座。

后一千八百三十三年,侯失勒约翰(即约翰·赫歇尔)造北天星云表,为二千一百五十五座;星林表,为一百五十二座。又在阿非利加(Africa,即非洲)南地造南天星云表,为二千二百三十九座;星林表为二百三十七座。

后一千八百十九年(疑为1839年),法兰西国阿拉哥(Franois Arago,1786—1853,今译弗朗索瓦·阿拉戈)以光分南北方向,用颜色相配,制南北线分光镜。

后一千八百四十三年十一月二十二日,法兰西腓乙(Hervé Faye,1814—1902,今译埃尔韦·法叶)推彗星轨道一周为七年百分年之二十九,轨道在土、火两星之间。

后一千八百四十五年,英国罗斯伯(Lord William Parsons Rosse,1800—1867,今译罗斯伯爵威廉·帕森思)——罗斯,地名,伯爵也——造反照光千里观星镜,长为五十三英尺,测星云为无数,小星者甚多。

后一千八百四十六年九月二十三日,英国拉斯拉(William Lassell,1799—1880,今译威廉·拉塞尔)测得海王星之第一月。

后一千八百四十八年四月二十五日,英国格来汉测得第九小行星,名"弥低斯"(Metis),译曰"猎师"(即颖神星)。

后一千八百四十八年九月十六日至十九日,合众国(即美国)本特(William Cranch Bond,1789—1859,今译威廉·克兰奇·邦德;George Phillips Bond,1825—1865,今译乔治·邦德。此二人为兄弟)测得附土星(Hyperion,土卫七)之第八月。九月十九、二十日,拉斯拉亦测见之。

后一千八百四十九年四月十二日,以大利特迦斯巴利(Annibale de Gasparis,1819—1892,今译安尼巴莱·德·加斯帕里斯)测得第十小行星,名"海其阿"(Hygeia),译曰"医女"(即健神星)。

后一千八百五十年五月十一日,特迦斯巴利测得第十一小行星,名"巴腿拿卑"(Parthenope,即海妖星,以《希腊神话》海妖帕耳忒诺珀命名)。是年八月十四日,英国拉斯拉测得海王星之第二月。是年九月十三日,英国欣特测得第十二小行星,名"维多利亚"(Victoria),译曰"胜女"(即凯神星)。是年十一月二日,特迦斯巴利(即加斯帕里斯)测得第十三小行星,名"哀及利亚"(Egeria,即"芙女星")。

后一千八百五十一年五月十九日,欣特测得第十四小行星,名"以来奈"(Irene,即司宁星);五月二十三日,特迦斯巴利亦测见之。是年,英国法拉抬(Michael Faraday,1791—1867,今译迈克尔·法拉第;邓亮、韩琦二先生的点校本将其写作"拉法抬")究明养气指南北方向,以噉铁石(即磁铁或吸铁石)能力加在养气之上为南北方向,其余诸气俱东西方向。并又究明吸养气之能,以热气大小、体之大小为准。

后一千八百五十二年十一月十六日,英国欣特测得第二十二小行星,名"加略必"(Kalliope,即司赋星)。

后一千八百五十三年,日耳曼阿多斯得路佛(即奥托·威廉·冯·斯特鲁维,其为 Friedrich Georg Wilhelm von Struve,1793—1864,今译瓦西里·雅可夫列维奇·斯特鲁维之子,后者是第一位测量织女星视差的天文学家)测定织女星(Vega),离地一百三十亿万英里,所射出之光应二十一年至地,又星光较多于太阳光十六倍。

后一千八百五十四年,英国约翰孙(Manuel John Johnson,1805—1859,今译曼努埃尔·约翰·约翰逊)测定天津五六两星中之定位星,用地轨道半年差,究明其星约离地六十亿万英里,所射出之光,应十年至地。此星与白西勒(Friedrich Wilhelm Bessel,1784—1846,今译弗里德里希·威廉·贝塞尔)查出之数相符。

后一千八百五十六年,巴黎斯哥勒斯迷(Hermann Mayer Salomon Goldschmidt,1802—1866,今译赫尔曼·迈尔·萨洛蒙·戈尔德施密特)测得第四十一小行星,名"大副尼"(Daphne,即桂神星),英国和其孙(Norman Robert Pogson,1829—1891,今译诺曼·罗伯特·普森)测得第四十二小行星,名"依昔斯"(Isis,即育神星)。两行星轨道俱在火、木二星之间,星等如第十一、第十二之恒星。是年,又有人究明正月内一小时见五流星,七月内一小时见九流星,八月内一小时见十三流星,九月、十月、十一月内一小时各有四流星,余月内一小时俱有三流星,如此诸流星降下数,时常有之。

后一千八百五十七年,泰西诸天文士测见第四十三至第五十小行星。

附:《格致新学提纲》译名对照表

王韬译名	可能对应的外文词语	今译
《磁石论》	*De Magnete*	《磁石论》或《论磁石》
《格物穷理新法》	*Novum Organum*	《新工具》
《格物原本》	*Philosophiæ Naturalis Principia Mathematica / Mathematical Principles of Natural Philosophy*	《自然哲学的数学原理》
《火星运动》	*Astronomia nova / New Astronomy*	《新天文学》
《视学》	*Opticks*	《光学》
《数学纪要》	*Mathematical Collections*	《数学汇编》
《天文重学大成》	*Mécanique celeste / Celestial Mechanics*	《天体力学》
《天象旋转考》	*De revolutionibus orbium coelestium / On the Revolutions of the Heavenly Spheres / On the Revolutions of the Celestial Spheres*	《天体运行论》
《土星考》	*De Saturni Luna observatio nova / About the new observation of the moon of Saturn—discovery of Titan*	《关于土星卫星的新观测——泰坦的发现》
《重学》	*De Motu Antiquiora / On Motion*	《论运动》
阿但史	John Couch Adams, 1819—1892	约翰·柯西·亚当斯
阿尔白士	Heinrich Wilhelm Matthus Olbers, 1758—1840	海因里希·奥伯斯
阿拉哥	François Arago, 1786—1853	弗朗索瓦·阿拉戈
哀及利亚	Egeria	芙女星
巴黎斯哥勒斯迷	Hermann Mayer Salomon Goldschmidt, 1802—1866	赫尔曼·迈尔·萨洛蒙·戈尔德施密特
巴理知思	Henry Briggs, 1561—1630	亨利·布里格斯
巴腿拿卑	Parthenope	海妖星
白拉格	Joseph Black, 1728—1799	约瑟夫·布拉克
白拉里	James Bradley, 1693—1762	詹姆斯·布拉德雷

续表

王韬译名	可能对应的外文词语	今译
白西勒	Friedrich Wilhelm Bessel，1784—1846	弗里德里希·威廉·贝塞尔
备根	Francis Bacon，1561—1626	弗兰西斯·培根
本特	William Cranch Bond，1789—1859；George Phillips Bond，1825—1865	威廉·克兰奇·邦德；乔治·邦德
比乙拉	Wilhelm Von Biela，1782—1856	威廉·冯·比拉
玻尔大	Giovanni Battista della Porta，1535—1615	吉安巴蒂斯塔·德拉·波尔塔
大副尼	Daphne	桂神星
大泥勒墨尔	Ole Christensen Rømer，1644—1710	奥勒·罗默
代加德	René Descartes，1596—1650	勒内·笛卡尔
到里直理	Evangelista Torricelli，1608—1647	埃万杰利斯塔·托里拆利
道伦德	John Dollond，1706—1761	约翰·多伦德
德路威	Otto Wilhelm von Struve，1819—1905	奥托·威廉·冯·斯特鲁维
弟谷	Tycho Brahe，1546—1601	第谷·布拉赫
恩格	Johann Franz Encke，1791—1865	约翰·弗朗茨·恩克
尔士德	Hans Christian Ørsted，1777—1851	汉斯·奥斯特
法拉抬	Michael Faraday，1791—1867	迈克尔·法拉第
肥乙大	François Viète，1540—1603	弗朗索瓦·韦达
腓乙	Hervé Faye，1814—1902	埃尔韦·法叶
风气车	vacuum pump	真空泵
佛兰格林	Benjamin Franklin，1706—1790	本杰明·富兰克林
弗伦好弗	Joseph von Fraunhofer，1787—1826	约瑟夫·夫琅和费
附土星	Hyperion	土卫七
歌白泥	Nicolaus Copernicus，1473—1543	尼古拉·哥白尼
革来	Stephen Gray，1666—1736	斯蒂芬·格雷
格来汉	Andrew Graham，1815—1908	安德鲁·格雷厄姆

续表

王韬译名	可能对应的外文词语	今译
格来罗	Alexis Claude Clairaut,1713—1765	亚历克西斯·克劳德·克莱罗
格勒哥里	James Gregory,1638—1675	詹姆斯·格雷戈里
葛西尼	Giovanni Domenico Cassini,1625—1712	乔凡尼·多美尼科·卡西尼
谷女	Ceres	谷神星
国里该	Otto von Guericke,1602—1686	奥托·冯·格里克
哈尔定	Karl Ludwig Harding,1765—1834	卡尔·路德维希·哈丁
海更士	Christiaan Huygens,1629—1695	克里斯蒂安·惠更斯
海其阿	Hygeia	健神星
海特里	John Hadley,1682—1744	约翰·哈德利
寒暑表	Thermometer	温度计
好里	Edmond Halley,1656—1742	爱德蒙·哈雷
好洛斯	Jeremiah Horrocks,1618—1641	杰雷米亚·霍罗克斯
和其孙	Norman Robert Pogson,1829—1891	诺曼·罗伯特·普森
亨该	Karl Ludwig Hencke,1793—1866	卡尔·路德维希·亨克
虹神	Iris	虹神星
侯失勒	William Herschel,1738—1822	威廉·赫歇尔
琥珀气	Electricity	电
花神	Flora	芙罗拉
火女	Vesta	灶神星
纪限镜仪	reflecting octant	双反射八分仪
加离略	Galileo Galilei,1564—1642	伽利略
加略必	Kalliope	司赋星
佳但	Girolamo Cardano,1501—1576	吉罗拉莫·卡尔达诺
佳生地	Pierre Gassendi,1592—1655	皮埃尔·伽桑狄
刻白尔	Johannes Kepler,1571—1630	约翰内斯·开普勒

续表

王韬译名	可能对应的外文词语	今译
拉白拉瑟	Pierre-Simon Laplace，1749—1827	皮埃尔-西蒙·拉普拉斯
拉格浪	Joseph Louis Lagrange，1736—1813	约瑟夫·拉格朗日
拉那	Francesco Lana de Terzi，1631—1687	弗朗西斯科·拉纳·德·泰尔
拉斯拉	William Lassell，1799—1880	威廉·拉塞尔
力佛理亚	Urbain Le Verrier，1811—1877	奥本·勒维耶
猎师	Metis	颖神星
罗斯伯	Lord William Parsons Rosse，1800—1867	罗斯伯爵威廉·帕森思
茅鹿理哥	Francesco Maurolico，1494—1575	弗朗西斯科·马若利科
弥低斯	Metis	颖神星
那比尔	John Napier，1550—1617	约翰·纳皮尔
奈端	Isaac Newton，1642—1727	艾萨克·牛顿
欧楼	Leonhard Euler，1707—1783	莱昂哈德·欧拉
奇白德	William Gilbert，1540—1605	威廉·吉尔伯特
清蒙气差	atmospheric refraction	大气折射
师纳拉	Willebrord Snellius，1580—1626	威理博·斯涅尔
史德文	Simon Stevin，1548—1620	西蒙·斯蒂文
特迦斯巴利	Annibale de Gasparis，1819—1892	安尼巴莱·德·加斯帕里斯
天后	Juno	婚神星
乞理师	John Wallis，1616—1703	约翰·沃利斯
维多利亚	Victoria	凯神星
武女	Pallas	智神星
欣特	John Russell Hind，1823—1895	约翰·罗素·欣德
亚必亚齐	Giuseppe Piazzi，1746—1826	朱塞普·皮亚齐
严女	Astraea	义神星

续表

王韬译名	可能对应的外文词语	今译
以来奈	Irene	司宁星
英爱理	George Airy,1801—1892	乔治·艾里
於咏士	Uranus	天王星
约翰	John Herschel,1792—1871	约翰·赫歇尔
约翰孙	Manuel John Johnson,1805—1859	曼努埃尔·约翰·约翰逊
稚女	Hebe	韶神星

西學原始攷

伊立勳觀尚

光緒庚寅　春季遜叟　手校印行

綱凡象緯麻數格致機器有測得新理或能出精意創造一
物者必追紀其始旣成一卷分附於中西通書之後今俱散
佚無從搜寬因於鉛槧之暇復爲編輯篇帙逾多爰授之剞
剛氏非敢問世也亦欲世之考求西學者知其濫觴之所自
爾然掛漏之譏知所不免他日容有續增未可知也光緒庚
寅閏花朝天南遯叟王韜自識於滬上淞隱廬時年六十有
三

西學原始考終

門人興國蔡嘉穀寶臣校字

西學原始考

長洲　王韜　紫詮輯撰

西國紀元前二千四百餘年希臘國有格致士曰大利司摩擦
琥珀能吸引輕物謂琥珀中有氣一經摩擦卽外發擦後其
氣仍收於體內輕物近之卽隨氣趨附其面故當時名爲琥珀
氣後經考察始知爲電氣此爲電學之肇端
二千二百餘年當帝舉三十一年甯綠王於百辣河畔始建巴
比倫城獨據四大城而立國始爲民之首領西古史謂甯綠英
武蓋世係挪亞次子舍之後裔洪水之後挪亞有三子曰四曰
含日雅弗在小亞細亞分王其地爲西洋諸國之祖按此爲西
土築城之始
二千一百四十七年當中國帝摯八年巴比倫始造文字始創
天文占驗法前一年埃及始造石塔按今泰西列國所傳巴比

《西学原始考》光绪庚寅春季遜叟手校印行版

三

华英通商事略[①]
（1857 年）

伟烈亚力　口译

王韬　笔受

王韬按语(1889)：

　　西士伟烈亚力口译，长洲王韬笔受。此即所谓东方贸易公司也。英之强，专恃商务，开疆拓土，以商人为先路指导。由五印度而达东南洋诸岛，以及通商粤东，皆商人为之主持。逮公司停而领事立，其势益横。道光十三年，英国公会始准诸商至中华贸易，不数年而蚌起。读《通商事略》一书，益叹当轴之昧于外情，而失驾驭远人之道焉。

　　韬按通商之局，至今日而一变，英与中国关系尤重。西人不患中国之练兵讲武以张国势，而特患中国之夺其利权，故致力于商务，在所必争。今日中国欲制西人而自强，亦莫如由商务始。欲商务之旺，莫如设立商务局始。[②]

---

① 点校自《六合丛谈》第 1 卷第 2、6、7、8、9、10 号（奥地利国家图书馆藏版）。其中，第 8 号名为"华英通商述略"，第 9、10 号以"畧"通"略"。该版与《西学辑存六种》（松隐庐活字版，1890 年）刊载有所不同，但其中多为王韬增改，故严格意义上讲，后者不完全属于译本范畴。

② 此按语为王韬晚年所加。参见王韬所著的《弢园著述总目》，载于《春秋朔闰至日考》（哈佛大学图书馆珍藏本），光绪己丑（1889）年七月。

编者按语：

《华英通商事略》叙述了不列颠东印度公司[The British East India Company（EIC），或 the Honourable East India Company（HEIC），East India Trading Company（EITC），the English East India Company 以及 the British East India Company 等]在华商业贸易发展史暨早期中英200年通商史，较为全面地记载了华英贸易中的若干大事件。文本的叙事起点，是1596年（明万历二十四年）英国女王伊丽莎白一世遣使访华。叙事止笔于1834年（清道光十四年）；是年，东印度公司在华垄断贸易结束。

全文读来，简略得当，言简意赅，比较全面，但到结尾处，又明显有戛然而止，意犹未尽之意。但如果我们明白伟烈亚力所译《华英通商事略》事实上是一部类似于马士日后所著五卷本《东印度公司对华贸易编年史（1635—1834年）》(*The Chronicles of the East India Company*，*Trading to China 1635—1834*)的一篇东印度公司在华贸易编年简史文章，而非一部完整意义上的中英通商通史作品的话，就会明白伟氏缘何止笔于1834，而不是1857年，即其完成本文的当年——这期间有着太多中英通商史上的大事件有待于叙述，比如律劳卑事件（The Napier Affair）、义律（Charles Elliot，1801—1875）单方面宣布《穿鼻草约》成立、两次鸦片战争中《南京条约》的谈判与订立和"亚罗"号事件的发生，等等。为方便读者阅读，现将本文所涉及若干重要事件罗列于此。

1596年，伍德使团访华。

1637年，威德尔船队抵达澳门；明英军事冲突或称明英战争（未提及1634年葡萄牙驻果阿总督邀请东印度公司来华贸易）。

1664年，英国东印度公司同澳门通商。

1668年，英国东印度公司同福州通商。

1670年，英国东印度公司同台湾通商。

1681年，英国东印度公司终止同台湾、厦门通商。

1683年，清收复台湾。

1685年，英国东印度公司恢复同厦门通商。同年，葡萄牙阻挠英国在广州通商。

1689 年,华英冲突之狄番斯事件。

1727 年,华英税则协商税负征收问题。

1728 年,清提高出口关税税率。

1734 年,因营商环境问题,当年只有"哈里森"号商船抵粤。同年,Grafton 驶往厦门后返粤。

1736 年,英国"诺曼顿"号商船开往宁波。

1741 年,英国人乔治·安森驾驶第一艘战舰"孙吐晓"号抵澳门。

1744 年,西班牙同英国交恶,在粤诋毁英国商人声誉。

1747 年,洪任辉任翻译。

1754 年,华英协商难事五端。同年,英法水手在粤械斗,英人希冀中国官员按照属地管辖原则,处理该案。

1755 年,英人哈哩逊和英国人洪任辉达到宁波。

1759 年,洪任辉事件。

1765 年,英国战船"阿尔戈"号和"库达洛尔"号抵粤。

1772 年,华英交涉事件。

1773 年,澳门华民遇害。

1780 年,华官处死犯事法国人。

1781 年,涉及域外管辖的重要案件抹拉利事件。

1782 年,英商请求英国驻印总督以武力威胁处理华英借贷纠纷。

1784 年,"休斯夫人"号事件。

1792—1793 年,马戛尔尼使华。

1795 年,乔治三世致书清帝。

1800 年,天佑号事件。

1802 年,英国驻印度总督以防止法国占领澳门为借口,派军舰抵达澳门。

1805 年,贡与非贡之争。

1807 年,"海王星"号事件。

1808 年,英国占领澳门事件。

1813 年,英国东印度公司广州特选委员会主席剌佛抵粤。

1814 年,美国商船被英国战舰俘获;阿耀事件等。英商罢市,小斯当东广州谈判。

1816 年,阿美士德使团访华。

1820 年,陀巴士事件。

1822 年,广州商馆大火。

1828 年,行商债务问题。

1829 年,议添设洋行,酌改船税。

1830 年,东印度公司与当局关系紧张。

1834 年,东印度公司在华垄断贸易终止。

除以上大事件外,本文亦不乏中英、中葡、英印、英法、英葡关系的重要论述,点出贸易之于国家利益的重要价值和国家利益对于国际关系的决定性作用。

明万历丙申(1596),吾英人始慨然有观光上国(指中国)之心。女主(即英国女王)以利沙伯(Elizabeth I,1558—1603,今译伊丽莎白一世)遣乌特(Benjamin Wood),统三艘,具书币,修好明帝,以通商舶。中途舟坏,事遂寝。①

崇祯丁丑(1637),舟长威忒(John Weddell,1583—1642,今译威德尔船长)率货舶五,航海西来,抵苏门答腊之亚珍(Atjeh,Acheh 或 Achin,今译亚齐)。三荷兰人居其地已稔,隐诮之于民,乃去之。澳门葡萄牙人据

---

① 1736 年至 1766 年在伦敦陆续出版的《天下史》(*Universal History*)第 10 卷,第 17 节和第 18 节的注释 H 中对于这次航行有简短记录,这支舰队的三只船的名字分别是"熊"号(the Bear)、"熊仔"号(the Bear's Whelp)和"本杰明"号(Benjamin),由船长伍德(Captain Wood)率领。该舰队由伊丽莎白一世女王的亲信罗伯特·达德利爵士(Sir Robert Dudley,1547—1649)提供装备。

此岛为己利,不利英人之至,与岛民群来姗笑。英人欲逾遣使求通于官,葡辄沮之,遂长驱抵虎门,得数华民,稍辨华言。既泊,守土官诣舟。舟长白其意,言欲通商缔和,置食物,与葡人等。守土官弗敢专,言将告大宪,六日而后覆命。英舟张白帜以待。

六日间,事忽变。葡人散流言,言英之诈,久必为害。华官惧,连夜戒严,环设大炮。英人登岸取水,即行轰击。舟长怒,拨白帜,立皂旆,扬帆乘潮,径逼炮台。华兵开炮数次,铅丸未及于舟,英舟亦燃炮相向。纵击二时许,华兵疲,乃登陆而战,炮台之卒尽遁。遂据之,立帜运炮,焚衙署,截商船二,更得小舟一。寓书以告大宪,言:事非得已,因胥吏欺诈之故。此来非寻衅,惟欲通商,与他国等。

投书之明日,小吏前诣英舟,舟长告之,一如书中所言。以礼物馈大宪,华官受所贶(kuàng,表馈赠之意)。夜逆英人至省,曰:开炮击舟,衅非我启,实系葡人进谗。今请返我炮,听尔鬻货。越数年,并无他舟继至。中国又乱甚,海中多盗。

康熙甲辰(1664),贸易公局(指东印度公司)始筹通商,赁屋澳门,将与华官立约:进口之舟,议纳船钞,每舟二千金。英以千金请,弗许。后华官以兵环其居,艰于出入。英人难之,往万丹(Banten,位于爪哇岛西部)。盖葡人为之梗也。

戊申(1668),荷兰国与英通好。英之公使驻扎葡都,与葡人议:凡英船至天竺之哥亚(Goa,即印度之果阿)、中土之澳门者,葡人当为捍护,毋阻毋逸。其时,万丹已立公局,寄书至英,白(即说明)公局长言福州可往,其地产生熟丝(指生蚕丝和熟丝)、白铅、黄金、土茯苓、茶叶等物,吾国以大尼、铅、琥珀、椒、珊瑚、檀香、红木、香料、桂皮、木香等物易之。

庚戌(1670),英始通台湾。台王郑成功于康熙元年(1662)逐荷兰,而恐其复仇,故喜英人之至。与英约曰:英公局至台售货,悉听其便。台民害英人者,王为平反;英人害台民者,宜告英公局长,为之剖断。英人觐王,不拘以时,有事则见。译写之员,自行遴选。毋许兵士环卫所居。出游无常所,不必台民为伴。王置货,关不取税,进口之米亦然。售物加税百分之三,出口之货无税。英船入口,火炮、兵械,尽交之官,回则给还。所议如此,然英无利可取。

辛酉(1681),公局止厦门、台湾之贸易。

癸亥(1683),台湾为大清所得,入版图,诏台民剃发易服。溯自有明末季,宽大无猜,英船入口较易。迨乎大清肇造之年,宁波、厦门帆樯(船帆与桅樯,意指英国商船)未至。

乙丑(1685),英船迭敕①抵厦门通商,而公局又欲在粤行贾,舟行靡定。葡人于中百计愚弄,日与华官訾论其短。

己巳(1689),英船狄番斯(Defence)至粤。河舶司度其船身,索钞殊奢。争辨(辩)时,英舟人击毙一华民。顷之华民逢至来敺(驱),伤毙数舟子、一医士。华官责银五千两赎罪。请以二千两,弗许,船主竟起锚而去。按今定例,凡英船至黄埔者,载货八百吨,税银约四千两。

自康熙末,迄雍正丁未(1727),英船在粤屡为官吏酷待,苛索万端。是年,英商欲减浮收(指额外征收)。旧例凡出货,于百中取十六,今裁。欲至英船售食物,必纳贿于官,今废。凡舟出入海口,输银一千九百五十两入官,曰礼物。在纳税外,今概停止。前粤抚专派一人,售西人货物。事多,一人难独任,数商汇立一行,建议以为货之贵贱,惟彼得定其价。舟长心弗善也,请于粤督。罢其议。英人谓纳税綦(文言副词,极)重,不少

---

① 原为"勅"。

减,将离粤他往。河舶司阳许,以羁縻之。

雍正戊申(1728),华官于出口之物加税什一。英人议其不公,置若罔听。盖华官云:印度商船,载物料夥,输关税多;而英船所携,不过器皿、尼布,物料少,输税寡,故增出货之税,以补其细。

甲寅(1734),税益增,浮收愈重,商人弗堪。是年,仅一舟至粤,曰哈利逊(Harrison)。此外,曰格辣顿(Grafton),驶往厦门,与华官商秉公贸易之法,而闽之官吏议察严厉,于定税外,复有所益。其请卒不果行,是以居数月即返粤。

乾隆丙辰(1736),挐蛮噸(Normanton,今译"诺曼顿"号)舟往宁波。宁之官吏,辄以威恫喝,凡英船进口,必交器械于官,否则勿许入港。挐蛮噸在宁二月,而抵粤时值乾隆御极(指即位),除所加什一之税,蠲免礼物,惟船钞不在免例。然朝廷虽免之,而官吏仍收之。继开读免税之诏,粤商偏告西人,必叩首谢恩,拜跪如礼。西人自思于其君,尚不屈膝,况他邦之主,遂固辞之。是役也。西舟在粤凡十:英四、法二、荷兰二、嗹国(Danmark,即丹麦)一、瑞颠(Sweden,即瑞典)一。

辛酉(1741),英师船(今舰船)孙吐喨(*Centurion* under the command of George Anson,指英国海军航海史上著名的乔治·安森环球航行历史大事件,今译"百夫长"号),环地球而行,抵澳门,是为英师船至华之始。既至,缮修罅漏而去。于海遇敌国吕宋(Spain,今西班牙;小吕宋常指菲律宾马尼拉一带)之船阿克波哥(Acapulco galleon,西班牙大型帆船),截而取之,舟载宝甚多。复返粤购食物,偕武弁安逊(George Anson,今译乔治·安森)俱至,居英人唐孙屋。时唐孙不在粤,粤商不许之居,曰:彼不在,我必环保,尔既虏舟舶,则吕宋必至粤讦告,官将治我罪矣。安逊曰:不购食物,我必不行,我舟无五日之粮尔。乃为之请于官。

不许。惧其久留,遂私遣人售之。

甲子(1744),吕宋以失船故,修怨于英。建战舰三,横截中流,阻英舶往来。公局船哈特威(Hardwicke),将抵海滨,有小艇持书,告以是事,遂往厦门。华官谕[先]将火器交纳,后议通商。英人见其地,无货可售,泊舟半月而行。时粤之贸易不广,官吏勒索,更甚于前。粤商又狡甚,其谓英人则曰:此官饬谕,制抚定议也。谓华官则曰:西人悍而无礼,愚而多诈。盖彼阻塞华西相见之路,播弄(指挑拨玩弄)其中,自肥其身,欲于是时流通货殖,亦甚难矣。然势值万难,杰士出焉。

英人咈林德(James Flint,约1720—?,即1759年洪任辉事件的主角洪任辉)始效华言,能与华人游。丁卯(1747),咈林德理翻译事。甲戌(1754),以难事五端,请华官裁止:一、英船到粤,停泊日久,货物不能出舱。二、港中多藏宵小,恒窃什物,官不置问。三、每岁华官授意商民,遍张揭帖,讪骂西人。四、海关胥吏,诛求无厌(指勒索诈取没完没了),佯增税额,以供食饕。五、中外隔绝,不能谒见;言语无由自达,书往未省(指未曾)。

是年(1754),英船多泊于外,环俟命下,而请卒不行。盖由英法微有不睦,议非佥同(指商议达不成一致意见),事遂中止。自后黄埔中,英法水手械斗之事起矣。英之舟子(指船夫),一杀一虏。时华官同胥役验伤,令法释英人,法从之。言交哄时,英实先欧[殴],第(表但是)法杀英人,非由猝怒击毙,按律当死。英人心各怀忿,籲(指呼吁)华官代为析冤。华官谕法将罪人絷献,否则毋许在粤。无何(即不久),华吏执一人至城,自言为杀人者,乃寘(置)之狱。明年大赦,遂出之。而虑黄浦中或有争斗激变之虞,乃与英人以大尼(Danes)岛;又以一岛与法人,曰佛兰西冈,恣其游览,令释前憾。

　　乙亥(1755)，英人哈哩逊(Samuel Harrison,1802—1867)偕咈林德至宁(指宁波)，知税轻于粤。浙抚(指周人骥)亦许其来，继而英船荷特奈斯(Holderness)至宁。闽督(指喀尔吉善)谕将兵械交官，循粤定例纳税。浙抚意不欲行，而不能重违闽督之命，故言将驰告京师，往返需时，谕以火炮半交于官，与船钞外更加税银、浮收诸项，皆倍于粤，舟人不得居岸。华官之意谓丝、茶等物，从陆运往粤东关，征其税；今在宁贸易，节去此税，故英在宁通商，非国之利。于是，西人货价骤增。是船离宁时，禁勿再往。抵澳门，华官即以帝诏之曰：西人惟准在粤通商，此外勿许。

　　己卯(1759)，浙抚毁英旅廨，远徙通英之华商。设师船，禁英舶往舟山售食物。咈林德重往宁波，粤官禁之。不从。遣之返英，亦不从。竟诣宁无人为介，径之天津。上知之，简大臣偕咈林德由陆路至粤。咈居城十日，而回英公局。西人闻大臣至，群来谒见。大臣定河舶司罪，免浮收。货税取百之六，礼物一千九百五十两，永为定例。未几，粤督召咈林德、公局长老偕往。见时，左右强之跪，不屈。粤督宣读帝诏，命咈林德先返澳门，后归英国。初上不许英人至宁，咈林德重违帝诏，以是得罪。又言为西人书启者(指起草书信等)例当斩，谬指一人，置之法，并暴(即曝)河舶司贪婪之罪。是日，幽咈[林德]于城，继迁于香山(指广东香山县)置狱。越数日，法、嗹、瑞颠、荷兰同集英国公局，致书粤督，责其不能柔远。咈林德在狱三年，释于黄埔，登英舟好孙嗬(Horsenden)而返国。

　　乙酉(1765)，师船挨哥(Argo)偕小舟克大啰(Cuddalore)至粤。小舟载公局银五十万，师船翼护之。华吏以船有眷属，例当查覈(指查核)。英人不从。华吏云：但容至舟两巡即已。英人答以运银之后，惟命是听。华官闭糴(指禁止买入)，乃于运银时，一任华官往巡，继欲量度师船。舟主亚弗勒(Philip Affleck,1726—1799)曰：壬戌(1742)，孙吐嚘舟(即上述"百夫长"号)来，粤官欲测度，舟主安逊(即上述乔治·安森)不之许。兹我请援斯例，华官乃谕罢海市。公局愿照最巨船只输税之例为请，不许。

英人计无所出,遂听量度。

壬辰(1772),西人与华民斗,伤之甚,乃弗许英船庚吨出口。受伤者多迁于公局。华吏前来诘问,谕必献伤人之首犯,乃可启行。后被伤者痊,遂无事。癸巳(1773),澳门华民遇害猝死,伪言为英人肆各(Francis Scott)所杀,执之控于葡人公署,欲定罪而苦无证。华官云:如不献之出,必毁澳门一邑。葡官难之,集长老议其事。一曰:如其人无罪而献彼,使之受戮,必无是理。第聚论盈廷,言此者惟一人而已。一长老曰:凡暴君欲诛无辜,不与则民受害,舍一人以救众,似亦可为。更一人曰:华官若阻塞通商,我将饥而死,与以英人,所以保全我也。乃与之,华官即杀之。

庚子(1780)冬,英船色锡斯(Ceres)抵澳门,其舟于有系法人者,欧[殴]毙葡人,遁于法之领事署。匿之数日,送于华官,未询曲直,即缢之死。辛丑(1781),印度船从孟加腊(Bengal,即孟加拉)至,遇吕宋舟自澳门来,获之(被俘获的是吕宋舟,即西班牙船Spanish vessel)。舟主抹拉利[McClary,是印度船"达达罗依"号(Dadoloy)的英国籍船长]令舟吏挽之入口。(被俘船主诉称该船并非西班牙船,而是葡萄牙船,于是将案件)先诉于葡之大吏。大吏置抹[拉利]于狱,谕释吕宋舟。使命方至,风起练断,舟半沉于水。抹拉利在狱,有司(指官吏)待之酷。后以银七万圆,偿船价以赎罪,而后获免。越数月,抹拉利泊舟黄埔,与荷兰船首尾衔接。闻英与荷有隙,遂执其舟(指抹拉利又俘获了一艘荷兰船"好望角"号Goede Hoop)。粤官谕释之,对曰:是非贵国事也,请毋相彼。关税无缺,否将率之出口矣。弗听且索之急,抹[拉利]遂挂帆而去,驶近虎岛(Boca Tigris,即虎门岛)。华人鼓噪而前,先以厉词恫喝,后以甘言慰藉,抹[拉利]皆不可。卒之,粤商与抹[拉利]约,令许华兵登舟,作凯歌然后旋。

初西商贷银于华人,以权子母(以资本经营或借贷生息为"权子母")。递至壬寅(1782),累积日多,约计百余万,屡索不获。西商中有贾于印度者,禀驻扎印度之总督,求遣水师提督浮嫩(Rear-Admiral Sir Edward Vernon)助之,以索此银。遂遣师船至粤,呈书粤督,诉以贷银之事,令扩清积弊。粤督疏奏京师,诏令尽偿,毋许再贷。

甲辰(1784)岁杪(指岁末),英船莱提休斯(Lady Hughes,今译"休斯夫人"号)泊于粤,举炮贺岁,误伤旁舟三人。明日,其一人伤重而殒。举炮吏闻之,惧而遁。华官索人于公局长皮哥(Frederick Pigou,1711—1792,今译东印度公司大班庇古)。对以可在公局,同定其罪。越二日,华之委员,偕粤商再至,索如前。公局曰:是船属于邻邦,非由公局统辖,不能强为折狱。如肯辱临公局,查核是事,岂敢不固请于货长四美(George Smith,"休斯夫人"号大班或贸易代表,今译乔治·史密斯)。俾遣其人,前来质讯,华官不允所请,惟令四美泊舟待此。夜间委员至,以诳辞谓公局曰:此案将诣尔所同鞫(指审问)。乃诱四美入城,后街道列栅禁往来。西商闻之咸集,思华官之待西人也虐,遽以小艇载兵械,游奕[弋]自卫,而遍愬各船。华官谕之曰:尔毋畏;事白,即释若货长。遣兵阻截小艇,小艇遵军令,不反[返]一炮,乃陈师于西人旅廨前,致书云:如尔船开炮,即翦灭尔众,无噍类(指不留活口)。既夕,召西人入见,乃咸至署。旋遣通事至公局,持四美书达船主,令遣举炮者来。越日驰书至城黄埔,举炮之吏至。年已老,公局与众商咸白其无罪。遣之诣城,华官犹以善辞遣使者。顷四美归公局,言华官待之如礼。后九日,华官谕缢举炮之吏。此英受诳之最甚者。

是时,英之大臣议于华贸易,当渐拓规模,特遣使臣马甘尼(George Macartney,1737—1860,今译马戛尔尼)恭诣京师。时在乾隆壬子年(1792)也。初戊申(1788),武臣克迦(Charles Cathcart,1759—1788,今译加茨喀特或卡斯卡特)率船佛斯泰(Vestal)奉命觐帝,抵噶罗巴(Kelapa,即今印尼雅加达),卒于舟。王命未达于皇都,使船即返于故国。至是马甘尼继之。为马之辅者曰斯当东(副使本是 Sir George Leonard

Staunton,但这里所言为使团见习侍童、斯当东之子小斯当东 Sir George Thomas Staunton),熟谙华事,明练通达,深究华言,稽考书籍文学,暨政体、律例、禁令、兵刑诸大务。(咸丰丁巳六月朔日　以上第 7 号)

马(指马戛尔尼)至京邸,所求各款,首在求通商于宁波、舟山、天津等处。朝议寝其事。惟覆书于英主曰:除广东、澳门地方,仍准照旧交易。外所有尔使臣,恳请向浙江、宁波、舟山及直隶天津地方,泊船贸易之处,皆不可行。又云:定当立时驱逐出洋,未免尔国夷商,枉劳往返,勿谓言之不预也。然偕马往之公局船印度斯单(Hindustan),许一次,带往舟山贸易,免关税,异数也。舟山官民遇之善,丝、茶贱于他处。第商贫货少,售物则缺,消货则滞。丝茶之商,惟索银,不欲易货,废然而返。

乾隆乙卯年(1795),英主以书币(指修好通聘问的书札、礼单和礼品),由本国达于清帝。英之大臣及公局首,亦以书币寄粤督。粤督为转达京师,以清帝所答书币回,而粤督之书币不受。云:中国臣子无外交也。中国礼官书云入贡。暨后嘉庆乙丑(1805)年事,亦云入贡。近粤有司移文云:英向例入贡。公使答云:旧惟书币往来,未尝有贡也。盖英于他国,从未进贡。后数年,粤相安无事。有司待西商稍善,一切费累之重,尚有未减。以土商之贪利无厌也,中有公所钱最重。有司勒索于土商,土商取盈于客船,又有进出口钱数项。

嘉庆庚申(1800),英之樸维顿斯(Providence,今译"天佑"号)师船,泊于黄埔。夜有疑来割船缆者,问之不应,放枪击之。一中伤,一惊堕于水。华官欲罪其人。师船麻打拉萨(Madras),武员逊勒格斯(John Dilkes)请于华官,欲执割缆之人,而定施枪者之罪于本船上。后被伤者痊,议乃止。

壬戌(1802),英之印度总督挖勒斯力(Richard Wellesley,1760—1842)疑法人欲取葡属。英素与葡和,于是遣孟加拉兵来戍澳门。葡人许诺。粤督惧,谕去之。适英之特立克拉船至澳,报知欧洲法、葡已和,兵乃撤回。无何葡人献谗于有司,言英将不利于中国。有神父者,法人能效华言,英用之以通事,葡人忌而逐之。自此货艇之先至澳门者,尽移伶仃,繁盛之区变为萧条之域矣。后在华之南海,群盗出焉。海中小岛重叠,多为渔人所居。其人赤贫无业,膂力(指力气)刚猛,恒聚为盗。华官不能制,商旅苦之。盗擒英人二,一忒乃尔,一格拉斯婆,强之为盗,后其友醵金赎之。二人在盗中久,言其事甚详。盗藐视华之师船,惟见欧罗巴商舶,则不敢动。嘉庆庚午(1810),盗船大小共六百艘。大者载炮十二门,或售自西船,或掳于华舶。大船可载百人至二百人,时遣其小艇至镇市劫掳。盗目死,其妻代统厥众。群盗多遵其令,盗律甚严,违者斩;得物均分之,嫁娶以正;犯奸者,有严刑。商船来投诚者,给票以便往来。惟师船被掳者虐待之。盗势猖獗,时濒海之城乡、市镇,皆许纳税,蔓延几至粤东。公局船从粤至澳,每以师船翼护。缘是二师船,从孟买(Bombay)来防盗,在海中无事。日周行,测海深浅。俾后来航海者,不遇危险,其功非细。于时盗当自斗,一立皂旂,一树红帜,互相攻击。皂旂者败,势蹙就抚,朝廷即优加爵赏。渠魁之妻,既失大援,势遂微弱。华官遣降盗入海,捣其巢穴。每战辄捷,悉残旃。是时虽通商已久,而华英之民,尚未能耦居无猜。西人登岸沽饮者,肆主必置毒酒中,令其昏眩。

嘉庆丁卯(1807),英师船奈敦(Neptune,今译"海王星"号)至粤。舟人登岸沽酒既醉,与华之游民斗。乃于公局暂避,匿空室中。无赖之徒踵至,以石击门。见西人过,飞石如雨。粤商出劝,弗听。舟中水手忽怒吼,夺门而出。华民辟易(指退避),一人伤重而毙。华官令闭市,谕保此船之土商。着此船交出凶手,迄不获。又以前入城就讯之不公也,抗不赴质。故华官后又至公局,与公局长及水师弁罗勒思(Robert Rolles)同鞫。鞫时,见十一人特悍于众,究未知凶手是谁。华官必欲指一人,以偿命,乃以一人名"伸"者,幽于公局。始思以金赎罪,既而公局长离粤时,欲携去。华官弗许。罗(指罗勒思)告公局曰:若不许,我将强致之。华官不得已,上爰书于朝,改为坠物误伤。吏议罚银十二两,宥其罪,释之。

戊辰(1808),英驻扎印度总督(Lord Minto,1751—1814),闻法欲取小吕宋海岛,恐澳门亦有失。英葡故有约,以英商之在粤也,宜预为计,遂遣兵戍之。葡人屡谮于华官,官谕速去,闭粜罢市。告英人曰:尔知葡人所居,此中国帝王之土也,法(指法国)安能举兵犯我海疆。若其果至,我兵勇自能驱除。提督致书粤督请见,不答。传曰:此间有事,惟公局长是问,他人可毋庸。于是提督图礼(William Brian Drury)抵粤城外,声言逾半时,不纳我,城将自启,亦不省。提督归船,恐伤华人。稍俟。越数日,发兵备械,再至粤。华官以师横截江面,提督驾小舟欲与之言。不许。燃炮伤英人一,英船不施一炮,遽退。是役也,图礼仁而不武,粤人轻之,后遂多事。英议罢戍兵,粤督旋以褫职去。

癸酉(1813),英故公局总司喇佛(John. W. Roberts)来粤,以前事故衔之。华官移檄公局,不许入境。时喇佛已卧病澳门,公局长移文有司。若不宽其禁,请绝通市。后又启于粤督,议宽之,而未答。喇佛死。公局复理前说,以事关两国局面,非喇佛一人。粤之有司,乃讲解。通市如故。

初使臣马甘尼至京,见大臣松筠(1752—1835)。松待之厚,后为粤督,以礼延纳远人,及登揆席。癸酉(1813),英人由国中,以书及金函入贺,松受之。使者以名刺返粤。粤之有司,罪以通番,执而戍之。俄而(指不久)松被黜,所受之金函,仍还于粤之公局内。松官卒不显。然其人,君子也。英人亦惜之。

甲戌(1814),英以独利师船(H. M. S. Doris),截合众国(指美国)商船(the Hunter),毋许近粤,获一船于万山海岛,拽入澳门。华官移文公局,令遣回师船,不可。既而师船又以小舟,袭合(指合众国,即美国)商之船。自澳门至黄埔获之。合船之在黄埔者,咸来夺取。自此华官深恶公局,毋许役使土人。有则执之。公局船行于内港,时有所扰,离间师船之

相应援。于是公局愤甚,将去之。华官见罢市,则遣人与公局使者斯当东议。斯当东至粤,条议数款:

一、不应坐前使人以通番之罪。华官对以他故,久之不决。粤督令罢议。公局令商船离粤。粤督悔之,复令土商招来。斯当东再诣粤。粤督又欲食言,再四共议,而英商所欲,即得矣。

二、立约定议:往来文书,始许用汉文字。

三、嗣后,毋许华官遣人擅至公局。

四、华人为英启[供]役使者听。

此外尚有数款。英国中闻之,嘉斯当东之能办其事也。然通商一事,华人上下相蒙,事例未尽归一致。时有变端。

丙子(1816),英主遣大臣亚默尔思(William Pitt Amherst,1773—1857,今译阿美士德),以国书贻清帝。陈明在粤情事,兼欲中外自此和好,商贾流通益广。(咸丰丁巳七月朔日　以上第8号)

嘉庆乙亥年(1815),亚默尔思(即英国使臣阿美士德)秉亚尔雪(Alceste)船,离英国,与赖拉(Lyra)小船,及公局船,夏间同抵澳门,遇士[斯]当东、壹末(Henry Ellis,1788—1855,今译埃利斯)、马礼逊(Robert Morrison,1872—1834)等人,遂与俱入京师。行半月余,至直隶泊舟十二日,行三日抵天津。清帝遣大臣来问,赐宴。有司设黄幔,令循例叩首。对言:昔马甘尼末尝行此礼也,余亦弗能行。案前马甘尼尝云:若中国臣子官爵等于我者,行叩首礼于吾王御像前,或中国使者,入吾国叩首于吾王座下,则我亦可行此礼也。兹故引为故事,然不特此也。粤中大府,不利英使者之入告,多方阻之,争叩首事,特其一端耳。此时,廷见之事,卒亦无成。

第十六日夜半,中国押伴使者,偕行抵都城东门,沿城而北,天黎明,乃抵圆明园。黑夜崎岖,车行颠簸,昏眩烦倦。至行在所,停车求宿。不可。有来请者云:往见和公。盖户部尚书和世泰也。突然引至一处,见诸王大臣,盛服将朝,方知被绐(指欺骗),已入阙廷矣。俄又有来告者云:期(指本来预定)以明日引见,奉旨改早一日。或来曰:和公立侍,引尔见上。英使者言:余来仓促,衣冠不具,国书未携,且道途况瘁,乞以缓日见。忽和尚书(指户部尚书和世泰)来云:朝廷立俟尔见。然在英使者,势终不能入见,因暂假馆憩息。俄又一大人来云:上震怒,命仍押回通州,即是日申刻折回。

当是时为粤督者,蒋攸铦(1766—1830)一切为难。层层布置,线索通神。此三船者,先行回粤。粤有司待之尤苛,以为此贡船也,不许上岸贸易。除公局船外,将大小二船,屏黄埔外,视暹罗(今泰国)贡船尤轻。英人驾亚尔雪船,直驶入内。军士砲台开砲御之,船上仅发一砲,而砲台之砲遽止。无何。船砲一面齐发,砲台军士奔散。粤有司乃权辞逊谢,许买食物。出示云:前之开砲,系是敬客之礼。英使者亚默尔思押由内地运河回粤。

在路四阅月,西历正月元日至粤。粤督已奉廷寄书币,致英之监国。设黄幔,粤督首顶御书,恭授于英使者。此一役也,虽未得见清帝,而中外通市,相安无事,较有异于前日矣。自丙子(1816)至己丑(1829),市不改肆,惟壬午(1822)有师船滋事一节。粤之有司,极意拊循(指安抚)。

庚辰(1820),公局船遣小舟上岸取水,华人以石击之。英水师弁见事,欲惊散其众,望空放枪,误伤隔河一童子。华官索抵命,公局长老言此在危急中,非故杀,不应抵罪。相持论间,忽公局船一屠者死,官乃伪验此人行凶结案。人言籍籍。此童子之父,亦不服。官缚其父,并旁人皆下狱。

是年(1820),陀巴士(HMS Topaze,今译"土巴资"号)师船抵伶仃岛左右,水手上岸取水,土人以兵械及长竹击之。师船上见事急,即遣兵上岸助之。见土人聚一小市上,乃向市施砲,阻其出,护水手回船。水手带伤回者十四人,土人死者二人,伤四人。船主致书粤督,求理此事。不答。告公局言:英人不抵命者停市。公局见华官枉法,即离粤上船开行。督复出示云:咎不在公局,但请回粤。惟师船上不送出人抵命者停市,公局亦不能从。文书往返逾月,迄无定议。洋行家以船主所云是否交出人犯,必禀明本国之说告粤督。不准。公局仍开船益远。洋行家使公局移文,言水手逸去,令华官以此水手当凶手。公局又不许。行家又使兵船,潜开出港数日,事当中止。公局言粤中局事及兵船,如不分别办理,永不来粤。而兵船主云:余瓜期将及而行,无容有潜逸名。既而有一华官至伶仃,上兵船,见有受伤之水手,意始释然,与船主及公局长往来拜谒,期满,兵船竟去。华官遂言:兵船事不关公局,可通市如故。公局船离粤,四十余日乃返。此初次粤有司知公局不预兵船之事也。

癸未(1823),粤中仍究此事。此船回英本国,讯明无罪。本国公局,寓书粤督,申辨(辩)其枉,不知达否。特事本末,已有成案。

(道光)壬午(1822)岁冬,夜民家失火,去西行三里许。火起风猛,虑延烧公局。飞书粤督,许水龙人役救火。明日,西行火(指十三行大火)。除一二处外,已全烧。公局之货存栈者,悉毁,惟银窖得无恙。华房连烧,无家可归者,计五万人,焚死无算。公局船遣人,轮班防堵,官役日夜巡逻。货物有搬运上小船者,华商以其室赁于公局。越七日,开市如故。后数年,粤中无事。特粤省洋行多诈,致生他虑。粤省旧有十一行家,其最小之二三行家已败。向来国家功令,一行逋欠,各行均赔,毋许亏负西商,卒格不行。粤商公所挟赀颇富,故西商甚委信于洋行,听其赊贷,而洋行之逋负愈多。

戊子(1828),有一行败,逋欠百万。有司定拟,边远充军,未至戍所而死。明年己丑(1829),又一行败,所亏约百万,其人携赀而归。因其人阀阅家(指有功勋的世家),故有司未置于法,因此令粤商公所循例赔银。盖自二行败,亏银綦多,西商甚不便之,乃于粤商公所约,刻期偿还。洋行以十年为请,每岁偿十之一。西商约以六年,计至癸巳(1833)而逋负清。然华官以公所赔狡商之银,于理不合,出示令停此例。事于商有益。以公所之银，本出于西国也。嗣后止有六行家，不胜公私诸事之繁，愿欲专利。惟公局议增，时行家多为官困，故愿充者少。

己丑(1829)，公局移文粤督，议添设洋行，酌改船税。黄埔纳公私税费，每一船小者已有三千余两。关吏尚贪利无厌，粤督惟许添立洋行，他不问。公局移文往返，泊舟以守回文。弗省。谓贸易从贵国之俗，法度宜守中国之礼。历四月议不决。公局求英之印度督，代申其情于中国帝都。印度督以非出自本国指挥，不许。越月，粤督移文，许添设一行，后将复增。前存行之银，概行归还。至税费一事，已入奏于朝，候旨定夺。公局船欣然，进泊黄埔。越月，增立三行。

会有瑞士国作时表(指怀表)者，薄阜与巴西人同居，出入共一后门。薄阜性躁，杜门(指闭门)拒繁。是夜一船主在内，闻后门有声，暗中取棒乱击，未知即巴西人也。巴西人聚而拒击，船主伤重死。公局移巴西人至孟买质讯，粤有司言此事宜归我地方官办理。当是时粤督出示，公局长有家眷在省者，不便居住。缘此二事，非理相干。英人乃以水手百名，炮二位，置公局内，防变。继而粤有司自明无相害之意，乃撤回水手及炮于船。火灾后，一切烬余，俱堆英行前河内，积成平陆。斥地稍广，辟为苑囿，花木蔚然。粤人见而恶之，令废去。不可。会英商离粤，辄来拆毁。

庚寅(1830)，公局诸长皆迁易，商船悉回澳门，粤督亦因公离省。粤抚至公局所，问行家及通事人等，何故擅成此围。俱答言不知。粤抚怒，即锁拿通事下狱。首行跪祈免究，河泊司代为叩求，乃命首行及通事，仍平此围为滩，否必重处不贷。出示颁行新例八条，例甚严刻。夏日不许西人留省，粤人之在行生理者，概行约束(指受束缚)。西人毋得远离行家。身无路照，不得往来河道。废前甲戌(1814)所定文移，用中国文字章程。以上诸事，行文各衙门，遵照办理。公局闻之，乃亦出告条云：若此条例必行，秋间必罢通市。明年夏，督回省，见抚院所定条例。是之，闻于朝。公局知奉有朝旨，无如何，寄书英印度总督商办。粤地方官见事招众怨，不甚奉行此例。

是年(1830)冬,师船从孟加拉至,以印督移文,达粤督。粤督回文,多不经语,公局不受。后英本国寄书公局,令勿论此事。壬午(1822),鸦片土船,自澳门进泊伶仃,售销甚利,以粤有司不行严禁也。有司官欺罔贪婪,不能杜弊除害,中国人屡次为鸦片船炮伤命。尸亲陈诉于官,官既与船商暧昧,无颜讯明。公局不预其事。有思贸易道广,何必专于一粤海口。于是,公局遣一印度船劳亚默尔思,以各货物与能华言者,俱泛海入厦门、福州、宁波、上海,绕道至高丽、琉球,往返六月有余。各处土人,相待颇善。惟货物不售,仅以奇巧玩物,与有司相酬酢而已。英本国公局闻之,不以为善,移书责之。

甲午(1834)春,英东方贸易公局,已届二百年期满,向例惟公局商船得至中国。今废之,令嗣后各商每船,自行行运。(咸丰丁巳九月朔日以上第10号)

附:《华英通商事略》译名对照表

王韬译名	可能对应的外文词语	今译
阿克波哥	Acapulco galleon	阿卡普尔科帆船
挨哥	Argo	"阿格"号
安逊	George Anson	乔治·安森
独利师船	H. M. S. Doris	"皇家多丽丝"号
大尼	Danes	丹麦人
狄番斯	Defence	"防卫"号
佛斯泰	Vestal	"维斯塔"号
哗林德	James Flint,约1720—?	洪任辉
浮嫩	Rear-Admiral Sir Edward Vernon	爱德华·弗农
噶罗巴	Kelapa	雅加达

续表

王韬译名	可能对应的外文词语	今译
哥亚	Goa	果阿
格辣顿	Grafton	格拉夫顿
哈哩逊	Samuel Harrison,1802—1867	塞缪尔·哈里森
哈利逊	Harrison	哈里森
哈特威	Hardwicke	哈德威克
好孙嗰	Horsenden	霍森顿
荷特奈斯	Holderness	霍得尼斯
虎岛	Boca Tigris	虎门
克大啰	Cuddalore	库大罗尔
克迦	Charles Cathcart,1759—1788	加茨喀特或卡斯卡特
喇佛	John. W. Roberts	约翰·罗伯茨
莱提休斯	LadyHughes	"休斯夫人"号
赖拉	Lyra	莱亚
嗹国	Danmark	丹麦
罗勒思	Robert Rolles	罗伯特·罗勒斯
麻打拉萨	Madras	马达亚斯
马甘尼	George Macartney,1737—1860	马戛尔尼
马礼逊	Robert Morrison,1872—1834	马礼逊
孟加腊	Bengal	孟加拉
抹拉利	McClary	麦克拉里
拏蛮嗰	Normanton	诺曼顿
皮哥	Frederick Pigou,1711—1792	庇古
樸维顿斯	Providence	"天佑"号
瑞颠	Sweden	瑞典
色锡斯	Ceres	塞雷斯

续表

王韬译名	可能对应的外文词语	今译
斯单	Hindustan	印度斯坦
斯当东	Sir George Leonard Staunton	斯当东
斯当东	Sir George Thomas Staunton	小斯当东
四美	George Smith	乔治·史密斯
肆各	Francis Scott	弗朗西斯·斯科特
孙吐哮	Centurion	"百夫长"号
逊勒格斯	John Dilkes	约翰·迪尔克斯
图礼	William Brian Drury	威廉·德雷
陀巴士	HMS Topaze	"土巴资"号
挖勒斯力	Richard Wellesley, 1760—1842	理查德·威列斯里
万丹	Banten	万丹
威忒	John Weddell, 1583—1642	约翰·威德尔
乌特	Benjamin Wood	本杰明·伍德
亚尔雪	Alceste	阿尔塞雷斯
亚弗勒	Philip Affleck, 1726—1799	菲利普·阿福列克
亚默尔思	William Pitt Amherst, 1773—1857	阿美士德
亚珍	Atjeh/Acheh/Achin	亚齐
壹未	Henry Ellis, 1788—1855	埃利斯
以利沙伯	Elizabeth I, 1558—1603	伊丽莎白一世

甫里逸民刊
於淞北寄廬

華英通商事略　茝齋署

述其生平游歷之蹤跡嘉詳歐洲人得悉中華之風景皆此數
人爲先路之導也近日西國航海之學日益精進汪洋巨浸中
幾於無遠不至由亞美利加洲直北及東北其水程皆可抵中
國其能探悉而貢獲者於道光二十五年則有弗蘭華林於光
緒七年則有瑞典人其好學殫思不憚艱險至於如此商務有
不蒸蒸日上哉是所當取法者已

華英通商事略終

門人興國蔡嘉穀寶臣手校

華英通商事略

英國　偉烈亞力口譯
長洲　王韜　仲弢著

英人與我中國通商自明萬歷丙申年始於時歐洲諸國覽土
東來各擇埠頭競講貿易其重視中朝若匈奴之仰漢如在天
上而英人亦慨然有觀光上國之心女主以利沙伯遣島特統
三艘具書幣愈好明帝以通商舶中途舟壞事遂寢然書難未
達而向往之情愈好崇禎丁丑舟長威武率貨舶五自西航
海而來抵蘇門答臘之亞珍三荷蘭人居其地已稔隱譏之於
民乃去之澳門葡萄牙人據此島爲己利不利英人之至與島
民羣來嫉笑英人欲遣使求通于官葡舟長阻之遂長驅抵虎門
得數華民稍耕華言既泊守土官詣舟長白其意言欲通商
緒和置食物與葡人等守土官弗敢專言將告大憲六日而後

《华英通商事略》甫里逸民刊于淞北寄庐版

四

西国天学源流①
（1957—1858 年）

伟烈亚力　口译

王韬　笔受

王韬按语(1889)：

　　西士伟烈亚力口译，长洲王韬笔受。天算之学，中国开其端，西国竟其绪。西国考第一次日食，在周平王五十一年，较中国畴人家测算幽王时日食，相距无几时，可知其学必先由东而西。逮后历法愈精，遂不能与西国争衡。读之可以讨源沂流，而知其学之由来古矣。②

编者按语：

　　《西国天学源流》与《格致新学提纲》中关于天文学的部分内容有相似之处，但前者更为详尽，系统地陈述了西方天文学的发达史及西方宇宙观的演进过程，内容讫于 1846 年发现海王星。

　　天算之学由来古矣。最奇特者，能导人离地球而至天空最远之处。

---

① 点校自《六合丛谈》第 1 卷第 5、9—13 号(奥地利国家图书馆藏版)，第 2 卷第 1—2 号(《官板六合叢談(第二卷删定本)(二)》，東京：老皀舘，刊年不详)。该两版与《西学辑存六种》(松隐庐活字版，1890 年)刊载基本一致。

② 此按语为王韬晚年所加。参见王韬所著的《弢园著述总目》，载于《春秋朔闰至日考》(哈佛大学图书馆珍藏本)，光绪己丑(1889)年七月。

考察世间万物之理,俱能使心量扩充;而考察地球以外诸事,扩充心量,能令大极至不可喻。凡测量行星之远近、大小、轻重,及彗星之道,窥定星无数而甚远,因此能渐知造物主大能全智,亦知人在天地间为一小物。以上诸事若已了然,便能知耳目闻见,未足为凭。故向谓地球不动,而不知实动。目见诸行星左旋,而实右旋。昔以地球为六合中甚大之物,今知为六合中一微尘。当上考载籍,而知天算之学,肇自古昔。

《旧约·约伯记》,为万国最古之书。屡言天星,则此时已知观天矣。又相传希腊王亚力山大(Alexander III of Macedon,365 BC—323 BC,今译亚历山大)破巴比伦(Babylon)时,其师亚利斯多(Aristotle,384 BC—322 BC,今译亚里士多德),受日食表于嘉腊提(Galatea,希腊神话中的海洋女神之一),表具载巴比伦一千九百零三年中所见之食。此说虽未有据,然非无因。多禄某(Claudius Ptolemaeus,英译 Ptolemy,约100—170,今译托勒密)书中载迦勒底(Chaldea)六次食,或即本于嘉腊提表也。第一次在周平王五十一年(720 BC),其时约当(指大概是)亚述(Assyria)王掳以色列族之岁也——见《旧约·列王纪》略下(原文小字解释)。近代好里(Edmond Halley,1656—1742,今译哈雷)因考古表,始觉月行变速,而拉白拉瑟(Pierre-Simon Laplace,1749—1827,今译拉普拉斯)证明其故。多禄某(即托勒密)言:迦勒底治天学者,多而精,盖彼地人已知六千五百八十五日三分日之一为一会,共二百二十三月。每会中诸食,次第与浅深恒同。又传彼地亦有十二宫,每日分十二时云。古时候天以拜星,今详考之,知上帝之道,久已衰息,古人已疑天星为主宰而拜之,流传至今。各国拜星者尚不少,如中国拜斗其一也。

古时又占天以判休咎。盖昔人见耀流辉射地,又见太阳高弧每日不同,而地面之四时应之。又见天有冬夏,而草木之荣枯应之。疑皆太阳所为。因疑太阳为神,地面之事必悉知之。故国事一听之占望,重之以祭祀,设官司其事,考星定其仪。《旧约·以赛亚书》云:迦勒底有人仰观天象,占察星辰。每值月朔,以卜未来,以定吉凶——四十七章十三节(原文小字解释)。是也。

天学之起,最古者,或云中华,或云埃及,或云自度,或云迦勒底,其说不一。然此诸国,在古昔实已考察日出入、中星、日月食、行星合日诸事,以授民时。印度历,在古时已立元。周伐纣之前一千九百九十一年,得日月如合璧,五星如连珠。然以今法上推,其年表多不合,而金星之差尤大,则此表乃后人上推之数,非当时实测也。中国日食,见于商书者为最古,而自幽王五年(777 BC)后,至今凡有食,皆载于史。又中国天分十二宫,其来已久,不知始于何时。

希腊天算学之起,约计当在春秋初年。时有二人,以时名世,曰海修达(Hesiod,约 8 BC—7BC,今译赫西俄德),曰和马(Homer,约 9 BC—8 BC,今译荷马)。其所著书,屡言天星。如海修达言:"昴星隐四十日而复见"。今上推尔时彼地之纬度,昴星近太阳时,合隐四十日也。又论农事,言:"昴星隐时当割麦,见时当耕田"。海修达生子于周孝王(约 950 BC—886 BC)时,以岁差上推,此时昴星见,当今立夏后二日。今希腊割麦,当春分后九日,中间四十,昴星近太阳不见,其说恰合。海修达又言:"昴星出暗海,海中行船危"。出暗海者,言日没时出地平也。考此时,昴星日没时出地平,在秋分后。今秋分后,希腊海洋有飓风,行船最险,其言亦合。和马书中,亦有数星名,如《阿陀塞亚》(书名)(*Odysseia / Odyssey*,今译《奥德赛》)中,述阿陀苏(Odysseus,今译奥德修斯)论昴壁紫参,及青龙七宿、北斗星诸星。太阳长行不息,月之望,诸恒星若冕旒,云云。又曾考论天狼(Sirius)。海修达亦曾考论大角(Arcturus)。然二人俱未言行星。古人恒言天狼星色红,今色白,不知何故。

以阿尼(Ionian,今译爱奥尼亚)部人,喜察天,为希腊天学之最。创始者曰他勒(即托勒密)。他勒,米利都(Miletus)人也。相传其童时,夜间观天,误落沟中。保母援其手出之,谓之曰:"他勒何为远察天,不近视地耶?"此时希腊人士多喜吟咏,善议论,讲求经济,习武艺或好谈性理(指哲学),无治天学者。独他勒与其徒,好谈天。凡天地之理,其所创①获者,多与今合。初希腊航海者,皆以北斗为北极。他勒始斥其疏②,而以极星为北极。又推得太阳平径,亦密合。始倡言地为球体。预推某年,日当食,至时果验。此前人所未有者。黑陆独都(Herodotus,约 480 BC—425/413 BC,今译希罗多德)史,言:米太(Media,今译米底亚)与吕氏亚(Lydia,今译吕底亚)战(今译米底—吕底亚战争),当昼时,忽昏黑如夜,遂罢战。盖他勒预推此年当日食也。近时天文家倍律(Francis Baily,1774—1844,今译弗朗西斯·贝利),上推周匡王三年(610 BC)秋分后七日,午前日食,月影中线,由小亚西亚(Asia Minor Peninsula,今译小亚细亚)东北,过亚美尼(Armenia)至波斯(Persia)。案:小亚西亚东北,当时二国战地也(原文按语)。

他勒(即托勒密)之前,希腊未知测天,此必本之他国历表,盖非久测,不能预知。或曾得迦勒底表,未可知也。自他勒后,学者有所心得,时与今理合。有亚那西慢突(Anaximander,610 BC—546 BC,今译阿那克西曼德)者,言地自传,又言月光借日而生。有亚那煞各剌(Anaxagoras of Clazomenae,500 BC—428 BC,今译阿那克萨哥拉)者,传他勒之学于雅典,言月面必有山谷、平原,与地面同。闭他卧剌(Pythagoras of Samos,570 BC—495 BC,今译毕达哥拉斯)合诸新理考论之,推阐益精,因知地球必绕太阳。后非禄老(Philolaus of Croton,470 BC—385 BC,今译菲洛劳斯)本其说,恒畅论于广座。闭他卧剌(即毕达哥拉斯)之门人,皆言五星、彗星,俱绕太阳,非飞行空中无定则焉。人多不信之,因与亚利斯多(即亚里士多德)之说异也。历一千八百余年,无信闭他氏(即毕达哥拉斯)之学者。是时诸游学士,群立一说,言地为心,诸星皆行平圆,以平速绕地球,彗星乃地气中所生。亚利斯多本其说。人以其与目见合,皆信之。或言亚利氏之师百拉多(Plato,427 BC—347 BC,今译柏拉图)晚年颇悔其说,

---

① 原为"朸"。
② 原为"疎"。

谓地球非最大,不当为天心,天心必别有大于地球者。然当是时,有信他勒及闭他氏之说者,有司辄收之。有亚那煞各刺(即上述阿那克萨哥拉)者,坐此当死,赖彼力格里(Pericles,495 BC—429 BC,今译伯里克利)救之而免。然犹流之希力斯奔(Strato of Lampsacus,今译兰普萨库斯的斯特拉图),终身不赦。非禄老坐言地球绕日,亦见逐。盖在上者,恐此说流传,因之人心好异,变乱旧章焉。

亚利斯多(即亚里士多德)既殁,而埃及天学,遂为西国冠。希腊王亚力山大于尼罗河口筑城,以己名名之,后为埃及都城。多禄某第一王(Ptolemy I Soter I,367 BC—282 BC,今译托勒密一世),于城中建大书库。时未有印本,库中书甲地球。后嗣王于库立格致学,聘国人聪俊者居之。付以测量精器,令互相讲求。学中诸教授,俱名播西国。其学分数科,中有究天察地之科,定恒星之位,测行星之道,考日月之迟速,用三角法,量弧角诸度。当是时,学中所定历法星度,冠于地球。由今论之,殆不及闭他氏之真确。然多实测而得,故后学能知其误,辄复改正。学中所创①,最善者,测地球距日,及地球大小云。亚里达古(Aristarchus of Samos,310 BC—230 BC,今译阿里斯塔克斯),撒摩(Samos)人也,立测地距日法。如图,申为日心,寅为月心,戊为地面测处。候月光恰半,日月俱在地上时,自戊作线至寅,与自申至寅之线成直角,乃测得戊角。以推戊申与戊寅之比例,即知日地相距,十九倍于月地相距。今人知其未密,所差尚多。然其立法之意,亦甚巧矣。所以未密者,因未能求月光恰半之真时刻,且测天之器亦未精也。近时测日地距,立法更精,非古人所能梦见也。亚里达古(即上述阿里斯塔克斯)从闭他氏(即今译毕达哥拉斯)说,谓地球绕日。有诘之者曰:如此恒星何以无视差。答曰:地绕日之轨,较恒星之距,如一微尘耳。

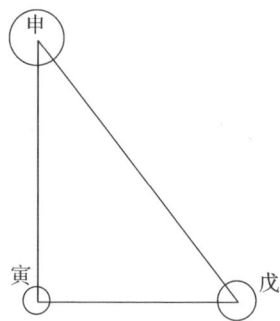

———————————

① 原为"刱"。

此言与今理合。是亚里氏(即上述阿里斯塔克斯)胸中之天,大于古人胸中,无量倍也。然史官不为立传,生卒无考,但知其考定冬夏二至。在周赧王三十五年(280 BC),所著书,传者惟日月大小远近说。康熙二十七年(1688),英国华力(John Wallis,1616—1703,今译约翰·沃利斯)校而重刻之,其日径三十分,较今差二分。

欧拉独提尼(Eratosthenes of Cyrene,276 BC—194 BC,今译埃拉托斯特尼),古利奈(Cyrene,今译昔兰尼)人也,生于周赧王五十七年(258 BC)。多禄某第三王(Ptolemy III Euergetes,约280—222,即托勒密三世),征为掌库。寿至八十,不乐居世,不食而死。欧拉独提尼(即上述埃拉托斯特尼)立测地球大小法。埃及西隐(Syene or Aswan,今译阿斯旺)城,夏至日过天顶,当午正,深井中水面光满,距井四周三百步,物无影。亚力山太(Alexandria,今译亚历山大,埃及地名),与此城同经线。当西隐午正时,于亚力山太测太阳距天顶度,即二城相距度——以二地相距度与二地相距里数比例得地球周里数(原文小字注释)。如图,戊为地心,亚为亚力山太,申为太阳,西为西隐城。测亚戊西角,为五十分周之一,即七度十二分,为亚力山太西隐二天顶相距。当时以地为正员[圆]球,故以二城相距里数,五十乘之,为地球周里数。有司命人度量二城相距,得五千步。推得地球之周,二十五万步。当时步率今无考,故不知其测量确否。其立法之意,与今理合。而法未精,既未知太阳地半径差,而西隐又非正当昼长圈下,差北五十分,与亚力山太亦非同经线,偏东三度。今测天较密,既知诸差,而所用之器,又远胜于古,故今推地球大小得数较确云。

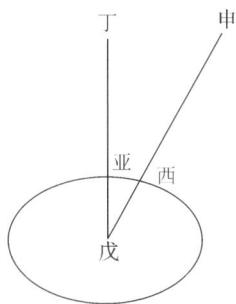

古天学家最著者,曰依巴谷(Hipparchus of Nicaea,190 BC—125 BC,今译喜帕恰斯,方位天文学之父)。今尚论之,真不愧天学先师焉。依巴谷,庇推尼(Bithynia,今译比提尼亚)之尼西(Nicaea)人也。其测天,多

在地中海罗底岛（Rhodes，今译罗得岛，爱琴海上的一个岛屿）。初用弧三
角法，或云即其所造，未可知也。时所用岁实为三百六十五日四分日之
一。依巴谷测夏至，与一百四十五年前撒摩人亚里达古（即上述阿里斯塔
克斯）旧测相较，始知微强，改定为三百六十五日五小时五十五分十二秒，
较拉白拉瑟（即上述拉普拉斯）所定真岁
实，大六分十三秒。拉白氏推当时岁实，
小于今岁实四秒二，所差甚微。盖古时测
天，但用浑天仪，无远镜，亦无分微器，故
未能密合。亚力山太仪器较精，测北极，
尚差四分度之一。今天学家，能察一秒下
之小分。古时一度下之小分尚未能定。
故或所差度分，至等于日月之全径焉。依巴谷测天，新见一恒星，因思作
星表，谓测日月及行星，全凭星表。星表成，始知有岁差，则以表中所定角
宿第一星，与一百七十年前亚力山太城中旧测相较，旧测离秋分点八度，
新测离六度。未知星东行，或秋分西行，乃遍考诸星皆然。纬度不便，经
度俱变，所以定为春秋分西行也。此理至奈端（Isaac Newton，1643—
1727，今译牛顿）始详解之。依巴谷星表，共一千零八十星，既定诸星经纬
度，乃作天球。依其度刻于上，并作地球，定各国经纬焉。生卒无考。其
测天诸事，当在汉文帝（203 BC—157 BC）、武帝（156 BC—87 BC）之时，
后世称其实事求是，不惜劳苦，可与今之天学名家并驾齐驱焉。依巴谷后
三百年，天学无可纪，而多禄某（即托勒密）出，立异说以惑人。

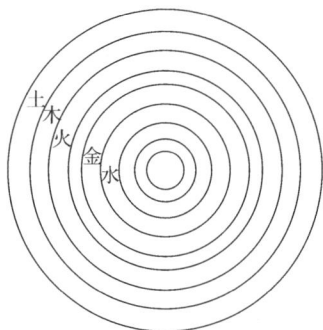

多禄某，埃及之亚力山太人也，其生约在后汉中叶时，颇立异说，然亦
有功天学。同时讲学者，以多禄某为最。多禄某善推步，精测候，亦深于
地理。初测知月体向地心半面，或左右侧，或上下侧，时变动，非常同也。
亚力山太书库遭兵燹。依巴氏所著书，仅存一种，余俱烬焉。未烬前，多
禄某尽见其书。故所著书，多引依巴氏说，因之名遂大显。其书独行一千
五百年，欧罗巴洲皆主之。书中引历代积事，证以当时所测，以解己立法
之理。言地为球体，定居天心。日月五星列宿，每日俱以平速，绕地约一

周,轨道俱平圆。准目所见,此理似合。观太阳每日绕地,行平圆一周。太阴(指月亮)及诸星或过一周,或不及一周,亦行平圆轨。古人俱甚信其说。然此时希腊人已知日月诸星,有自西至东之行度;亦知日行黄道,月行白道;亦知五星有变行之法。

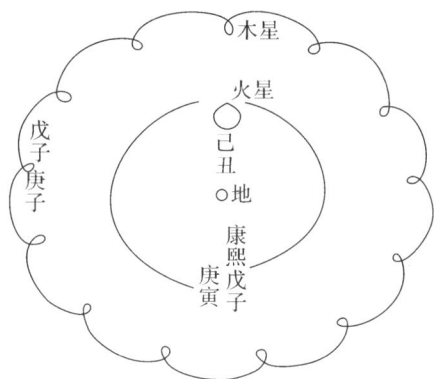

盖人在地面,视五星之行,最难解。或疾,或迟,或留,或退,或勾己。火木二星之道,自地面视之,如上图。观此图之状,则古人信行星之轨为平圆。有不可解者,依巴氏知目所见不足凭,故不敢立说,但言太阳绕地行平圆轨,而地不在中心。盖测知春分至夏至,九十四日半;夏至至秋分,九十二日半;春分至秋分半年一百八十七日;秋分至春分,半年一百七十八日。视年不平分,则云:太阳之道为平圆,而以平速行;地若在中心,必不合。故依巴氏谓:地必不在中心也。如图,甲乙丙丁平圆为太阳道,戊为地球心,己为圆心,与地不同点。戊己为两心差,庚辛为最高卑点,壬为夏至点,癸为冬至点,子为春分点,丑为秋分点。

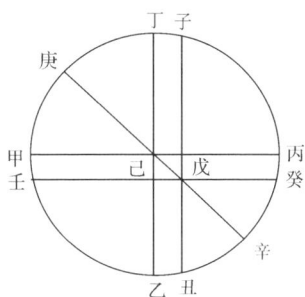

如此,则年虽不平分,而太阳以平速行平圆,理亦合。盖子至丑、丑至子,二圆分不同。所以人在地面,视日近辛点,行必速;近庚点,行必迟。古人皆置地于中心,依巴氏始变其说。多禄某不从依巴氏说,谓地球恒居天心,终古不动。七政俱以平速行平圆,精思造法,与实测合。日月五星有迟速,用小轮以齐之。凡不平之动,变为无数平动。此理本于希腊旧说,谓合二平动。视之,成曲折动,即彼说所祖也。譬如有船平行近岸,舟中人视岸边物,反若平动,与船同速。若舟中人在船面,以平速往来,则视岸边之物,皆非平动矣。从尾到首时,视岸上物速于船;从首至尾时,视岸上物迟于船。设岸有人向前行,速于船，则舟中人视之，反若逆行。所以若不知船动，则岸上物或迟，或速，或逆，无平动时。实则合二平动，一为船，一为人也。此明地动之理。多禄某小轮之说，亦有二平动，一小轮心，一小轮周也。如图，戊为地，寅为小轮心，行星行于甲′乙′丙′丁′小轮周，同时寅点行于甲乙丙丁大圆周。故人在戊，视星之行，有顺，有留，有逆，然尚有他变行。此说不能通，则轮上又加均轮，次均轮，及不同心诸轮。阿［亚］利斯多言平圆之动，为宇宙之公理。多禄氏从其说不疑，故作此繁重之法，以释平圆之理，以合诸星之行。观此亦见古人用心之巧。然学者当知无确证者，虽立法甚巧，不足凭也。历数千百年，多禄氏之徒，世守其法，或不合实测，辄加次轮，不同心轮，以合天行。又谓天有层数，每层有硬壳，质如水晶，能透光，每壳上一行星居之。诸行星天外，有恒星天，亦如水晶，透光其外。又有宗动天，磨动诸天，每日一周。其外有天堂焉。此皆其徒附会之说，非多禄氏本意焉。

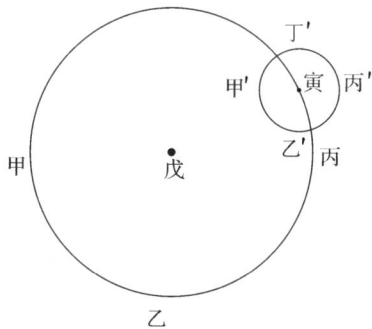

从多禄氏者，皆士多亚学（疑为 The Stoics，今译斯多葛学派）中人，好臆说，而不知实事求是之学。其人善辨论，格致之功阙焉。然多禄某精测望，其说虽非，亦有可取者。如言：清蒙气能映卑为高，映小为大。故测高度，须减此差，乃得真度。愈远天顶，其差愈大。故日月近地平视体较大，盖因此焉。此说至今承之。

多禄氏前有埃及之天学，费多费（Marcus Vitruvius Pollio，80 BC～70 BC—约 15 BC，今译马尔库斯·维特鲁威·波利奥）传其法，较多禄氏为近理焉。其言：金水二星俱绕太阳，随太阳以绕地球。又言：金水二星最近日，以日为心，行十二宫，有顺，有逆，有留。然信之者少，其徒不多。盖古人未尝测见二星之弦望，故不知其说之确焉。若亦有远镜如今时，当必信之矣。古人列火、木、土诸星离地球次序，与今合。然仅能测其光与速，余不知焉。以迟者为远。土星最迟，故为最远；木次之，火又次之；日、月、金、水俱在火星轨之内。月最近地球焉。日月交食之外，如月掩食诸星，如月与行星犯恒星，如彗星，俱测候焉。亚利斯多书有月掩火星一条，多禄氏书亦有秦王政十九年月（227 BC）掩土星一条。后代天变，古书多有之，惟金钱食未见焉。古人测天之器，多不甚巧。最古用石表测日影，列国皆然。古测岁实法最易。冬至午正影最长，至春分而得中，已而渐短；夏至影最短，至秋分而得中，已而渐长。故测岁实法，太古已有之。盖此于农事为最要。若于表之下作诸时线，亦可测一日之时焉。埃及诸国有古时极高石柱，不知何用，意亦日影表。亚古士督（Augustus，63 BC—14 BC，今译奥古斯都）徙埃及二石柱于国都，亦用以测日焉。凡测天文，必先正时。古人昼则用诸种日晷，夜则用水漏、沙漏；而希腊、罗马诸士讲理，用漏以定程课。今雅典城有楼，号风楼，亦号时表楼。亚力山大为王时所建也。其楼八面，意当时每面皆置日晷焉。其壁上有穴，自能大小。日长则渐小，日短则渐大。意当时必有水漏，昼与夜恒俱分为十二时焉。亚力山太人在当时能造诸巧器，亦有浑天仪以测日星。其后亚喇伯（Arabia，今译阿拉伯）所造，更大而精。当时或亦有助目窥筒，未可知焉。盖古书有云：空中有小体，浮行往来，似指木星、土星之月也。正昼测天，有数器，能使目不眩。亚利斯多有用镜法，时未有玻璃，或磨金板为之。多禄某有盘油测日食法。实尼加（Lecturt Seneca，约 4 BC—65，今译卢修斯·阿奈乌斯·塞内卡或辛尼加）有烟熏玻璃法。

多禄某（即托勒密）之后数百年，亚力山太之学院虽存，而声称渐衰，后王不好学故也。后诸国共灭罗马而亚喇伯（指阿拉伯）尤横虐。初入罗马，即焚亚力山太学院书库，论者或比诣中国之始皇焉（指秦始皇焚书坑儒事件）。然其后王渐向学，与罗马定约：罗马所有希腊书，亚喇伯每种皆取其副，用骆驼负归。中有迦林（Claudius Galenus of Pergamum，129—199，今译克劳狄乌斯·盖伦）医学、亚利斯多性理（即哲学）、多禄某天文，诸种藏于王宫，延名流翻译焉。亚喇伯文教之盛。在唐末时，有三王甚好学,曰阿曼所(Al-Mansūr,714—775,今译阿尔曼索尔),曰阿拉实(Harun al-Rashid,763—809,今译哈伦·拉希德)、曰阿麦门(Al-Ma'mun,786—833,今译阿布·阿拔斯·阿卜杜拉·马蒙·本·哈伦,哈伦·拉希德之子,其与父亲被并称为阿拔斯王朝最著名的两位哈里发),皆广立学校,分科教士。天文以多禄某为主,造仪器更大于多禄某所造。校勘多禄氏书诸题,益求密合。测岁实仅差数秒,于白蜜腊(疑为 al-Madīnah,英译Medina,今译麦地那)郊外测黄道一度,应地几里,以考欧拉独提尼(即上述埃拉托斯特尼)之说合否。测定黄赤交角,测木土二星之盈缩,列于星表。时已知蒙气差(atmospheric refraction,即大气折射),故测候较密于希腊(指教希腊天文学家所得数据更为真确可信)。一时格致学,以亚喇伯国都巴加达(Baghdad,今译巴格达)为宗,流传于埃及、摩洛哥、吕宋诸国。故亚喇伯既亡,而学不绝。蒙古入中原后,于波斯筑观星台。又筑观星台于撒马儿罕(Samarqand,今译撒马尔罕),造恒星表。其书今犹存。序言多禄氏表中有八星,今无。此或多禄氏之误,否则其故不可解。

传亚喇伯之学者,莫盛于西班亚(Spain,今译西班牙)。当时,欧洲诸国讲学者,惟亚喇伯。其学至今犹传焉。西王亚而封(Alfonso X of Castile,1221—1284,今译阿方索十世)所作星表言日五星之道较密,又详考岁实,俱宗亚喇伯焉。后数百年无可纪。间有立新说者,然皆谓地球不动云。

歌白尼(Nicolaus Copernicus,1473—1543,今译哥白尼),普鲁士国之韬纳(Thorn,今译托伦)人也。生于成化八九年间(1472—1473),童时承父业治医。闻人谈天学,辄喜,稍稍习之。弘治十年(1497),至以大里(Italy,今译意大利)薄罗那(University of Bologna,今译博洛尼亚大学),学天文于马利亚氏淘米尼(Domenico Maria Novara,1454—1504,今译多梅尼科·玛丽亚·诺瓦拉),于罗马传理学。其叔父为天主教教主。歌白尼学益进,加神父爵。后即真,在叔父管下,居复安堡(Frombork,今译弗龙堡)天主堂终身焉。在堂或当职事,或出施济行医,暇即讲求天学。慎交游，重然诺。性温和，缄默寡言。于教事及格致学外，不论他事。复安堡，濒海孤村也。天主堂在山顶，一望海天无际。独居无事，辄深思天地之理。谓：己所心得，后世必有知之者。云：天地万物之理，皆简而易明，而世人所论，往往相反，以是知其必愦①也。著书曰《天体环绕》(*De revolutionibus orbium coelestium*，英译 *On the Revolutions of the Heavenly Spheres*，今译《天体运行论》)，成于嘉靖九年(1530)，皆自论所立法，以地球为行星，绕太阳行，轨道在金火二星之间。又每日自传，成昼夜。视日月星辰，一如东出西没焉。凡行星之视动，参差变化，乃合本星地球二动而生也。读其书，想见其敏悟，于理无不透彻。然甚慎不敢轻以语人。盖是时人信旧法久，骤阅新说必大惊，反以为妄，故仅与其故人言之。故人有习天文者二人，曰莱诺(Leino)、勒的哥(Georg Joachim Rheticus，1514—1574，今译雷蒂库斯)。又有大教主双保(Paulus PP. III，1468—1549，今译教宗保禄三世)、教主开斯(Tiedemann Giese，1480—1550，今译泰德曼·吉斯)，俱是之。谋传其书，各与所知言之，信者渐众。有爱儿堡(疑为 Ergoldsbach，今译埃戈尔茨巴赫)者，不信，大为妄，令优人为歌白尼状，以姗笑之。然诸人信益坚，皆劝歌白尼刊其书以行世。不许。凡历十年，劝者益众，勒的哥(即雷蒂库斯)更劝之不已。乃许摘刊其纲领。既出，见者是之，始许刊布全书。其赀皆出自双保，而牛令堡(Nürnberg)人阿山大(疑为 Andreas Osiander，1498—1552)司校雠(指校勘)焉。工未竣，歌白尼病甚。迨见初印本，遂卒。时嘉靖二十二年(1543)夏也，即葬于复安堡天主堂之下。葬甚简，墓碑刻球象数具。又洼肖(Warsaw，今译华沙)有城内空地，有歌白尼像。

自歌白尼死，至今三百年，合地球皆重其为人，讲学之士，过其地者，必往吊其基，想见其风采焉。尝读歌白尼书，凡立新说，必曰或当然。盖未有确证，不敢自必焉。其后白拉里(James Bradley，1693—1762，今译詹姆斯·布拉德雷，英国天文学家)测得星之光差。律德(Jean Richer，

---

① 原为"愰"。

1630—1696,今译让·里歇尔)测得赤道吸力(gravity,今译引力),小于两极,始知地动有据云。歌氏自序言古人诸小轮,以推七政之行;今言地动,以证七政之变动,俱无确证,则无不同焉。由今论之,二者虽俱无确证,然地动之说,似较可信。盖繁简异也。人或难歌氏:地若动,且如此速,地面之物不尽散飞空中乎?答曰:地面之物散飞,则诸星之行更速,不更当散飞乎?此答虽甚辩,然未得真诠焉。又言天空无穷大,无人疑其自转之难,而微小地球,反疑其不当自转,何不以星之绕地为视行,实则地球自转之为近理乎?古诗云:舟人以岸为动兮,盖以为岸行而舟不动,其误一也。古人谓太阳行于黄道。其说亦通。盖地球一岁,绕日一周。人视之,若日一岁,绕地一周。然地小日大,自当以小绕大为是。行星顺逆、迟速、留伏诸行,多禄某之徒,累世思之不得其解。歌氏谓合两动而成,涣然冰释矣。如图,申为太阳,甲乙丙丁为地道,甲′丁′丙′乙′为外行星道,寅卯为天空圈。地在甲,行星在甲′,人视星在戊。地自甲至乙,星自甲′至丁′顺行,人视星似逆行自戊至己。地自乙′至丙,星自丁′至丙′,人视星似逆行自己至庚。地自丙至丁,星自丙′至乙′,人视星顺行自庚至辛。地与星各于本道再前行,则视星必若留。次复顺,次复逆焉。歌氏虽自云或当然。观此图说,知甚合天也。第虽云合天,不足为证,而此时无测望精器,又不能得他事以证之,故未敢自必。然亦自知后世必得证,而益信其说云。

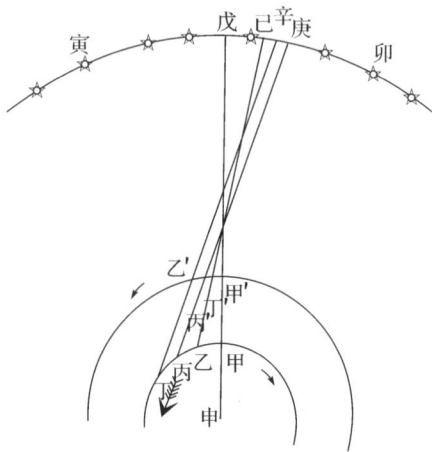

第谷姓勃拉(Tycho Brahe,1546—1601,今译第谷·布拉赫),嗹国(Danmark,今译丹麦)之那忒斯叨(Knutstorp castle,今译斯堪尼努斯托城堡)人。地濒波罗的海,生于明嘉靖二十五年(1546),时歌白尼死已三

载矣。三十九年(1560)秋间，日食。第谷尚幼，观之，始慨然思习天文焉。继入太学读书，每至夕乘师熟睡，仰观乾象，彻夜不寐。第谷产自豪族，无骄奢余习。惟自孳孳媚学不倦，长而著书，且以天学教人。第谷恶富贵习，闺门尤甚。娶小家女为妇。其族皆轻侮之，乃避于黑西加塞(Landgraviate of Hesse-Kassel，今译黑森-卡塞尔伯国)，小国也，其君维廉(William II，1469—1509，今译威廉二世)，亦治天算，爱重之。维廉尝夜测天，观新增星，乐甚。有小臣以宫中失火告，不顾，测如故。其好学如此。第谷言地球不动，而五星俱绕太阳，太阳率之以绕地球。盖第谷欲合多禄氏、歌氏两家说，故立术不能尽合天。后人讥第谷造此法，为不明于理。然此时第谷与歌氏二家之说俱无确证。而第谷言地若动，则人于高楼下石，及地时，当距所下之处数百尺。此亦本之多禄某所谓"地若动，则云与飞鸟，顷刻之间，与本处相失也"。盖未知物下坠时，有二动：向地心之动，生于坠；绕地心之动，未坠之前本有之。

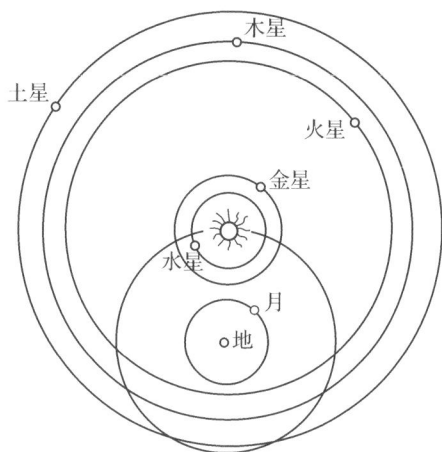

佳生地(Pierre Gassendi，1592—1655，今译皮埃尔·伽桑狄)曾验其说于法兰西马赛里(Marseille，今译马赛)海口。当船行时，于桅顶下石，果至桅足，与船不行同。不特此也。凡物下坠时，绕地心之动，必更速于地面之自转。以图明之。如图，戊己为地面赤道圈，酉为高楼，与地心呐为垂线。寅为楼顶申随地球自转一周所成之轨

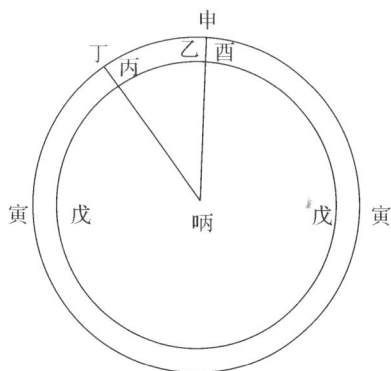

道。设楼之足为乙,行至丙,则楼顶必至丁。楼顶之圈大于地平之圈,故石绕地之动更速也。盖地自转,其面与楼俱向东行。石自楼顶坠,有楼顶之速率,必速于楼足。故石至地,必在丙之东。奈端(指牛顿)始悟得此理。言三十丈高,以石球下坠至地,必偏东半寸许。旱堡(Hamburg,今译汉堡)礼拜堂最高楼二十三丈,用球三十枚试之,皆偏东四分,又偏南分半,意风使然,乃于煤穴深二十六丈试之,俱偏东五分,无偏南北者。此地动之确证也。第谷不从地绕日之说者,盖疑地绕日,则于地轨道上径线之二界点,视恒星当有差角。不知恒星极远,视地轨道如一微尘,故差角不可见。然有远镜时,此论似不合。盖恒星之径,用远镜测之,无过一秒者,而凭目视,则最大者二分,最小亦十二秒。第谷意谓,地若动,于径线二界,视恒星又无差角,则星径不应若是之大,故定为地不动。虽废歌氏之说,不谓无见也。第谷法虽误,然测天有功。

隆庆六年(1572),欧罗巴于中夜共见一大星,俱甚异。第谷在田中行见之,其光甚大。若本有此星,昔何不见,疑目花误视。有众农夫共见皆然,遂测定其分秒,记于簿。未几在其国都太学中,与格致之士言,皆未知。时方共饭,群笑之。因与之偕出庭中望之,果有此星,乃群异之,因作书论此事。又有格马(Francesco Maurolico,1494—1575,今译弗朗西斯科·马若利科)亦见此星。前二夜,曾细测,本无此星。自初见至末,光日微,凡十六月而没。初出时,星之光能生表影。最明时光白,后变黄,后与火星同色,最后如土星色。自初出至没,不移分秒,在地轨道,亦无差角,故其远与恒星等。第谷之前三百年,亦见客星,古人亦屡言之。第谷疑天河之光,聚而成星云。万历五年(1577),有彗星出,第谷细测之,绝无地道差角。知其甚远,非在月之下,又见其出入行星诸天,始知诸天皆空。旧说如玻璃层层包裹者,谬也。此理今已大明,无须说,然在当时,则为创[①]见。故奈端亦尝论之。第谷作星表,定七百七十七星之位数,较旧表少,而所定之度分较密。又测行星,作表。后刻白尔(Johannes Kepler,

---

① 原为"刱"。

1571—1630,今译约翰内斯·开普勒)本此表造新法。第谷测知行星有迟速,月道之交点行亦有迟速,且测得黄白大距。用新测较古测,知黄赤大距。古今渐易,又用清蒙差,改定七政、诸星。天学中此差最要,不知加减此差,则所测非真矣。如图,甲乙、甲乙、甲乙、甲乙为诸层蒙气,愈近地面寅卯,则愈重。申为星,其光自入蒙气至地面,必成未未未呷曲线。其入目之度即目见物之方向,所以人在呷,视申之星,如在丙。其差角恒为高低差,而视物恒高于本处。故物在地平辛辰下丁点,视之如在辰点。

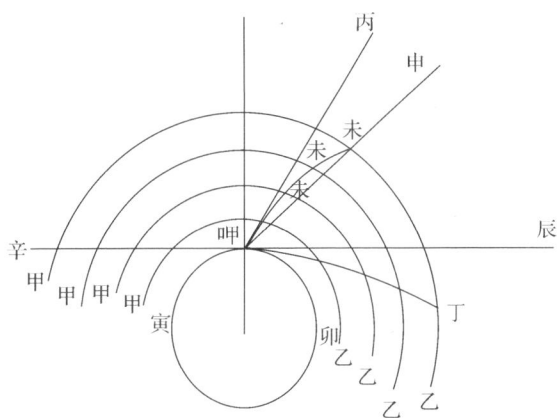

多禄某论视学已言之,而于测天不用,盖当时未知也。亚喇伯亦因多氏说而知。在第谷时,无人知其用。第谷立法,改星之高度,初作差角表。推地平线上之物,其差角三十四分,于率

近。至云高四十五度,当无差角,此则不合。盖当时所用之器,未能密测也。其小国君谓嗹国君言第谷系明理之人,于是嗹君请第谷归国,为之筑精室并观星台。第谷欲归,并许以波罗的海中一小岛赐之,每年俸银二千,食瑙威(Norway,今译挪威)若干户,于小岛筑室,及观星台。状其奇玮,名星城,测星极精细。第谷既居岛中,甚贵重、自负。然为人胆怯,而其造作,规模甚大。观其台者,可以想见其为人。其台长六丈,高七丈五尺,周以围墙高二丈二尺。基址正方,每边三十丈。中开大门,门内有室,阍者(即守门人)居之,其内皆称是。有天球,其星皆依新表刻之。球径六尺,架高五尺,造窥天仪器,约费银钱二十万。第谷居此岛二十一年。观星之外好饮酒,而畜一小犬,坐卧必以随。是时,第谷之名远播四方,常有国王,亲造其岛候焉。英国君若迷斯(James VI and I,1566—1625,今译

詹姆士一世)往啴国亲迎,亦造其岛,八宿而去。啴国君既死,第谷遂及于祸则朝中勋爵,多忌其宠,谮于嗣君。故也,初有大臣击其小犬,第谷怒,遂成雠隙。至是,夺其俸食,逐出海岛,遂离本国,终身愁苦。第谷既逐,客游诸国。后至奥地利(Austria,今译奥地利)巴拉加(Prague,今译布拉格),其君路道弗(Rudolf II,1552—1612,今译鲁道夫二世)厚待之。死于万历二十九年(1601)。其测天为西国第一焉。死后五十七年其岛入瑞颠国(Sweden,今译瑞典),室与台毁焉。今过其地,惟蔓草荒烟而已。

第谷去本国。虽愁苦,然因此遇刻白尔(即上述开普勒),后学受益不浅。盖刻白尔能用第谷测定诸数,成密法焉。先是第谷见刻白尔所著书,爱其敏悟,聘之至巴拉加邑(即布拉格城),为己副。刻白尔甚贫,厚给之,教以精测之法。临没[殁],尽以平生测量簿授之,刻白尔名约翰,瓦敦堡(Baden-Württemberg,今译巴登-符腾堡)国之维勒(Weil der Stadt,今译魏尔代施塔特)城人也,生于隆庆五年(1571)。读书为神父,后弃之,习天算。万祟[历]二十二年(1594),为葛喇剌(Graz,今译格拉茨)书院教习。为学务速成,用心过锐,所得多虚理,不合实测。及交第谷,告以当先求真实之根,则学可渐进,能得所以然之理。刻白尔然之,乃弃虚理,从事实测,学始有门径。初歌白尼重古说,不敢改平圆道,而火星道两心差最大。刻白尔于火星冲日时,见其行度有异,遂细测之。又检第谷所遗测量簿,有测诸行星细数,推求其轨道。其始尚泥平圆法,多用诸小轮以合天。继思火星或行椭圆道,而日为椭圆二心之一,不惮劳苦,考定其理。刻白尔自言,当推算时,如大帅临阵。火星道,敌军之帅也。初得胜,获之。以火星表为牢,囚禁之。以诸方程式为铁索,锁其项而系之,我以已无事矣。忽报敌帅力甚猛,铁索俱绝,牢亦破,已逸去,将复入其营。此时吾忧甚,幸得格物诸理,皆新募健卒,故终获而囚焉。观其喻,知其用心,亦良苦矣。火星表已定,密合天行,则知诸行星皆行椭圆道,乃以次考定之。以视歌白泥之言行星,皆以平速行平圆,其理较真焉。如图,甲丙庚椭圆为行星轨道,申为太阳所居之一心。作甲申、乙申二线,则乙申甲为椭圆面积之一分。星从甲至乙,其时分与面积有比例。设时为一月,乃于星道丙丁戊己庚诸点,俱作线至心。每二线内之面积,俱相等,则星从甲至乙,从乙至丙,从丙至丁,皆为一月,余仿此。是为刻氏第一新法。但面积等,而星所过之度,必不等。从甲至乙一段为最速,后诸段以渐而迟,故行非平速。此刻氏第二新法也。古人测量亦知不以平速行,而刻氏能考定其用何行法,与此速率合,可谓能改无法之行为有法焉。其第三新法,推行星与太阳相距。初意行星与日必有相属之理,日夜思之不得,心如负疚。后忽悟得,如重门洞开,澈底了然。知二星行同度时平方之比,如距日立方之比,心中乐甚。自疑梦中,此实为开辟来格致学中要理之一焉。以四率比例推之,既知二星距日,及一星之周时,即可知余一星之周时。观此,知行星非率然而生,漫然而行,俱有至理焉。如火星距日四倍水星,四之立方为六十四,开平方得八,则水星之速八倍火星。得此三新法,而歌白尼之说多有证。刻白尔亦愈信歌氏焉。后为奈端新术之根,其源实本于第谷之测簿。所居岛中,台名星城,预兆之矣。万秝[历]三十二年(1604),有新星见于天市垣。一年光渐微,又一年而隐。最明时,若金星。初见色黄,次变紫,次如火色,无地轨道差角。刻白尔谓空中有质之物,被火焚而然。然究不知何物焉。万历三十五年(1607),彗星见,后代名"好里"(Halley,即哈雷),刻白尔测其行度。四十六年(1618),又一彗星出,亦测之。然尚未知彗星之道与行星有同例焉。暮年贫困甚,时大臣多贪,侵其俸入,而王信休咎,占卜家反多食厚禄。英国公使在日耳曼者,怜其贫,招之入英。刻白尔重离故土,不肯。崇祯三年(1630),卒于腊底盆(Regensburg,今译雷根斯堡)城,即葬于城之天主堂侧。其墓今已湮没,后国王于其地立石像,刻火星之道于其座。

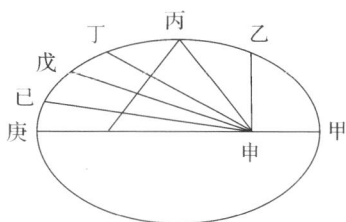

伽离略(Galileo Galilei,1564—1642,今译伽利略),以大利之皮撒

(Pisa，今译比萨)人也，生于明嘉靖四十三年(1564)，其所测定者，人人能晓。发明歌白尼之说，较刻白尔尤显易。创造远镜，见天空之界更远，测天更精，故能得歌氏之确证焉。万历三十七年(1609)，至威尼斯，适刻白尔论火星之书初出。偶与人谈论，忽悟远镜之根。时闻荷兰人造器能测远，因思仿此作测天之器，遂以精思造成之。既成，自言视物大一千倍，近三十余倍。昔亚利斯多(即亚里士多德)言：天空诸体皆正圆，自发光无少微翳。伽离略用远镜测太阴(即月亮)与地同，知古说非是。见太阴面有平野，有山，有高原，有谷，有影，有光。又测他行星，所得新理甚多。万历三十七年冬，夜测木星，见三小星近其体。后又见第四星，始知木星亦有月焉，则古人以地球居中不动者，不可信矣。治古说者病之，言木星旁无小星，不可信。伽离略使窥远镜验之，皆不肯，乃寓书刻白尔曰：世人守师说，而不通，一至于此。君与我当付之一笑也。又测土星不甚明皙，而窥金星有弦望与月同。初哥白尼言：金星绕日，当有弦望。然非目力所能见。至此始瞭然，知古人言不误也。时歌氏殁已七十年，其说始有证。前以歌氏之说为大谬者，今皆信其确然不可易也。又歌氏始言地自转，今以远镜窥太阳，见面有黑点，时时移动，则太阳必自转。古人言地球甚大，不能自转，必为定体。今太阳更大，且能自转，则古说之谬，不攻自破。古人又言：地球若自转，则地面之物，皆当散飞空中。伽离略于桅顶坠石，以破其说，言地气与地面之物，皆随地而转也。伽离略幼时，亦以歌氏之说为愚。既得诸证，始知歌氏具独见，远胜他家也。伽利略学愈精，嫉者愈甚。年七十，教大长谓其习异端。强令反其说，闻者悲之。后所遇益迍邅，爱女死，哭之丧明，病甚。欲至弗禄伦(Florence，今译佛罗伦萨)就医，吏禁勿许，既而耳复聋。积年患心痛，崇祯十五年(1642)卒。临死不昏愦。伽离略不修边幅，爱交游，宴会无虚日，心无忧戚。人乐与之游，时行田野中。自习农事，种葡萄。葬于弗禄伦大天主堂前，后迁葬天主堂中，有石像存焉。迁葬时，有人窃其一指骨，今以玻璃匣贮之，藏书库中。

伽离略未生时，英国迦思空（Gascoigne），已用远镜于象限仪（quadrant，即四分仪）。迦思空死后二十余年，无人知用者，而法兰西有某者造之,夸为创事,且造分厘镜。某死,二器亦无传,而伽离略复创为之。至顺治间,更造新器,事有名者为钟摆,测时最密,为天学重器焉。荷兰海更士(Christian Huygens,1629—1695,今译克里斯蒂安·惠更斯)实造之。又有器定星之经纬度,则嗹国勒墨尔(Ole Romer,1644—1710,今译奥勒·罗默)所造也。而伽离略远镜冠诸器,为今大远镜之祖焉。夫伽氏之镜,铅管不过长数寸,两端镶以凹凸二目镜,如今小儿玩物而已。然物虽微,而能破古人数百年旧说,得见月之平原、山谷,金星之弦望,木星之月,土星之异状。呜呼,亦奇矣。

格致学中诸精妙理,非一人所能悟,必历代通人,互相研究始得也。始刻白尔(即上述开普勒)测得诸行星之公理,其源由于第谷之精测。又赖若往讷白尔(John Napier,1550—1617,今译约翰·纳皮尔)所造对数。故数月之功,数日可毕。刻白尔所止之地,为奈端可起之地。奈端所未就者,拉白拉瑟成就之。诸畴人(指天文学者)亦非一邦之产。歌白尼生波兰,第谷生嗹国,刻白尔生日耳曼,伽离略生以大利。迨康熙时,而荷兰、法兰西、英吉利复生诸畴人。英特超众,今取其最著者录焉。但集(疑为Danzig,今译但泽或格但斯克)有商人曰:合未利(Thomas Harriot,1560—1621,今译托马斯·哈里奥特),创作月球图。

康熙三年(1664),测彗星,知其道在月道外,且略知其道之状。同时有海更士作远镜,精于前。测得土星一小星,即今第四月,且见土星状愈明晰。康熙五年(1666),夜偶测天,见参宿中有大星气。未几,法兰西葛西泥(Jacques Cassini,1677—1756,今译雅克·卡西尼)又测得土星四小星,即今第一、第二、第三、第五月也,且见土星之光带中有黑界,分为二道。此时英法二主俱筑星台,聘畴人测天。

康熙元年(1662),英初立格致工会(Royal Society of London for Improving Natural Knowledge,简称 Royal Society,今译皇家学会),奈端亦会中人也。五年(1666),法兰西格致太学(Académie des sciences 即 The French Academy of Sciences,今译法国科学院)成。法主雷第十四

(Louis XIV, 1638—1715, 今译路易十四)聘海更士于荷兰,聘葛西泥于以大里,俾居于中。葛西泥之子及孙,皆有声太学焉。葛氏测得行星诸月之周时,又定木星为扁圆球。而勒墨尔(即上述奥勒·罗默)造器,测星过经度。康熙十四年(1675),测定光行,且测定光行速率。光行一事,因久测木星之月始知之。盖推定木星月食初亏复光之时,与实测之时恒不合。或迟数分,或早数分。求其故,则因地木二体相距远近而生。远则迟,近则早。因此悟光行之理焉。如图,癸为木星,甲乙为地轨道,其径约五亿五千万里,为一年中地木二星相距之大较。地在甲点距癸,大于在乙点时,其较五亿五千万里。设光非行,则在甲与在乙,所见无时差。而勒墨尔测得甲乙二点之时差十一分,后精测得十四分。今测器更精,测得十六分又四分分之一。准此即知光行速率,历时一分,约行三千三百八十五万里,一秒约行五十六万四千余里。历时八分秒之一,可绕地球一周。自太阳至最远行星,约行二点钟;而至最近定星,须历五年。又光行速于砲弹一百五十万倍,而不能测其有力否。

英星台中,新星表之详密,冠地球诸国。星台初设,本为便商船行海,故定例:凡船至他国,必细测月之度分,归时以测簿送台中,与台测相较,以定各地里差。创议定例者求赏。英主令格致士议其当赏否。弗浪德(John Flamsteed, 1646—1719, 今译约翰·佛兰斯蒂德)曰:此法无用,不当赏。而是时月表、恒星表俱未密合,须久测改正。英主曰:如此,则我船至他国者,急当助之测望。于是始造星台,设台正官。时康熙十四年(1675)也,既成。勒碑于台,大旨言台之设,所以测天,便海舶焉。台官著名者,曰弗浪德,曰好里,曰白拉里,曰勃力斯(Nathaniel Bliss, 1700—1764, 今译纳森尼尔·布利斯),曰马思吉林(Nevil Maskelyne, 1732—1811, 今译内维尔·马斯基林),曰邦特(John Pond, 1767—1836, 今译约翰·庞德),曰爱理(George Biddel Airy,1801—1892,今译乔治·比德尔·艾里)。爱理今尚存。凡入台者,俱勒敏。昼夜测日月行星,定昴过经度,无一日间断。每年成行星历巨册,台正或有事出台,其副代之。中间惟白拉里、勃力斯相代时,停测三十三日。勃力斯、马思吉林相代时,停测五十三日。马思吉林、邦特相代时,停测四日。邦特、爱里相代时,停测二日。惹克(不详)尝言曰:英有此台,天下诸星台皆可废也。近英国大臣,令台中立表,表上置球,每日午正,令球下降,使四面望见之。

弗浪德最初为台官,不立新法,而尽通旧法,精于测验。拉白拉瑟曰:测天细密,无过弗浪德者。弗浪德,英国人也。家木寒素,力学不倦,遂为天算名家。王举用之,然家屡空、身常病,同僚多轻之。俸入止银四百,时或不与。国家始许给仪器,然终不给,自出俸购之。康熙十五年(1676),初入台,所用铁纪限仪,其半径七尺。象限仪,半径三尺。时钟二具,远镜二具。皆其家物也。用此诸器,仅能测诸星距度、方位而已。康熙二十八年(1689),复出俸造器,始能测定诸星经纬度。积三十年精测之功,成星表。定三千星之位,测月及诸行星迟速、远近。其后奈端藉此表悟得诸理焉。康熙五十八年(1719),弗浪德死,名不甚著。后人见其与友人论天诸书,始知奈端诸说,多本于弗浪德。

然奈端之学,虽因弗浪德而成,亦其用心之精,有以发之也。自刻白尔推得行星之比例,至奈端而能究明其所以然,夫岂易事哉。奈端之书,初刊行,诸格致家多不能解。或藐视之,或大笑之。书成四十年而死。是时英之外能读其书者,不过二十人。后各国畴人,见行星多参差动,不可解,因取索端书读,始服其理之确。拉白拉瑟曰:古今人所著书,当以奈端为第一焉。顾世俱以奈端求得吸力之理,有功格致学为最大,不知更有大于此者。初刻白尔谓太阳中有吸力,故能令诸行星绕之;又谓吸力或与相距之平方有反比例。而薄勒里(Robert Boyle,1627—1691,今译罗伯特·波义耳)及呼格(Robert Hooke,1635—1703,今译罗伯特·胡克)谓行星绕日,其不离本道,必有吸力。奈端之功,不在悟得此理,而能得此理之证。盖前人但空思其理,至奈端始知其确实之数,先论力之法(指力的定律),

以显力之用。故奈端较前人功尤大焉。

康熙五年(1666)，伦敦大疫。奈端避居郊外，于园中见果堕下，因思月亦必由地力吸之，故常绕地球，不直行空中也。月果如此，则诸行星绕太阳，理当皆然。自后屡思之，知有确证。然求其证最难，且有时一若其理不合。如此者十六年。先求地面之吸力，次求离地面若干，其力变小若干之比例。

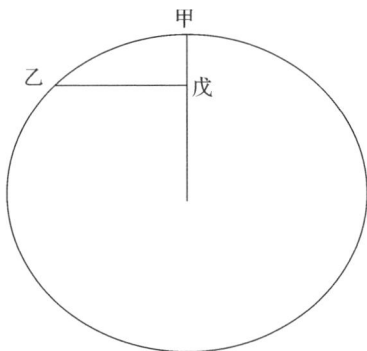

既得此比例，用以推月之动与所测合否。凡距地心之平方，与其吸力有反比例，故地之吸力加于月者，小于地面当三千六百分之一。乃立题曰：设如月行自甲至乙，别有物自甲坠至戊，必同时而到。测量甲乙弧之矢戊甲，设小于地面吸力当得之矢，为三千六百分之一，则吸力为有证。依此题，用弗浪德所测得行星诸事，立诸精法，悉推之，乃尽得其证。知物在月道于一分时中所行弧线之矢，与地面物下坠一秒中所过之界等，遂得远近吸力之定例。奈端积思既久，一旦得证，喜极，晕绝，复甦，不能终算，乃请其友依法推就之，则知此为公理。用此推诸行星及彗星，必皆合也。其理曰：若有物抛于空中，无阻力必终古以平速直行。

设又有他力加之，必行斜路。如图，设地球惟一推力使之动，则行甲乙直线。设无此推力，而仅有日之吸力，则地必向日而行，而日之吸力与推力恒并加，故成弧线行，二力恒不停，故弧线之行亦恒不变，而地之轨道成焉。行星诸道理皆同，吸力大小，与体大小，及距日远近，恒有比例。吸力之理与光同，散则小，而聚则大，其力之大小，与远近之平方，成反比例。设有行星距日倍于地球距日，则其吸力为地

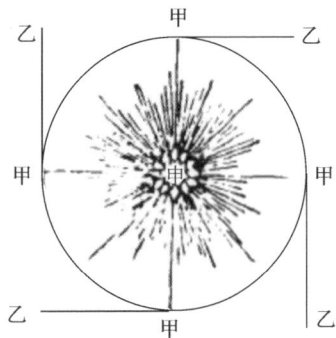

球吸力四分之一,二之平方为四故也。故吸力有二理:与远近平方成反比例;与大小成正比例;若长索系物而旋舞,日即手也。故最远行星,皆为日所属。推而上之,有太阳,即有造物主位置之,且定其法。自上古来,皆造物主主持之也,可不敬而畏之乎。诸球有交互相吸之理,其吸力轻重,视远近大小而异,故日吸诸行星,诸行星亦吸日,而行星之力,甚小于太阳。诸行星又互相吸,而其相距刻刻不同,则生不平之差。虽其差甚微,积之久,则有数可推,而后之不平差,必恰补前之不平差。前后相补,乃吸力之确证。奈端尚未知,赖后人发明之。奈端曰:有此不平差,久之诸轨道必大变,而行星必尽灭。后欧楼格来罗(Alexis Clairaut,1713—1765,今译亚历克西斯·克莱罗)、达浪勃(Jean le Rond d'Alembert,1717—1783,今译让·勒朗·达朗贝尔)、拉格浪(Joseph Lagrange,1736—1813,今译约瑟夫·拉格朗日)、拉白拉瑟,五人俱细究不平差之理,知前后必恰相补,则变而仍不变也。然则诸行星有灭坏之期,必不因行度之差,而惟造物主之命也。

好里(Edmond Halley,1656—1742,今译爱德蒙·哈雷),奈端之友也。家本富商,童时即弃其业而习天学。时合未利(即上述哈里奥特)、弗浪德(即上述佛兰斯蒂德)测天北半球,乃航海至阿非利加(Africa,今译非洲)①南海岛,测天南半球,欲定南极诸星,欧罗巴所未见者。而海滨蒙气太重,历一年,仅定三百六十星。当船过赤道时,见钟摆略迟,归语奈端。奈端曰:此因地心吸力略小故也。弗浪德死,好里代为台正,年六十四矣,而每夜测月,终十九年。交点一周,见月所次二千余处也。康熙十九年(1680),游法兰西,大彗星见,已过最近日点。时已闻彗星行极长椭圆,因精思得其理,以求各彗星复见之时。先以诸彗星行度列表,以备稽考。康熙二十一年(1682),有彗星见,检表,知景秦七年(1456),及嘉靖十年(1531)、万历三十五年(1607),三次所见,相距之时略同,意即一彗星也。

① 阿非利加行省是罗马共和国及其继承者罗马帝国在今北非的一个行省,范围约在今日的突尼斯北部及利比亚西部靠地中海沿岸的地区。

因言后七十五年,此彗星当复见。好里死后十七年,果复见,与所言合,因名"好里彗星"(Halley's Comet,即哈雷彗星)云。好里既死,白拉里为台正。

　　白拉里未入台时,先考定光差,谓地与光俱行,必生视差,此事须测方知。是时地绕日之理,人已不疑,皆欲测定星差角为证。盖意地之轨道极大,则于轨道相对两点,视定星必有差角焉。白拉里与其友摩利牛(Samuel Molyneux,1689—1728,今译塞缪尔·莫利纽兹),取天棓第二星同测之。其星略近天顶,于雍正三年(1725)起,测之屡,觉此星有向南之势。如图,地在甲,视星乙如在丙。设有差角,则地在丁,视星当如在戊,而测得在己,与差角理正相反。始疑测器有差,审定测器,再测之,仍如前。自十一月至三月,星差而南;三月至十一月,星又差而北。一若绕一小椭圆而行。如图,乙为天顶,甲为北极,小椭圆为见星所行之道,长径四十秒。白拉里思其故,久而不能得。一日偶坐小舟出游,桅上有小旗,其舟溯回川上,每当转橹时,见小旗微变方向。验之三四次皆然,乃问篙工(指掌篙的船工)曰:每转橹,风必变方向,何也。对曰:非风变方向,乃船变方向耳。言下忽悟星之差南、差北,乃地球行道变方向,与光动合而成也。准此理推星之差皆合。如图,体自甲至乙,同时光自丙至乙,合二动。故光入目时,一若目在乙点不动,而光自丁至乙也。所以星实在丙,视之如在丁焉。譬诸坐车行雪中,值天无风,雪向下直坠,车不动则雪至盖顶。车疾行向前,无论向何方,雪必扑面,如斜风飘也。光入目之方向,即为目见星之方向,故视星皆有差角也。此为地球

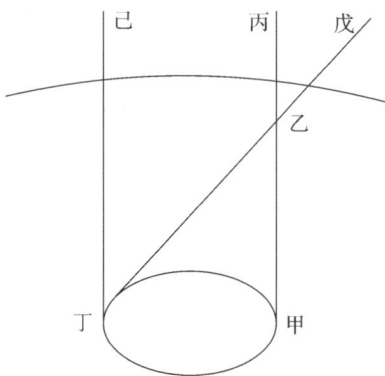

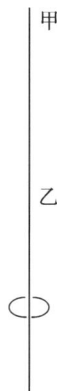

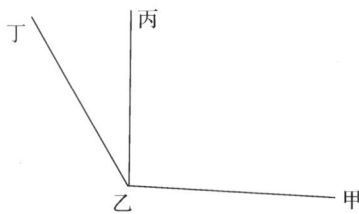

绕日之确证,乃天学中一最大要事也。既为台正,又测得地轴成尖锥动,十八年一周,测北如行小椭圆焉。初人以此为由于月之摄地球而生,白拉里始言由于地轴动,非关月也。为台正时,与其从子(即侄子)同测。凡一年共测一万八千次,而自乾隆十五年(1750)至二十七年(1762),共测六万余次。白拉里精心改正英国历法,侔于他国。乾隆十七年(1752)时,减去英八月中十日以合天。白拉里死,民言上帝所定之日,妄改之,故死也。其同僚或出,民必竞呼曰:夺我十一日,何时偿还耶。乾隆时,梅合(Tobias Mayer,1723—1762,今译托比亚斯·梅耶)造月离表,最精密,可推各海面经度。死后,王以银一万二千两,赐其妻。自是至今,每年预推三年后每三小时日月经纬度度。又测地球之形状、大小更密,测器亦更精。

侯失勒威灵(William Herschel,1738—1822,今译威廉·赫歇尔),阿诺威(Hannover,今译汉诺威,德国地名)人也。生乾隆时,其父精音律,少时迁居英国,以音律授徒,又以精思作视学诸器,且治天文,遂著名当世。初侯失勒欲测天,家贫,不能得远镜。既习视学,乃自造之。乾隆三十九年(1774),造五尺长回光远镜。后屡造回光镜,成五百多枚,以售人,择最精者留以自用。既测得天王星,名遂著。筑室于宫侧,制大远镜,各国天算家皆来观之。筒长四丈,回光镜径四尺,厚三寸半,重约二百斤,视力率一百九十二,较目力听及,远一百九十二倍也。地面所见最明者,老人星,然亦极远。其余诸星,皆小于此,则更远。目力所及之最小星,则最远;而侯失勒之镜,其力所及,较最小星更远一百九十二倍。成于乾隆五十四年(1789),露置无遮盖,久而雨日淋炙,架坏。道光三年(1823),其子遂毁之。其后罗斯伯(Lord William Parsons Rosse,1800—1867,今译威廉·帕森思,第三代罗斯伯爵)所造远镜,更大于此。

罗斯伯,阿尔兰堡(Ireland,今译爱尔兰)人也。其大远镜造之甚难,以坚忍大力,费赀不少,卒成最精之器。自创始至告成,皆独力任之。既成,天学家受益不少,故群称之,且感之。其回光镜,径六尺,其面大于侯失勒(即上述赫歇尔)之镜,约四倍,重约八千斤,铸于道光二十二年

(1842)夜中。罗斯伯亲督功，身当其危，略不畏避，成而精，宜也。其筒长五丈，架于二墙之间，器虽大，然人可以一手任意转之。有此镜而视天更明焉。自葛西泥测得土星第五月后，百年来，无新得星。侯失勒初测天时，日所属之诸行星、诸月，及好里彗星，十八而已。侯失勒独测得九星，乃天王星并六月，及土星一月也。合前共二十七星。乾隆四十六年(1781)，测天，见井宿诸星中有一星，光能变大。后二夜又见其易处，意为彗星。诸天文家亦为彗星。久测乃知系行星，即天王(Uranus)也。侯失勒初以英王之名名之，曰惹尔日(George III, 1738—1820, 今译乔治三世)。诸天文家又以侯失勒之名名之。后因其道在诸行星之外，定名曰天王焉。得此星而日所属之界倍远。盖其距日倍土星也。始用四丈远镜时，即见土星第六月，后又得第七月，而侯失勒之最大功，在测定星，始明天河为无数远星。又新测得诸星气，或如微云，或如未成星之气。又见定星，亦有绕之。每夜中测天，其妹助之。有所见，令其妹书之。次日细录之，不避寒暑。道光二年(1822)卒。二十八(1848)，其妹亦死。侯失勒在时，曾言普天之星，皆向女藏星而行，今人皆谓恒星绕昴宿，实侯失勒发之焉。

初，火木二星道间十亿余里，未见他行星，人颇疑之。由火至地，地至金，金至水，各二道间，约七千余万里至一亿四千余万里而止。刻白尔言，水土二道间，必有行星，方与诸行星远近比例合。远近比例者，伯灵(Berlin, 今译柏林)人波特(Johann Elert Bode, 1747—1826, 今译约翰·波得)所悟得者也。谓每行星与外星二道之距，恒倍于与内星二道之距。如金地二道之距，倍于金水二道之距，而半于地火二道之距。是也。初得此理时，天王尚未测得。后得天王，与此理合。诸行星轨道比例，以级数显之如下。日耳曼推步家(指天文历法家)，亦谓火木二道相距如是之远，中间必有未测得之行星，于是精心测望。嘉庆五年(1800)，推步家二十四人，以周天经度分段细测之。未几即

水		$= 四$
金	$四＋三$	$= 七$
地	$四＋三×二$	$= 一〇$
火	$四＋三×二$	$= 一六$
水	$四＋三×二^{四}$	$= 五二$
土	$四＋三×二^{五}$	$= 一〇〇$
天王	$四＋三×二^{六}$	$= 一九六$

测得四小行星,一谷女,一武女,一天后,一火女,俱绕日行。其轨道大小略同,距火道约三亿里。然皆非目力所能见,必藉远镜始见之。测得者为必亚齐(Giuseppe Piazzi,1746—1826,今译朱塞普·皮亚齐)、阿尔白士(Heinrich Wilhelm Matthias Olbers,1758—1840,今译海因里希·奥伯斯)、哈尔定(Karl Ludwig Harding,1765—1834,今译卡尔·路德维希·哈丁)三人。四星行法,异于他行星,其道甚相近,一也,道相交,二也。四星中最小者,略如西班牙国土大小。或谓此必系一大行星所分者,似亦合理。然未有确证。

近时天文之最新奇者,道光十三年(1833)十月中,见流星如雨。道光十五年(1835),好里彗星复见。道光十八年(1838),白西勒(Friedrich Wilhelm Bessel,1784—1846,今译弗里德里希·威廉·贝塞尔)定天津中无名小星地道差角。又自十四至十八年(1834—1838),侯失勒约翰(John Herschel,1792—1871,今译约翰·赫歇尔,区别于威廉·赫歇尔)至阿非利加好望角,测南半球。二十六年(1846),亨该(Karl Ludwig Hencke,1793—1866,今译卡尔·路德维希·亨克)又测得一小行星,名严女。二十七年(1847),又得其一名稚女。是年(1847),欣特(John Russell Hind,1823—1895,今译约翰·罗素·欣德)又测得其二,一虹女,一花女。二十八年(1848),格来汉(Andrew Graham,1815—1908,今译安德鲁·格雷厄姆)又测得其一,名慧女。二十六年(1846),又测得大行星海王(Neptune)。二十八年(1848),又测得土星第八月,乃英拉斯拉(William Lassell,1799—1880,今译威廉·拉塞尔)与合众(指美国)本特(William Cranch Bond,1789—1859;George Phillips Bond,1825—1865,今译邦德兄弟)同时所得也。

初畴人测天王行度,有极不平处,以土木二星之吸力推之,亦不尽合。法兰西力佛理亚(Urbain Le Verrier,1811—1877,今译奥本·勒维耶)细推天王之根数。道光二十六年(1846),著一书行世。言天王不平行者,空中必尚有一行星。细推其行度诸根,且定其大小,及所居之经纬度。此书既出,一月后,嘉勒(Johann Gottfried Galle,1812—1910,今译约翰·格弗里恩·伽勒)在柏灵,果测得之,即海王也,而英国亚但史(John Couch Adams,1819—1892,今译约翰·柯西·亚当斯)已先推之。道光二十三年(1843),推星所在度。二十四年(1844),细推日心之经度,及星道两心差,并最卑点之经度。二十五年(1845),以细草送太学天文师爵李(James Challis,1803—1882,詹姆斯·查雷斯),又送星台正爱理(即上述艾里)。事在力佛理亚(即上述勒维耶)书未出前六月,亚但史(即上述亚当斯)所推,亦密于力佛理亚。爱理见二人所推略同,令人细测之。而爵李(即上述查雷斯)测之七夜,已得此星。后八夜又见之,误谓恒星。故未细测其度,且未记簿也。然海王距天王,非倍天王距土,与波特(即上述波得)例不合。

附:《西国天学源流》译名对照表

王韬译名	可能对应的外文词语	今译
《阿陀塞亚》	*Odysseia / Odyssey*	《奥德赛》
《天体环绕》	*De revolutionibus orbium coelestium / On the Revolutions of the Heavenly Spheres*	《天体运行论》
阿尔白士	Heinrich Wilhelm Matthias Olbers,1758—1840	海因里希·奥伯斯
阿尔兰堡	Ireland	爱尔兰
阿非利加	Africa	非洲
阿拉实	Harun al-Rashid,763—809	哈伦·拉希德
阿麦门	Al-Ma'mun,786—833	阿布·阿拔斯·阿卜杜拉·马蒙·本·哈伦
阿曼所	Al-Mansūr,714—775	阿尔曼索尔
阿尼	Ionian	爱奥尼亚
阿诺威	Hannover	汉诺威
阿山大	Andreas Osiander,1498—1552	安德烈亚斯·奥西安德

续表

王韬译名	可能对应的外文词语	今译
阿陀苏	Odysseus	奥德修斯
爱理	George Biddel Airy,1801—1892	乔治·比德尔·艾里
巴比伦	Babylon	巴比伦
巴加达	Baghdad	巴格达
巴拉加	Prague	布拉格
白拉里	James Bradley,1693—1762	詹姆斯·布拉德雷
白蜜腊	al-Madīnah/Medina	麦地那
白西勒	Friedrich Wilhelm Bessel,1784—1846	弗里德里希·威廉·贝塞尔
百拉多	Plato,427 BC—347 BC	柏拉图
邦特	John Pond,1767—1836	约翰·庞德
薄勒里	Robert Boyle,1627—1691	罗伯特·波义耳
薄罗那	University of Bologna	博洛尼亚大学
倍律	Francis Baily,1774—1844	弗朗西斯·贝利
本特	William Cranch Bond,1789—1859；George Phillips Bond,1825—1865	邦德兄弟
彼力格里	Pericles,495 BC—429 BC	伯里克利
必亚齐	Giuseppe Piazzi,1746—1826	朱塞普·皮亚齐
闭他卧剌	Pythagoras of Samos,570 BC—495 BC	毕达哥拉斯
庇推尼	Bithynia	比提尼亚
波斯	Persia	波斯
波特	Johann Elert Bode,1747—1826	约翰·波得
伯灵	Berlin	柏林
勃力斯	Nathaniel Bliss,1700—1764	纳森尼尔·布利斯
达浪勃	Jean le Rond d'Alembert,1717—1783	让·勒朗·达朗贝尔
大角	Arcturus	大角
但集	Danzig	但泽或格但斯克
第谷姓勃拉	Tycho Brahe,1546—1601	第谷·布拉赫

续表

王韬译名	可能对应的外文词语	今译
多禄某	Claudius Ptolemaeus,约 100—170	托勒密
多禄某第三王	Ptolemy III Euergetes,约 280—222	托勒密三世
多禄某第一王	Ptolemy I Soter,367 BC—282 BC	托勒密一世
非禄老	Philolaus of Croton,470 BC—385 BC	菲洛劳斯
费多费	Marcus Vitruvius Pollio,80 BC～70 BC~约 15 BC	马尔库斯·维特鲁威·波利奥
弗浪德	John Flamsteed,1646—1719	约翰·佛兰斯蒂德
弗禄伦	Florence	佛罗伦萨
复安堡	Frombork	弗龙堡
伽离略	Galileo Galilei,1564—1642	伽利略
歌白尼	Nicolaus Copernicus,1473—1543	哥白尼
格来汉	Andrew Graham,1815—1908	安德鲁·格雷厄姆
格马	Francesco Maurolico,1494—1575	弗朗西斯科·马若利科
格致工会	Royal Society of London for Improving Natural Knowledge	皇家自然知识促进学会
格致太学	Académie des sciences/ The French Academy of Sciences	法国科学院
葛喇剌	Graz	格拉茨
葛西泥	Jacques Cassini,1677—1756	雅克·卡西尼
哈尔定	Karl Ludwig Harding,1765—1834	卡尔·路德维希·哈丁
海更士	Christian Huygens,1629—1695	克里斯蒂安·惠更斯
海王	Neptune	海王星
海修达	Hesiod,约 8 BC—7 BC	赫西俄德
旱堡	Hamburg	汉堡
好里	Halley	哈雷
好里	Edmond Halley,1656—1742	爱德蒙·哈雷
好里彗星	Halley's Comet	哈雷彗星

续表

王韬译名	可能对应的外文词语	今译
合未利	Thomas Harriot,1560—1621	托马斯·哈里奥特
和马	Homer,约 9 BC—8 BC	荷马
黑陆独都	Herodotus,约 480 BC—425/413 BC	希罗多德
黑西加塞	Landgraviate of Hesse-Kassel	黑森-卡塞尔伯国
亨该	Karl Ludwig Hencke,1793—1866	卡尔·路德维希·亨克
侯失勒威灵	William Herschel,1738—1822	威廉·赫歇尔
侯失勒约翰	John Herschel,1792—1871	约翰·赫歇尔
呼格	Robert Hooke,1635—1703	罗伯特·胡克
华力	John Wallis,1616—1703	约翰·沃利斯
佳生地	Pierre Gassendi,1592—1655	皮埃尔·伽桑狄
迦勒底	Chaldea	迦勒底
迦林	Claudius Galenus of Pergamum,129—199	克劳狄乌斯·盖伦
迦思空	Gascoigne	迦思空
嘉腊提	Galatea	加拉太亚
嘉勒	Johann Gottfried Galle,1812—1910	约翰·格弗里恩·伽勒
爵李	James Challis,1803—1882	詹姆斯·查雷斯
开斯	Tiedemann Giese,1480—1550	泰德曼·吉斯
刻白尔	Johannes Kepler,1571—1630	约翰内斯·开普勒
拉白拉瑟	Pierre-Simon Laplace,1749—1827	拉普拉斯
拉格浪	Joseph Lagrange,1736—1813	约瑟夫·拉格朗日
拉斯拉	William Lassell,1799—1880	威廉·拉塞尔
腊底盆	Regensburg	雷根斯堡
莱诺	Leino	莱诺
勒的哥	Georg Joachim Rheticus,1514—1574	雷蒂库斯
勒墨尔	Ole Romer,1644—1710	奥勒·罗默
雷第十四	Louis XIV,1638—1715	路易十四

续表

王韬译名	可能对应的外文词语	今译
力佛理亚	Urbain Le Verrier, 1811—1877	奥本·勒维耶
利奈	Cyrene	昔兰尼
嗹国	Danmark	丹麦
路道弗	Rudolf II, 1552—1612	鲁道夫二世
罗斯伯	Lord William Parsons Rosse, 1800—1867	威廉·帕森思,第三代罗斯伯爵
吕氏亚	Lydia	吕底亚
律德	Jean Richer, 1630—1696	让·里歇尔
马利亚氏淘米尼	Domenico Maria Novara, 1454—1504	多梅尼科·玛丽亚·诺瓦拉
马赛里	Marseille	马赛
马思吉林	Nevil Maskelyne, 1732—1811	内维尔·马斯基林
梅合	Tobias Mayer, 1723—1762	托比亚斯·梅耶
蒙气差	atmospheric refraction	大气折射
米利都	Miletus	米利都
米太	Media	米底亚
摩利牛	Samuel Molyneux, 1689—1728	塞缪尔·莫利纽兹
那忒斯叨	Knutstorp castle	努斯托城堡
奈端	Isaac Newton, 1643—1727	牛顿
瑙威	Norway	挪威
讷白尔	John Napier, 1550—1617	约翰·纳皮尔
尼西	Nicaea	尼西亚
牛令堡	Nürnberg	纽伦堡
欧拉独提尼	Eratosthenes of Cyrene, 276 BC—194 BC	埃拉托斯特尼
欧楼格来罗	Alexis Clairaut, 1713—1765	亚历克西斯·克莱罗
皮撒	Pisa	比萨
惹尔日	George III, 1738—1820	乔治三世
瑞颠国	Sweden	瑞典

续表

王韬译名	可能对应的外文词语	今译
若迷斯	James VI and I,1566—1625	詹姆士一世
撒马儿罕	Samarqand	撒马尔罕
撒摩	Samos	萨摩斯岛
实尼加	Lecturt Seneca,约 4 BC—65	卢修斯·阿奈乌斯·塞内卡或辛尼加
士多亚学	The Stoics	斯多葛学派
天狼	Sirius	天狼星
天王	Uranus	天王星
洼肖	Warsaw	华沙
瓦敦堡	Baden-Württemberg	巴登-符腾堡
维勒	Weil der Stadt	魏尔代施塔特
维廉	William II,1469—1509	威廉二世
西班亚	Spain	西班牙
西隐	Syene or Aswan	阿斯旺
希力斯奔	Strato of Lampsacus	兰普萨库斯的斯特拉波
象限仪	quadrant	四分仪
小亚西亚	Asia Minor Peninsula	小亚细亚
欣特	John Russell Hind,1823—1895	约翰·罗素·欣德
亚但史	John Couch Adams,1819—1892	约翰·柯西·亚当斯
亚而封	Alfonso X of Castile,1221—1284	阿方索十世
亚古士督	Augustus,63 BC—14	奥古斯都
亚喇伯	Arabia	阿拉伯
亚里达古	Aristarchus of Samos,310 BC—230 BC	阿里斯塔克斯
亚力山大	Alexander III of Macedon,365 BC—323 BC	亚历山大大帝
亚力山太	Alexandria	亚历山大
亚利斯多	Aristotle,384 BC—322 BC	亚里士多德

续表

王韬译名	可能对应的外文词语	今译
亚美尼	Armenia	亚美尼亚
亚那煞各剌	Anaxagoras of Clazomenae，500 BC—428 BC	阿那克萨哥拉
亚那西慢突	Anaximander，610 BC—546 BC	阿那克西曼德
亚述	Assyria	亚述
依巴谷	Hipparchus of Nicaea，190 BC—125 BC	喜帕恰斯
墺地利	Austria	奥地利

西國天學源流

源流　西國天學　純齋署

已丑秋淞隱　盧邈叟校印

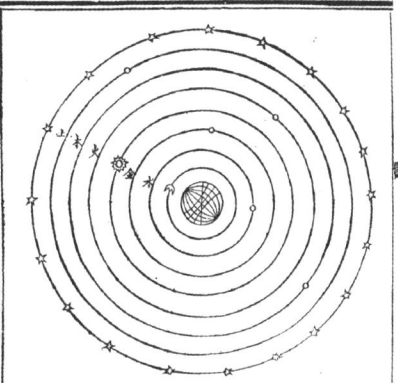

西國天學源流

英國　偉烈亞力口譯
長洲　王韜　仲弢著

天算之學由來古矣最奇特者能導人離地球而至天空最遠
之處考察世間萬物之理俱能使心量擴充而考察地球以外
諸事擴充心量能令太極至不可比喻凡測量行星之遠近大
知造物主大能全智亦知人在天地間爲一粒芥一微塵渺乎
其小也以上諸事若已了然於胸中便能知耳目聞見未足爲
小輕重光暗遲速及彗星之道窺定星無數而甚遠因此能漸
憑故向謂地球不動而不知實動目見諸行星左旋而實右旋
昔以地球爲六合中甚大之物今知一星一地球虛空界中無
數行星實有無數地球而小於諸行星數千百倍蓋嘗上考載
籍而知天算之學肇自古昔

依巴氏說因之名遂
大顯其書獨行一千
五百年歐羅巴洲皆
主之書中引歷代祘
事証以當時所測以
解己立法之理言地
爲球體定居天心日
月五星列宿每日俱
以平速繞地約一周
軌道俱平圓準目所
見此理似合觀太陽
每日繞地行平圓一
周太陰及諸星或過

《西国天学源流》己丑秋淞隐庐邈叟校印版

五

重学浅说[①]
(1858 年)

伟烈亚力　口译

王韬　笔受

王韬按语(1889)：

西士伟烈亚力口译，长洲王韬笔受。西人于器数之学，殚精竭思；其最奥者曰重学。以轻重为学术，行止升降，必藉乎力；高下疾徐，必因乎理；而所以制器测象者，非此不可。凡助力之器有六：杠杆、轮轴、滑车、斜面、螺丝、尖劈。赖此可以举重若轻，其中各有算学比例在。是书向编入《六合丛谈》中，亦有单行本，后乃冠于艾约瑟所译《重学》之首，余与伟君皆未署名。[②]

编者按语：

《重学浅说》是近代中国翻译的第一部关于西方力学的专著，具有开创性意义。原版包括"重学总论"(设有杆、轮轴、滑车、斜面、劈、螺旋等六

---

① 校自 1858 年《六合丛谈》第 2 卷第 1—2 号(奥地利国家图书馆藏版)。1890 年《弢园著述所存书》中《重学浅说》新增"重学原始"一节(约六页半)，注明英国伟烈亚力原译，长洲王韬紫诠笔著。考虑本书是以译者王韬的逻辑来点校整理，所以不选 1890 年版本，而选最早 1858 年版，为点校对象文本。

② 此按语为王韬晚年所加。参见王韬所著的《弢园著述总目》，载于《春秋朔闰至日考》(哈佛大学图书馆珍藏本)，光绪己丑(1889)年七月。

节），"总论（重学之理）"等两大部分。

本书源于苏格兰钱伯斯兄弟即威廉·钱伯斯（William Chambers，1800—1883）和罗伯特·钱伯斯（Robert Chambers，1802—1871）编纂的《钱伯斯国民百科全书》（*Chambers's Information for the People，A Popular Encyclopedia*）第一卷。从本书点校者查阅的第五版（1858 年，第162—173 页）来看，伟烈亚力和王韬依据的是该书的"Mechanics-Machinery"一节。

总　论

凡物用力与动推其理，名曰重学（mechanics，今译力学）。重学中之力，与化学中之力异。重学之力加于实体，不能令本质变化。化学之力，则能变化本质也。如青石或用碪击，用水冲，可令碎为粉。然本质不变，此重学之力也。若用磺强水令化为粉，则本质尽变。此化学之力也。重学中之器，分为二科：一曰简器，如杆与锄之类；一曰繁器，则合数器为一器。重学论器，或论其理，或论其用法。

凡器皆为用力之巧法，其大端不过受他力加于物，而所得力较本力更简便。有时用法令发出奇巧力，一若器自能生力者。重学之大要，乃用为抵定对面之力，所用之力曰"力"（power），所抵之力曰"重"（weight）。

仅用手不用器，所生力不多。故凡工作皆用器助己之力。野蛮用一木治田，与最奇巧之器，理归一致。深于格致者，能详细言之。助力之器有三种：曰杆（the Lever，今译杠杆），曰滑车（the Pulley, or Cord，今译滑轮），曰斜面（the Inclined Plane），是谓原器（the Primary Mechanical Powers）。又有三种：曰轮轴（Wheel and Axle），曰劈（Wedge，今译楔子），曰螺旋（Screw，今译螺杆），轮轴即杆类，劈与螺旋即斜面类，是谓次器（the Secondary Mechanical Powers）。凡繁器大率（指大概）合此六器而成。

杆

诸器中常用者为杆。杆以坚质为之,其用凭于坚物或轴上转动之。杆有三点:曰力点(the power,今译动力)、重点(the fulcrum,今译支点)、倚点(the weight,今译阻力)。加力之处为力点,所凭之处为倚点,加重之处为重点。分力与重者,论杆之用耳,其实力与重皆力也。倚点距力点,曰力倚距,距重点曰重倚距。

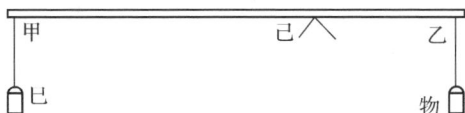

杆有三种,俱为直杆(straight bar)。力之方向俱与杆正交。一、倚点在力重二点之间;二、重点在力倚二点之间;三、力点在重倚二点之间。

第一种杆,倚点在力重二点之间。如图,直杆甲乙,凭于倚点己。乙为重点,物即重物也。甲为重点,巳为小重。甲己距大于乙己距,巳物二重恰相定。若去巳重,用手压于甲代之亦可。手愈近己点,则用力必愈多。

又图,己为地上坚物。杆凭之,加力于甲,以乙起重物。甲距己远,乙距己近,则起重易。甲距己愈近,必愈加力。此名速率力

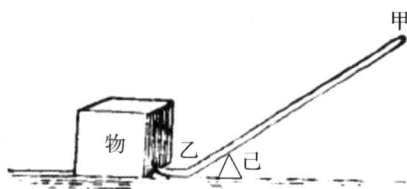

(virtual velocities)。其理简而易明。设款如左。同时中运小重过路远,运大重过路近,所用之力同。盖速率增,力亦增;速率减,力亦减也。

又二重相定,加动力令杆动,则一端为力所过之界,一端为重所过之界,界之长短,必与力重成反比例也。此理可以地心吸力发明之。凡重若干,即吸力乘体质诸点之和。盖诸点皆被吸力摄向地心,故若一点上下行一尺,或十点上下行一寸,其收发地心之吸力相等。准此用一斤力过十尺

界,可起一斤重过十尺界。又十斤力过十尺界,可起百斤重过一尺界。无论用何助力器,不能以十斤力过一尺界,起一斤重过十一尺界,亦不能以一斤过九尺界,起十斤重过一尺界。凡杆及一切器所发之力,必准所加之力,不能略增减也。

以杆言之。如前二图,同时分中,以力加于甲,或以倍力加于力倚距甲己之中点,杆于乙点所发之力相等,故杆若极长而坚,加力于其端,可令其发极大之力也。或问曰:远倚点加小力,近倚点加大力,历时能相等否。曰:小杆不能觉。若长杆,则远倚点加小力,历时必多。近倚点加大力,历时必少。盖杆长,远倚点,所过之界,必大。较近倚点,时必更久,故小儿用长杆超重物,或壮年用短杆起之,所发之力同。然小儿历时必多,且甚劳,以身所过之界大也。

凡力倚距愈长,力之能愈大。力与重之比,恒如重倚距与力倚距之比。凡重乘重倚距,力乘力倚距,二得数相等,则力重相定。

假如杆上一端有重一百斤,重倚距八寸;一端有重八斤,重倚距一百寸,则二重必相定。盖八乘一百,得八百;一百乘八,亦得八百。二数相等故也。

假如重与重倚距已知,亦知力倚距,求加若干力。令力重相定,法以重乘重倚距,以力倚距约之,所得即力数也。如重十斤,重倚距十寸,相乘得一百,以力倚距二十寸约之,得力五斤。此力之能率若一与二,重倍于力也。凡木工用木杆移木,石工用铁杆移石,皆是理也。

凡器有二股者,皆合此种杆理。日用所恒需者,为剪刀。所剪之物,即重,指力即力,销即二股之公倚点也。

阛阓(指街市)中所用天平(scale beam,今译秤杆),亦合此种杆理。杆之两边相等,点恰当重心,故两边相定。如

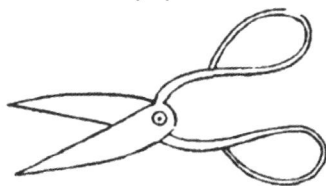

图,申为线,着于小轴,以悬甲乙杆。己为倚点,倚点两边甲己、乙己相等,故杆转动于小轴甚易。

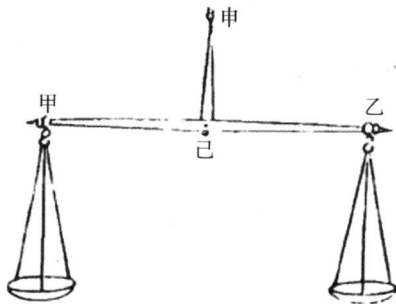

秤(steelyard,今译杆秤)亦此种杆也。重倚距与力倚距恒不等。重增,力倚距亦增;重减,力倚距亦减,以相定也。如图,丙为倚点,倚点一如轴,令杆易转。甲丙为重倚距,物为秤盘,所以承重。丙之右边必长于左边,分为若干等分,记以一二三四等字。巳为权,有一定重悬于杆,可任意进退。欲知盘中物重若干,则进退其权,令与物重相定,乃视力倚距若干,即知物之重。假如巳重一斤,定于三点,则物重必三倍于巳,为三斤也。余可类推。

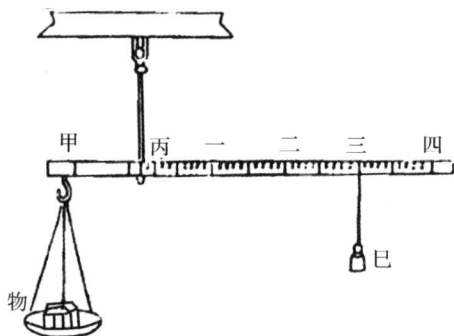

第二种杆,重在力倚二点之间(the power is placed between the power and the fulcrum)。如图己为倚点,物为重,加于乙。巳为力,加于甲。向上,甲至己为力倚距,乙至己为重倚距。此种杆用以起重,理如第一种。力愈远倚点,则力能愈大也。日用之器,此种最多。如以杆起货物,手即力,加于巳。地面己即倚点,物重在力倚二点之间也。

又如推车,轮着地处即倚点,车身及所载物为重,人执二柄之处即力,所执处距车身远近异,则轻重亦异。然推车之难易,又视倚点上之重而异,不尽关此也。

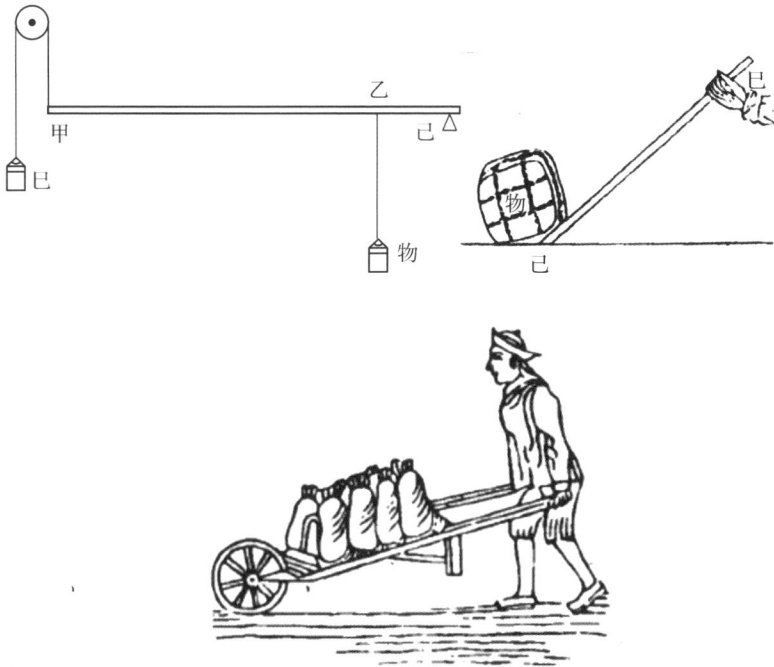

又如二人用杆扛物,物或加杆上,或悬杆下,不论。譬如肩舆,与半在杆上,半在杆下。或如图扛一箱,全在杆下,理无异也。凡扛物二人互相为力,亦互相为倚点,重在中间,则两端用力等。若移近此端,则此端用力,必多于彼端。愈近则用力愈多,两边之力,与两力重距,恒成反比例也。

设大人与小儿同扛一物,欲小儿不费力,当移物近己。又设车衡连于

车身之点,若非正中,则系马于两端,用力必不能等。

屋梁架于二柱端,亦合此种杆理。间有中间未加他物,因本质之重而自折者。凡绳或铁索举其二端,中必曲向下。虽最大力,不拉之令直。将近直时,必先中绝矣。风筝之线亦不能直,理皆同也。

小船之桨,亦合此种杆之理。着水处为倚点,船即重,手所加处即力。

夹剪亦合此种杆理。销为倚点,所夹之物即重,手指所加处即力也。二股皆为杆,故有双杆力。

此种杆或用于墙中挤物,杆端悬重即力,所挤之物,即倚点。西国农家或用此法挤牛乳饼。

第三种杆,力在重倚二点之间。如图己为倚点,巳为力,加于乙。物为重,悬于甲。此杆力倚距小于重倚距,力恒大于重,其能最小。然用得其所,亦甚妙。大约力不甚大,而欲杆之长端速动,则永之。

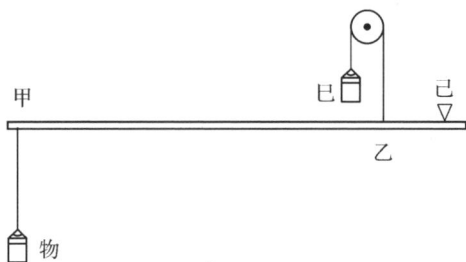

工匠车牀(turning-lathe)之踏板(footboard),合此种杆理。着地处为倚点,足所踏处为力,所拉绳申为重,足轻用力拉绳之端下行,过界甚大,足微起,纙即拉板上行,再踏再下,甚便也。

打麦杖(flail,今译连枷)之类,皆合此种杆理。一切动物之股,其动法尽合此种杆理。昔人称为费力杆,特未知其合用处耳。

叠　杆

叠杆者,以若干杆,联络用之。各杆之力点,在向原力一端,其力大小,等于相接杆所发之力,杆愈多则能愈大。如图,乃第一种,杆三个依直线相联络之叠杆也。各杆动于各倚点,可用微力与大重相定。推此器力重相定之率,亦如前法。重乘重倚距,力乘力倚距,二数相等,则相定矣。

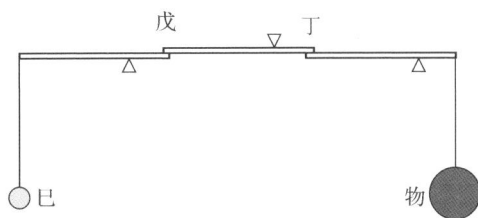

图中三杆,设力倚距六寸,重倚距皆二寸,巳力一斤,求物重几斤则相定。法以一斤乘第一杆力倚距六寸,得六;以重倚距二寸约之,得三斤,为第一杆戊点向下之重,即为第二杆戊点所发之力。次以三斤乘第二杆力倚距六寸,得十八。以重倚距二寸约之,得九斤,为第二杆丁点向上之力,即为第三杆丁点所发之力。末以九斤乘第三杆力倚距六寸,得五十四,以重倚距二寸约之,得二十七斤,即第三杆上所加之物重。是巳一斤,能与物二十七斤相定也。或巳为一两,则物为二十七两。无论若干,比例皆同也。此设重倚距、力倚距之比,为二与六,即一与三。其较尚小故力与重,相去尚未能悬绝。若令二距之比,若一与十,或若一与二十,则力之能更大。今再设力倚距皆十八寸,重倚距皆一寸,则巳力一斤。能定第一杆戊点十八斤。以十八斤乘第二杆力倚距十八寸,得三百二十四斤。第三杆丁点之力,再乘第三杆力倚距十八寸,得五千八百三十二斤,即物重是巳力一斤,能与五千八百三十二斤之重相定也。

推叠杆公法,以各杆力倚距连乘力,亦以各重倚距连乘重,二得数相等,则力重相定。无论各杆等不等,皆同。叠杆若用多,则以微力加于细杆,可举大重。国凡税关前,当路有活版[板],与路平,下承以叠杆之末一杆。此杆最大,其首一杆最小。在税房中,悬以小铁权,货车过活版[板]上略停,房中已秤得其轻重矣。

曲　杆

上所言杆,皆直杆也。力重俱正加,别有曲杆,力重俱斜加。

曲杆之能,视力重之斜度而异。斜度愈多,其能愈小。无论杆作何形状,力重何方向,但取过倚点之线,与力重之方向成直角,即显力重之能。

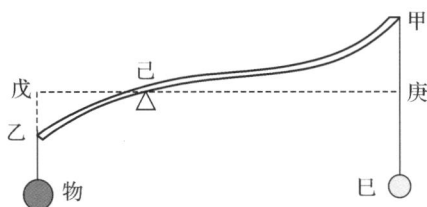

如图,甲己乙为曲杆,巳为力,加于甲点。物为重,加于乙点,乃过倚点己作虚线戊庚,与力重二方向俱正交,即显力与重之比,若戊己与庚己之比。

匠人起钉,合曲杆理。锤头着物处,即倚点。手所加处,即力点。齿衔处,即重点。钉在木中之阻力,即重也。

轮　轴

凡杆转于轴,若旋一周,即合轮之理。如图,甲乙为杆之二端,转动于倚点。即定轴己,压甲向下,则举乙向上。压乙向下,则举甲向上。故力重之体势,可

两边互易,而相定不变,如天平是也。此图显轮之本。

又图,甲乙、丙丁二杆,及轮周廓联为一体,转动于中心己。己点为全体内诸分之公倚点,故自己点任至周廓之一点,俱为杆之一端。虽无辐,作无虚线相联,理亦同。观此图,轮本于杆之理更显矣。别有一种轮轴,不在中心名偏心轮,今不论。

轮轴一器,大者为轮,细者为轴,轴与轮连为一体。轴之两端,凭于二柱端,可平转。用法,加大重于轴,近轴心;加小重于轮,远轴心。此器之理与杆同。轴心即倚点也。如图,甲为轮,乙为轴。轴心为轮轴之公倚点。辛为转器之柄,物为重,以绳连于轴,轴转则绳缠绕而引物上行。若不以手转而以绳悬小重巳于轮周,与轴之绳方向相反,则巳重引轮周之绳卸下,必令轴周之绳缠上,而引物上行。二力彼此相反,理与杆同。是以轮轴一名"永杆"(perpetual lever)。盖凡杆之两端转动,所过之界有限,用时转至限末,则撤而复始,故必屡用屡停。轮轴转动,所过之界无限,用时可永转不停,故曰永杆也。

此器从轴端视之,与杆同之理更显。如图,甲为轴周加巳力之点,乙为轴周加物重之点,己为轮轴之公心。作虚线联之,则甲乙即杆,巳即倚点。甲己轮半径即力倚距,乙己轴半径即重倚距也。轮愈大,则力倚距愈长,而与重物相定之巳力,必愈小。然巳力愈小,欲引物上行,则巳下行之界必愈大。有一利必有一弊也。

求重力相定,亦如杆法。重乘轴半径(即重倚距),力乘轮半径(即力倚距),二数相等,则相定矣。如悬一斤重于径十二寸之轮周,必与径一寸

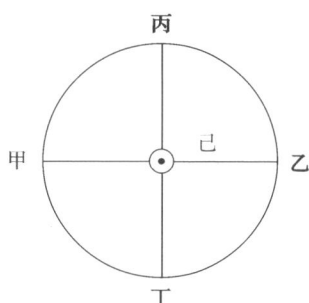

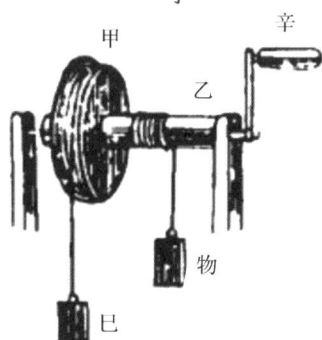

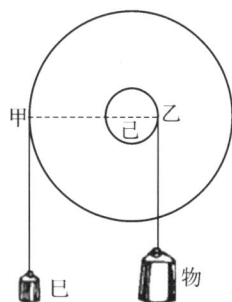

之轴周,十二斤相定也。用轮轴,当并推绳绕几周,盖此能令力倚重倚二
距生变也。然理不变,故今不详论。

日用之器,用轮轴者不少。如汲水之辘
轳,及煤矿中起煤之器,皆是也。轮上之力,或
用马,或用火机,皆可。大船上及坝上所用之
盘车,乃轮轴之平置者,纆横缠于轴,盘周有穴
若干,用时插诸杆于中,多人共推转之。杆愈
长,则轴上发力愈大,盖加力处即轮周也。

滑　车

滑车为助力原器之一。制如轮,其周有槽,轴
连于架。有定滑车,有动滑车。定滑车之架,悬于
高处,不能升降,以一长索过其槽。一端用力,一端
起重。如图,甲为滑车,乙为所悬处。巳甲物为索,
巳为力,物为重。此滑车如两端相等之杆,不能助
力。设一端有重一百斤,一端加力亦必一百斤。故
用此者,非欲省力,第便于拉耳。用索过一木,亦能
起重,但有两阻力能损索。滑车随索而转,无面阻
力,用之较便也。

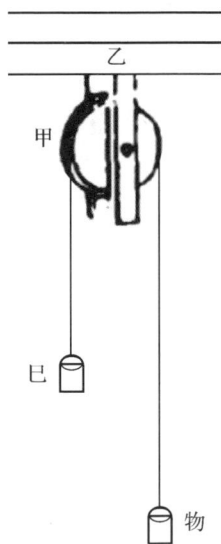

动滑车之架,非悬于高处,而系于重物,以索过
期槽,而拉令上升,重物亦随之上升也。如图,乙为
动滑车,丙为定滑车,定滑车与甲钩分悬于高处。
用长索,一端系甲钩,过乙车之槽,复过丙车之槽。以巳力拉其一端,则
乙车上升,而重物亦随之上升也。丙车不能动助力,不过变力之方向,而
乙车能省力之半。盖一重分悬于甲丙二处,二处出力等。故加半力于巳,
能超物之全重也。

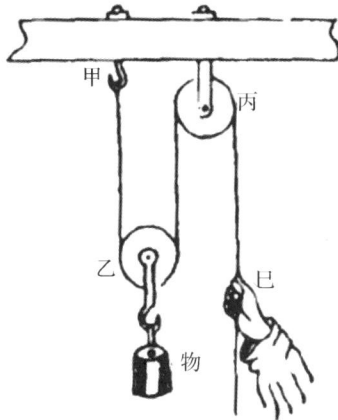

设物重十斤,则五斤为甲所引,五斤为巳所引。此二小儿共提一篮,彼此手执环,各任篮之半重也。或用绳络于篮底,各提绳之一端。理亦同。

凡用动滑车起重,恒以索之一端,著于高处,令任重之半,拉索者亦任重之半。然力省而时费,如起重至一尺高,拉索过滑车必至二尺也。

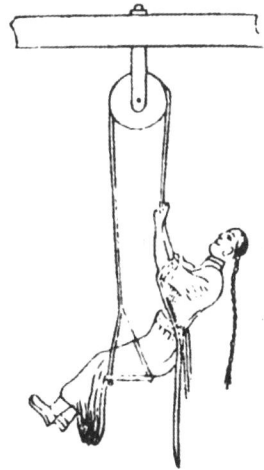

定滑车有一妙用。如图,有索过滑车,其一端作一套圈,人坐其中,而拉其又一端,能令己身上升。若再加一动滑车,则拉力更少一半。西国石工、泥工修高屋,恒用之。

滑车之功用,因索之各处力俱等,故能减小人力,又能拉力之方向。

滑车不能发力,其力全在索。索拉紧时处处等,故重物之力,散于索之各点。凡索拉紧,以令二物相近者,其理俱与滑车之索力同。如缝衣之线力是也。又如鞋匠上鞋一双,其数百次拉线之力,若并于一时用之,能举三四千斤也。

设用轮轴转滑车之索,则得杆与滑车二种器之和力,叠用无数滑车,可令其能至无穷大。故若以坚牢不坏之质作一助力器,阻力不大,则无

论若干重,不难举之。此器名曰连滑
车。连滑车有数式,或用一定滑车,或用数定滑车,群列
于左。

如图,连滑车第一式,用二定滑车,其索回还
四折,每折俱任重四分之一。第四折过第一定车
至人手,其力不分。盖一车仅能变力之方向,不
能助力,故手加于巳,亦任重四分之一。假如重
一百斤,则用力二十五斤,即能起之也。准此知
重之分数,恒倍于活滑车,而但用一分力,即能
起重。如此图,动滑车二,倍之为四,则重分为
四分,而手所加力为四分重之一也。他可类推。但用力愈少,则历时愈
多。因所拉之索尺数多也,又滑车多,阻力亦必加多。

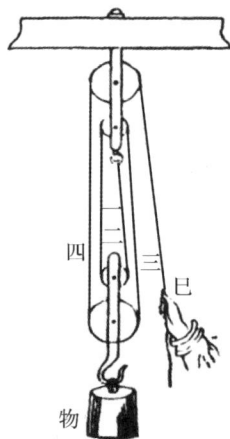

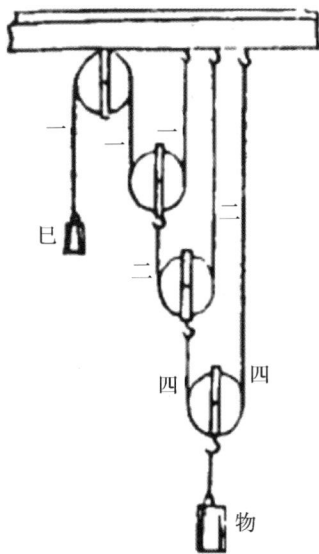

又图,连滑车第二式,用一定滑车,其动滑车每车一索,第一索之一端
巳,有一斤力,则其滑车必任二斤重。索之两端各任一斤也。推之第二
索,两端各任二斤重,其滑车必任四斤重。第三索两端各任四斤重,其滑
车必任八斤重。是巳一斤力,能起物八斤重也。若再加一动滑车,则能起

十六斤重。余可类推也。

凡加力于滑车，其方向或与索正交，或与索平行，则得正力。若斜加，则费力。离正交之方向愈远，则力愈费。

凡舶上樯之起倒，帆之上落，工匠建屋时起重，俱用连滑车。

又图，连滑车第三式。甲架有三动滑车，乙架有三定滑车，此为恒用之器。假如物重六百斤，巳力一百斤，即能起之。西国炙肉，欲令恒转，亦用连滑车悬重，重渐下，肉渐转也。

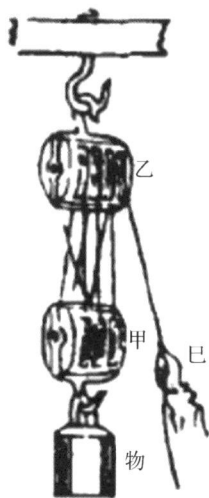

斜　面

凡平面与地平平行，谓之地平面。若一边高，一边低，则为斜面。如图，甲乙为地平面，甲丙为斜面也。

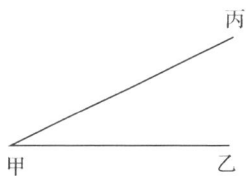

斜面为助力原器之一，用小力可令大重上升。凡用助力器，力省则时增。此器亦然。假加有物重一百斤，欲令上升，若不藉助力器，则用力必与重等，亦须一百斤。若令凭斜面徐升，则用力必少于一百斤。力减若干，视面之斜度而异。

凡面有免阻力，如引物或推车于地平面，所抵之力，即面阻力也。若其面极平滑，一无滞碍，则无面阻力。所引之物一动之后，可不更加力而自动也。凡引重物上斜面，则所抵者有面阻力，又有体质之重力。物在斜面上恒欲就下，即体质之重力也。但物于斜面上就下，较空中坠下，历时必多。其二时之比，若斜与高比，又若历时同，则所过之路不同，亦若斜与高比。譬如有物空中坠下，第一秒中过十六尺。设有斜面十六尺，其高一尺，物在斜面滚下，其第一秒中，必过斜面一尺也。余可类推。

凡引物上斜面，力之方向与斜面平行，其体质抵斜面之力，正交斜面。

如球置地平面,其球抵面之力向下,面抵球之力向上。俱正交地平面乙丙。甲乙即抵力线也。设地平面之一端丙移至丁,变成斜面,则球与面抵力之方向亦变,仍与面正交也。

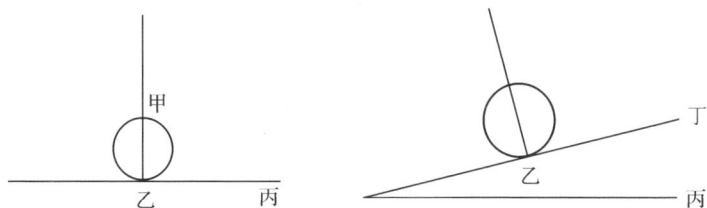

凡斜面非极平力,则必有面阻力阻物下行,亦可当作引物向上之力。

凡重与斜面诸力,时或增大,推得其例如下:

一、重力之大小,视面之斜度而异。斜面之度愈大,重力亦愈大。

二、运动迟,物之质阻力大,则加力必增多。

三、斜度愈小,则物压面力愈大。

四、以若干高为定率,则若干重与若干力之定率俱同。

设路斜长十尺,高一尺,则其斜率为十分之一。故重力减小,仅余十分之一,而用全重力十之一,即能引之上升也。又路斜长十尺,高一尺,则十尺之远,令物只上升一尺。故路上各点,仅举物全重十分之一也。设有二斜路:一长二十尺,一长五十尺,俱高一尺。车载物过二十尺,与过五十尺,面阻力不论,则费力必等。

如图,甲寅、乙寅二等高斜面,对合于顶点,其斜率不同,以索过顶上之滑车,系巳、午二重物,加于二面。设甲寅长二尺,乙寅长一尺,则午二斤,必能与巳四斤相定。面无

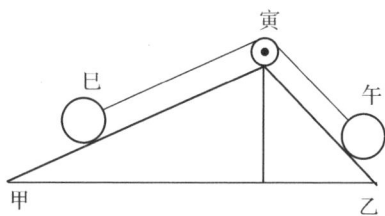

论若干长短,理皆同。西国铁轨,间有二斜面相合,用铁索连二车,令轻车下行,引重车上行也。古人不知斜面之理,作山路必跨岭蹦峦,上下直行,意谓如是较捷也。近时造路者,恒欲使路平,作山路,恒作斜坡,盘旋而度,或曲折数回。车夫过山路,必曲折行,能省马力也。

凡有大营造,必作斜面,令车运料上行。大桶入车,亦于斜面滚上。船成下水,亦用斜面。人家楼梯虽有级,亦斜面也。日用所需,用斜面助力者甚多,略举一二,难具述也。

劈

劈之理本于斜面。

斜面之用,面不动而重物动。劈之用,面动而重物不动。

劈为简器,以铜铁坚木之类为之。其形作三棱体。如图,乙为劈背,最厚;渐削至甲,为劈口。口之两边,或俱斜,则有两斜面之力。或一直一斜,则止[只]有一斜面之力。劈之用,或以开木,或以挤物令紧,或以起重。此为以劈开木之图。或以锤击劈背令入,或以重物压之令入,大率用锤为多。

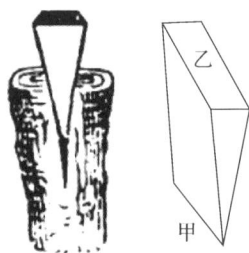

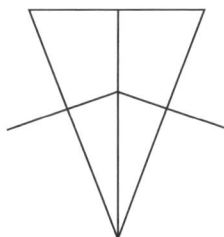

论劈之力,一如斜面。斜面角度愈大,阻力愈多,而用力愈大,故劈身短而背厚者,必费力也。劈之两边等势,则劈背所加力其方向与劈心线平行,而劈面抵物之力,其方向正交劈面,理与斜面同。如图,两横线与劈之两面各正交遇于中心,显抵力之方向。

劈力最难推,因锤击有轻重,斜面之角度有多少,所开之物抵力有大小也。劈所开之物,若二杆然。劈力所加处,即力点;将分之处,即重点。最下之点,即倚点也。

简器中,劈之用最少,而用物之有劈理者,最多。如针,如锥,如钉,如刀,如镰,如斧,如盘,皆是也。锯亦有劈理,每一齿为一小劈。

剃发之刀,刈草之镰,皆具劈理。窥以显微镜,见剃刀之锋,如锯齿,有无数微劈焉。

用上阔下狭二玻璃杯相套,以小力压上杯,能令下杯迸裂。此亦劈理也。盖上杯向下,其旁面加于下杯之口,有劈力。向下愈重,则劈力愈增。至下杯不能抵,则割然破矣。

螺　旋

螺旋亦为助力次器,其理本于斜面。

乃一线斜缠圆轴,如磴抱峰,斜盘而上,直至峰巅。此为常用螺旋图。缠轴之线,或方形,或三角形,理俱同。

其线缠轴一匝,为一层。

螺旋或无中轴,如开瓶塞之螺旋是也。此为开瓶塞之螺旋图。有斜面之力三:其线之末甚锐,向上渐粗,一也。其螺形削下丰上,二也。又螺旋之本理,出于斜面,三也。

螺旋之用,有斜面之理,观线之势自明。假如依轴心方向剖之,展圆柱面为平面,则逐层螺线,俱成斜面。其第一层为乙甲。若未展,则甲点在丙。故转螺旋一周,重物行于螺线。自丙至乙,与行于斜面。自甲至乙,无异也。

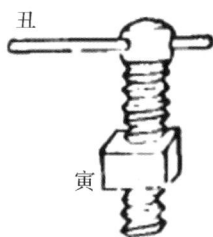

螺旋名牡螺线,与牝螺线相偕为用。牝牡二螺线,配合极密。用时此螺线为彼螺线所过之路,而互相压紧。如图,寅为牝线体,以坚杆转之。

螺旋之用,能加抵力于他物。其法牝牡二线,必一动一定。若牡线为定,则牝线转动;若牝线为定,则牡线转动,俱能挤物也。

凡用螺旋必兼用杆，杆或通过牝线轴之首，或着于牝线之外体，故螺旋有杆、斜面二器之合力。

凡斜面角度愈小，物上愈易，然历时愈久。此理推之螺旋，其螺线上下二层相距愈远，即斜面之角度愈大，用力必愈费。若相距愈近，即斜面之角度愈小，用力愈省。故螺线极密，所加之力必极小也。

设有甲乙二螺旋，甲线二层相距一寸，乙线二层相距半寸，则用相等力加之。甲转绕一周，乙转巳二周。设高下之界相等，则乙线层数必倍于甲线层数。甲杆以二人一转起重，乙杆以一人二转起重，重上升之数必相等。

螺旋转一周，线上之质点，所过斜路，分为平垂二路。平路等于螺旋之圆周，垂路等于螺线二层相距，故螺旋圆周，与线二层相距之比，若重与力之比。然用螺旋必兼用杆，则当以杆上力点绕轴心所成之圆周，代螺旋之圆周。

故力乘力点所成之圆周，等于重乘线之二层相距。欲螺旋发力大，当令杆增长，令线增密。若知杆之长短，线之相距，及所起之重，即可推用力当若干。又若知杆长、线距及力，亦可推能起若干重。

设有杆长四十寸，线相距一寸，起重八千斤，欲知当用若干力。约推之，倍杆长得八十寸，为圆径，三倍之，得二百四十寸。为圆周，以线相距，乘重八千斤，得八千，以二百四十约之，得三十三斤又三分斤之一，即当用之力也。然尚有面阻力，故当依所推力更加三分之一，方能起之。

大凡螺旋发力大，则不能令物速行。然惟单线之螺旋为然，若线之斜度大，相距甚远，中间更加数线以成密螺旋，则一轴上或有三四余线不等。诸线齐举物向上，发力大而速。西国印书架用之，能令二千斤之重，霎时起落，绝不费力也。

助力器发力最大者，莫若螺旋。螺旋有大抵力，恒不变。因牡线恒切牝线，故所发力，末尝或变也。

西国订书匠所用压书之架，最妙。如图，辛为不动之牝螺线，甲为转动之牡螺线。甲之下端有球，如乙。球之四面有孔，容杆以转螺旋。球下

有轴,镶入压板丙,能旋转而不能出入。螺旋
左转,则推压板下行;右转,则提压板上行。
压板之两边有缺口,与架柱凹凸恰相配,故随
螺旋上下,而左右方位不少变也。申为底板。
压书时,置书于底板,而左转螺旋,令压板向
下压之。书被压时,向上之抵力,与牝螺线向
下之抵力等。

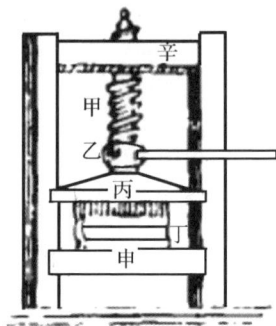

总论(重学之理①)

凡重学力,不能变化诸质,与化学力之功效异。重学力之功效,能令
体质移动,能变体之形状及方位。凡行星之绕日及自转,水与风之动法,
皆合重学力之理,而人造作,亦归重学。凡以力加于实体,乃重学力也。
日用之器皆然。人当尽心考察重学之理。此理日明,则器日精、日神妙。
若不明重学理,则器不能精,且用之多危险。

设数事明之。假如有檐或梁木,当三分之一处偶折断。若外
帮短木,用绳缚之,力必甚微。一遇外力加之必仍折,盖断木之一
段。若杆绳之力为重,重甚微,故不能胜所加之力也。若断木之二
段,各以锯剖之,为四段,乃以二短二长并凑缚之。如图,则或更固
于不断之木,盖木之刚柔恰相补也。

又如有板,半在楼内,半出楼外,人立于外端。若内无相当之
重,则外端必下行。人必坠落。盖板若杆,人身之重,若力在杆之一端,而
余一端之重太小,不能相定故也。人不知重学之理,往往犯此等危险事。

凡梁木之类,其力能抵横加之力。抵力之限,与广及厚之正方有正比
例,与长有反比例。故梁木愈粗愈短,则愈固。设长不变,其广倍,则抵力

---

① 《六合丛谈》版无"重学之理"四字,而在《西学辑存六种》出现。参见伟烈亚力原
　译,王韬笔著的《重学浅说》,袁俊德辑于《富强斋丛书续全集》,1901 年,小仓山房
　石印本,第 7a 页。

亦倍。若倍其厚，则抵力四倍。故体积加，抵力亦加，而抵力之加，其比例迟于体积。此为重学中最大纲领，营造家不可不知。

假如取长石一条，半入墙中，半在外，则在外一段，各点俱欲就下。有杆理焉。切墙之点，即倚点，墙即力，欲就下一段，即重。故加长外石，即加重，加至过抵力之限，石必折。

梁木或石条，若两端着柱，理与上同，但其折必在中点。两端着柱，中间之力，倍于一端入墙。若二端俱入墙，其力更大。

凡有纹理之质体，如木之类，以重直加之，其抵力大于横加。若斜加之，则方向愈近直加，其抵力愈大。假如木直植土中，其上墙任重之力为最大。一端入地，一端斜倚他物，其力次之。西国房屋之栋，恒作人字式。造桥梁恒令木斜倚，梁木下用诸木层叠，递相斜支，则最固。

大要造宫室、桥梁，重之横加者，改令近直加，使力不向下而两旁，为最妙法。

细察万物，知造物主于一切动植，用质少而得力大。故动植诸物，其体若更大，则本力必不能自胜其重。以小虫与大物比较，则体之比例，与力之比例不同。小虫之力更大，能受艰苦亦更胜。人之身体大小，相去不甚远，故行走甚便。若大数倍，则蹒跚难行矣。

凡器质增多，能力亦大，但比例渐小，故繁器之助力有限。凡屋与桥之梁，上压之重不过限，则甚固；过限，则不能胜而必折。

万象中式之最固者，为环形。工匠恒以巧法造之，环之凸面，恒任重。其形或正圆，或椭圆，或半圆，如桥，或全圆，如牖、如户，或卵形，其抵力之理皆同。大率环中诸点，互相挤紧，如无数小劈，其诸点恒欲向凹面，故凸面能抵大重，其抵力若正交环线，不过限，则愈多愈紧。

MECHANICS-MACHINERY
（重学浅说原文）

GENERAL DEFINITIONS

The application of the laws of motion and forces to objects in nature or contrivances in the arts, forms the branch of Natural Philosophy usually treated under the head MECHANICS, MECHANICAL POWERS, OR ELEMENTS OR MACHINERY. [①]

Machines are, under all denominations or circumstances, only instruments through which power may be made to act. They only convey, regulate, or distribute, the force or power which is communicated to them from some source of motion, and never create or generate power. But although a machine does not create power, or give more power than it has received, it practically applies the power which has been communicated to it, in so convenient and easy a manner, that a result ensues almost as surprising as if it had actually generated the

---

① In scientific works, the term *mechanics* is usually restricted to the action of *solids*, while *mechanical* or *mechanically* is applied to the action of both solids and fluids. For example, the wearing away of stone by the action of the water, is said to be *mechanical action*, or that the water acts *mechanically*.

whole or a portion of the power it exhibits.

The main purpose required in mechanical operations is to over-come, oppose, or sustain, a certain resistance or force. This purpose is obtained by applying another species of force. According to the usual phraseology, the resistance or force to be overcome is called the *weight*, and the force which is applied is called the *power*.

The ability of applying force by the human hands, without the aid of instruments or machines, is very limited. In almost all our opera-tions of art, it is found necessary to call in the aid of instruments or machines of some kind. All the instruments which mankind have a-dopted for their use—from the piece of stick with which the savage scratches the ground as a plough, to the most elegantly finished piece of mechanism—act upon certain fixed principles in nature, which a long course of experience and scientific investigation has developed.

The mechanical powers which exhibit the working of these princi-ples, are strictly only three in number, namely,— 1. the *Lever*; 2. the *Pulley*, or *Cord*; 3. the *Inclined Plane*. These may be called the Pri-mary Mechanical Powers; and from two of them, the Lever and In-clined Plane, other three are formed, as follow 1. *Wheel* and *Axle*, from the *Lever*; 2. *Wedge*, from the *Inclined Plane*; 3. *Strew*, from the *Inclined Plane*. These may be called the Secondary Mechanical Powers. The six altogether form the elements of every species of ma-chinery, however complex.

OF LEVERS

The lever is one of the most important and extensively used of all the mechanical powers, and its operation exhibits some of the leading principles in mechanics.

A lever is a rod, or bar of iron, wood, or any other material, which is movable upon or about a prop or fulcrum, or about a fixed axis. It is called a *lever*, from a French word, signifying to raise, and has been applied to instruments for raising or lifting weights.

Three elements contribute to the operation of the lever—the *power*, the *fulcrum*, and the *weight*. The power is the force applied, the fulcrum is the prop or support, and the weight is the resistance or burden to be lifted. The terms *power* and *weight* have merely a reference to the manner in which the machine is used strictly, both the power and weight are *forces* the same in character and action.

There are three kinds of levers, differing according to the relative situation of the power, fulcrum, and weight. Each of these kinds consists of a straight bar, and in theoretical calculations is supposed to be in itself destitute of any gravity or degree of heaviness. In theory, also, the forces which are applied are supposed to act at *right angles* to the fulcrum.

In the first or most simple kind of lever, "the fulcrum is disposed between the power and the weight." In the second kind, "the weight is disposed between the power and the fulcrum." In the third kind, "the power is disposed between the weight and the fulcrum."

In the first kind of lever, "the fulcrum is disposed between the power and the weight." Figure 1 is an example. A to B is a straight bar, resting on a prop or fulcrum F. From A to F is the long arm of the lever, and from F to B is the short arm. P is the power, or a certain force drawing down the extremity of the long arm at A. W is the weight suspended from the extremity of the short arm at B. The object is to cause P, which is supposed to be a small weight, to balance or overcome W, which is supposed to be a weight much heavier. Practically, the force of a man pressing upon the extremity of the handle of the level at A, will effect with ease, in lifting the heavy weight W, what it would require a much greater force to accomplish by pressing upon the long arm at a point half way betwixt A and the fulcrum.

Fig. 1

This is more clearly exemplified in fig. 2, which represents a lever placed conveniently for raising a square block W, which is the weight. On pressing down the extremity of the long arm of the lever at A, the point of the short arm B raises the Hock. F is an object lying on the ground to press against as the fulcrum. As in the case of fig. 1, "the force of a man pressing upon the extremity of the handle at A, will effect with ease, in lifting the weight W, what it would require a much greater force to accomplish by pressing upon the long arm at a point half way betwixt A and the fulcrum."

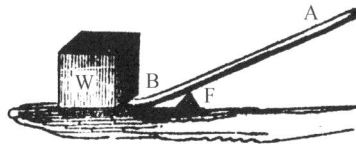

Fig. 2

The principle in mechanics which produces this phenomenon is very simple, and is explained by what is called the Law of Virtual Velocities, or, from its general application, the Golden Rule of Mechanics.

This law or rule is, *That a small weight*, *descending a long way in any given length of time*, *is equal in effect to a great weight descending a proportionally shorter way in the same space of time*. In other words, what is gained in velocity or time, is lost in expenditure of power.

Another way of stating this important law is as follows:—*In the case of equilibrium*, *if a motion be given to the mechanical power*, *then the power multiplied by the spate through which it moves in a vertical direction*, *will be equal to the weight multiplied by the space through which it moves in a vertical direction*.

This principle, which applies to every mechanical movement in the case of equilibrium, has been illustrated by a reference to the property of attraction of gravitation. What is called weight is only an effect of gravity on the atoms of matter. In figurative language,

every atom is drawn towards the earth by an invisible line or cord of attraction; and when one atom rises or falls ten inches, the same quantity of attraction is drawn out from, or sent back to the earth, as if ten atoms were to rise or fall only one inch.

Thus, by a proper mode of applying the power, we may cause a weight of one pound, by moving through a space of ten feet, to raise another weight of ten pounds, moving through a space of one foot; or (the reverse) by a weight of ten pounds moving through the space of one foot, we may make a single pound move through the space of ten feet. But by none of the mechanical powers shall we be able, by moving a weight of ten pounds through one foot, to move a single pound through eleven feet; nor, by a single pound moving through a space of nine feet, shall we be able to raise a weight of ten pounds through one foot.

Neither by the power of the lever, therefore, nor by any other of the mechanical powers, can we make any absolute increase of the power which is applied. In other words, the quantity of power expended in any great and instantaneous effort, is exactly the amount of the power which has been previously accumulated. All that we can do to procure mechanical advantage, is to accommodate the velocity, force, or direction of the applied power, to the purposes which we may have in view.

To apply this principle to the lever: in figs. 1 or 2, a small force at A is equal to double the force exerted at a point halfway betwixt A and the fulcrum, yet, in both cases, the same amount of mechanical power is expended. A slight push downwards at A, by being continued for one minute, is equal to a push of double the force at a point halfway towards the fulcrum, continued for the same time. Any amount of force, therefore, can be exerted with ease at the extremity of the long arm of the lever, provided we choose to make the arm long enough and strong enough.

It may possibly be said that it would be as expeditious to push down the extremity of the long arm of the lever, as to push down the arm at the point nearer the fulcrum. Practically, in small levers this may be the case; but when levers of considerable length have to be used, and a succession of depressions and raisings are necessary, it will be found that more time is spent in working with a long than a short lever. For when the sweep of the lever is inconveniently long, the person using it has to move his body quickly up and down over a larger space, and is sooner fatigued. For this reason, although a boy with a long lever may balance as great a weight as a man with a shorter one, yet, in raising weights successively by it, the boy would be sooner fatigued.

It is a general rule that "the force of the lever increases in proportion as the distance of the power from the fulcrum increases, and diminishes in proportion as the distance of the weight from the fulcrum diminishes." In making calculations to ascertain the proportions to be observed betwixt the power and the weight, regard must be paid to the respective lengths of the long and short arms of the lever. We must also fix what are to be the units of weight and distance, and let them be the same on both ends. If we state inches to be the unit of length of the short arm, inches must be the unit of length of the long arm; and in the same manner, if ounces be made the unit of weight of the short arm, ounces must be made the unit of power of the long arm.

Rule.—Multiply the weight by its distance from the fulcrum; then multiply the power by its distance from the same point; and if the products are equal, the weight and the power will balance each other.

Example First.—Suppose a weight of 100 pounds on the short arm of a lever, at the distance of 8 inches from the fulcrum, then another weight or power of 8 pounds would be equal to this, at the distance of 100 inches from the fulcrum. Because 8 multiplied by 100 produces 800, and 100 multiplied by 8 produces 800—and thus the weight and the power would mutually counteract each other.

Example Second.—Suppose we wish to calculate what power should be employed at the end of the long arm of the lever to balance a given weight at the end of the short arm. We multiply the weight by the length of its arm. This gives us a product; then divide that product by the number of inches in the long arm, and the result or quotient is the power. Thus, a weight of 10 pounds, multiplied by 10 inches as the length of the short arm, gives a product of 100. If the length of the long arm be 20, we find how many twenties are in 100, and there being 5, consequently 5 pounds is the power. In this instance, the mechanical advantage is two to one—that is, the power is twice as small as the weight.

The common spade used in delving in gardens offers a similar example of simple lever power, when employed in raising the earth from its place to turn it over. Fig. 3 represents an equally familiar example, namely, a wood-sawyer or carpenter moving a log of timber from its place, by means of a long pole or beam of wood. Stone masons use a lever of iron of this description, called a crow-bar.

Fig. 3

The power of the first kind of lever is frequently seen to operate in machines or instruments having two arms. The most common examples of this nature are pincers, scissors, and similar instruments. In the pair of scissors here represented, the two limbs are seen to be joined together with a rivet at the centre, which is the fulcrum of both.

Fig. 4

A common scale beam for weighing, used by shop keepers, is an example of the first kind of lever, formed with two arms of equal

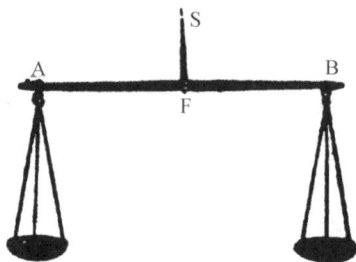

Fig. 5

length, and suspended over the centre of gravity, so that the two extremities balance each other. See fig. 5. S is a string or line suspending the beam A B at a central point F, which is the fulcrum. The point of suspension, or pivot, is sharpened to a thin edge, so as to allow the arms to rise or fall with as little friction as possible when anything is put in the scales.

There is another kind of balance called a *steelyard*, which consists of a lever with arms of unequal length, and acts upon the principle of distance from the fulcrum on the long arm compensating for weight on the short arm, as already defined. Fig. 6 is a representation of the steelyard balance. C is the fulcrum or pivot by which the beam is suspended, and freely plays as on an axis. A is the short arm, and the opposite end is the long arm. W is the scale for the reception of the article to be weighed. The long arm is graduated into divisions by marks, each mark denoting by a figure a certain number of pounds or ounces. P is a weight of a certain heaviness, and being movable by a ring, it can be slipped along the bar to any required point. The same weight is always used, and thus constitutes one of the principal conveniences of this kind of balance. In proportion as the article to lie weighed in the scale W is heavy, so is the weight P slipped along to a greater distance from the fulcrum; and when it is brought to a point where it balances the article, the figure on the bar at that point indicates the amount of the weight. If P be one pound, and if, when suspended from the division at 6, it balance[s] the weight at W, it is evident that the weight will be six times P, or 6 pounds. And so on with all the other divisions.

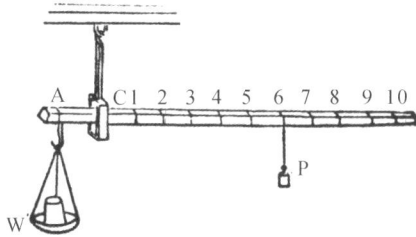

Fig. 6

The steelyard, though not so ancient as the common balance, is of considerable antiquity. It was used by the Romans, and has long been in use among the Chinese. Neither the lance nor the steelyard are[is] suitable for showing the varying weight or heaviness of an article at different latitudes of the earth's surface, because the weights employed are equally affected with the attraction of gravitation and centrifugal force, as the article to be weighed. For this reason, the difference of weight resulting from the causes mentioned, can only be demonstrated by a balance formed of a spring of elastic metal. By suspending the article from the spring, it pulls it out to a certain extent, and so indicates the weight on a graduated scale on the instrument. As the spring acts the same in all latitudes, it nerves as a fixed and unalterable power, while the article to be weighed is liable to an alteration in its weight or heaviness according as it is brought near or carried from the equator.

In the lever of the second kind, the weight is placed between the power and the fulcrum, as in fig. 7. The line from A to B is the long arm, B to F is the short arm. W is the weight, and P is the power. The object required by this lever is to lift the weight W by raising the extremity of the lever at A. In this, as in the case of the first kind of lever, the power is increased in proportion to its distance from the fulcrum.

Fig. 7

Examples of this kind of lever power are common. One of the most familiar is that of a man pushing or lifting forward a bale of goods, as represented in fig. 8, in which the [balance] weight W presses against the lever between the power P and the fulcrum F.

Fig. 8

Another example of the second kind of lever is that of a man using a wheelbarrow, as represented in fig. 9. A point in the wheel of the barrow where it presses on the ground, is the fulcrum. The body of the barrow, with its load, is the weight. And the two handles, lifted or held up by the man, form the power. In proportion as the man shortens or lengthens the handles in holding them, so does he increase or diminish the weight he has to sustain.

Two men carrying a load between them on a pole, is also an example of the second kind of lever. The load may either rest upon or lie de-

Fig. 9

pendent from the pole. In the case of two porters carrying a sedan chair by means of two poles, the load or weight is partly above and partly below the line of the lever. In the case of porters carrying a barrel slung from a pole, as in fig. 10, the weight is altogether below the lever. In both instances the principle is the same. Each man acts as the power in moving the weight, and at the same time each man becomes a fulcrum in respect to the other. If the weight hang fairly from the centra of the pole, each man will bear just a half of the burden; but if the weight be slipped along to be nearer one end of the lever than the other, then the man who bears the shorter end of the pole supports a greater load than the man who is at the long end. The weight increases precisely in proportion as it advances towards him. Sometimes, when a man and a boy are carrying a handbarrow between them, the man, in order to ease the weight as much as possible to the boy, holds by the arms of the harrow near to where they join the loaded part.

In yoking horses to the extremities of cross bars in ploughs, coaches, or other vehicles, care requires to be taken to hook the cross bar to the load at its centre, otherwise one horse will have to pull more than the other.

An inflexible beam resting on supports or fulcra at its two extremi-

Fig. 10

ties, acts similarly as a lever of the second kind. Should no weight be appended to its centre, the weight of the material itself, when the extension is considerable, will be enough to bend it down, and even to break it. Extended flexible cords or chains are from this cause always bent down in the middle, no power of extension being able to overcome the gravity of the materials, which will give way before they can be rendered perfectly straight. The bended string of a boy's paper kite is an example of this powerful influence of gravity of materials.

The instrument used for cracking nuts (fig. 11) is an example I of the second kind of lever with two arms or limbs. The fulcrum is the joint which connects the two limbs; the nut between them is the weight or resistance; and the hand which presses the limbs together, in order to break, the nut, is the power. As each limb is a lever, a double level action takes place in the operation.

Fig. 11

The oar of a boat in rowing is a lever of the second kind. The hands of the sailor who pulls constitute the power; the boat is the weight to be moved; and the water against which the blade the oar pushes, is the fulcrum.

The second kind of lever is sometimes employed as an instrument of pressure. The point of the short arm is. For example, pushed into a crevice or hole in the wall, the fulcrum is the object to lie pressed, and at the extremity of the long arm a heavy weight is applied.

In this rude but efficacious manner are cheeses pressed in some parts of the country.

In the lever of the third kind, the power is placed between the weight and the fulcrum (fig. 12). The fulcrum is at the extremity of the short arm at F; the weight W is dependent from the extremity of the long arm at A; and P is the power.

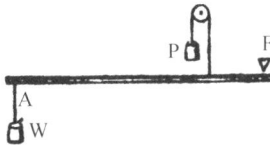

Fig. 12

In this kind of lever, the power acts with considerable disadvantage, or with small effect; but this disadvantage is compensated by an opposite advantage, which is frequently of great importance in the operations of both nature and art. The advantage consists in the velocity with which a small power will cause the extreme point of the long arm of the lever to move over a great space. This lever, therefore, whether in nature or art, is used only when a great space has to be traversed quickly by the long arm; but in this case the power must always be greater than the weight.

An example of this kind of lever is found in the foot board of the turning-lathe (fig. 13). The foot of the workman presses lightly on the board or plank near the end which rests on the ground, or fulcrum, and causes the opposite extremity of the board to move in a downward direction over a considerable space. A spring overhead, or a crank, pulls the board up again by means of a string 8; the workman again presses it downward, and so a constant action of the string or cord which works the lathe is easily produced.

Fig. 13

A man wielding a flail with two hands, and similar instances of u-sing weapons, are also examples of the third kind of lever action. A similar action was observable when we use fire-tongs; a small motion of the fingers near the joint of the instrument causes the legs, which are two levers, to open or shut over a consider able space.

Before the peculiar advantages of this kind of lever became known, or were appreciated, it was called the *losing lever*.

The movements in the limbs of animals are generally produced by the action of this kind of lever power.

When several levers of the simple kinds are connected together, and are made to operate one upon the other, the machine so formed is called a compound lever. In this machine, as each lever acts with a power equal to the pressure on it of the next lever between it and the power, the force is increased or diminished according to the number or kind of levers employed.

Fig. 14 represents a compound lever, consisting of three simple levers of the first kind, placed in a line, and each working on its own fulcrum. The desired object of the machine is for a small force or power at P to move or balance a large weight at W. The same rule applies, in calculating the action of this combined lever, which has already been given for the simple lever—namely, "Multiply the weight on any lever by its distance from the fulcrum; then multiply the power by its distance from the same point, and if the products are equal, the weight and the power will balance each other." Or, for the form of lever in the figure, "Multiply the length of the long arm by moving the power, and multiply that of the short one by the weight, or resistance."

Fig. 14

It is supposed that the three levers in the figure are of the same length, the long arms being six inches each, and the short ones two inches each; required—the weight which a moving power of 1 pound at P will balance at W. In the first place, 1 pound at P would balance 3 pounds at E; we say 3, because the long arm being six inches, and the power 1 pound, 6 multiplied by 1 is 6; and the short one being 2 inches, we find that there are 3 twos in 6, therefore 3 is the weight. The long arm of the second lever being also 6 inches, and moved with a power of 3 pounds, multiply the 3 by 6, which gives 18; and multiply the short arm, being 3 inches, by a number which will give 18; we find that 9 will do so (9 twos are 18); therefore 9 is the weight borne at the extremity of the short arm of the second lever at D. The long arm of the third lever being also 6 inches, and moved with a power of 9 pounds, multiply the 9 by 6, and we have 54; and multiply the short arm, being 2 inches, by a number which will give 54; we find that 27 will do so (twice 27 is 54); therefore 27 is the weight borne at the extremity of the short arm of the third lever. Thus 1 pound at P will balance 27 pounds at W; or 1 ounce at P will balance 27 ounces at W—the proportions being always alike, whatever denomination of weight we employ.

In this instance, the increase of power is comparatively small, because the proportion between the long and short arms is only as 2 to 6, or 1 to 3. If we make the proportions more dissimilar, as 1 to 10, or 1 to 20, the increase of force becomes very great. For example, let the long arms be 18 inches each, and the short ones 1 inch each, and 1 pound at P will balance 18 pounds at A, and the second lever would be pushed up with a power of 18 pounds. This 18 being multiplied by the length of the lever 18, gives 324 pounds as the power which would press down the third lever. Lastly, multiply this 324 by the length of the lever 18, and the product is 5832 pounds, which would be the final weight at W which 1 pound at P would raise.

The following is a general rule for calculating the advantages of a compound lever consisting of any number of levers, whether equal or not:—Call the arms of the different levers next the power the *arms of power*, and the other arms the *arms of weight*; then, if the lengths of the arms of power and the power itself be successively multiplied together, the product will be equal to the continued product of the arms of weight and the weight, when the power and weight are in equilibrium.

A similar result to that of a combination of levers might be produced by only one lever, provided it were long enough, but the operation would be both clumsy and inconvenient. By combining levers, and making them act one upon another, great weights may be balanced within a small compass, and with an exceedingly small power. On this account, machines are constructed with combinations of levers, for weighing loaded carts and other heavy burdens. The cart is wheeled upon a sort of table placed level with the ground beneath which the levers are arranged; and a small weight first lever, balances the load, which rests on the table above the last lever. This species of weighing-machine is often to be seen at toll-bars.

In the foregoing examples of lever powers, the levers or bars are supposed to be straight, and the powers and weights, or forces, are supposed to act at right angles with them.

Levers are frequently *bent* in their form, for purposes of convenience, and the powers and weights often act *obliquely*, or not at right angles.

In calculating the mechanical advantage of bent levers, the chief matter of consideration is *obliquity* in the direction of the applied power and weight. Obliquity in the action of the forces generally diminishes the mechanical advantage.

Whatever be the form of the lever, or the direction of the power and the weight, the mechanical advantage of the power or the weight is always represented by *a line drawn from the fulcrum*, *at right angles to the direction in which the forces arc respectively exerted*.

Fig. 15 is a bent lever, with the power of P hanging from A, and the weight W hanging from B. In this case, both the power and the weight act at right angles to an ideal line, drawn as from E to G across the fulcrum, which strikes the lines of direction of the forces at right angles.

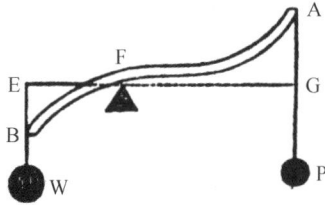

Fig. 15

OF THE WHEEL AND AXLE

A lever has been defined to be "a rod, or bar of iron, wood, or any other material which is movable upon or about a prop or fulcrum, or about a fixed axis." The illustrations which have been given, show the lever only in its character of a simple bar, which is movable in some part "upon or about a prop or fulcrum." It is now to be shown how it acts when movable upon or about a fixed axis. When a lever is movable upon an axis, and is susceptible of being turned completely round, it assumes the character of the diameter of a wheel.

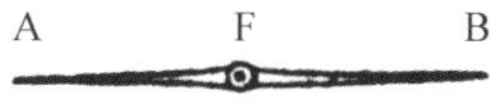

In fig. 16, the simple rudiments of a wheel are represented. A and B are the two arms of a bar or lever playing upon a fixed axis at F, and which axis is the fulcrum. If we push down A, we raise B, or if we push down B, we raise A. In this manner the situation of the power and the weight is transferable from

Fig. 16

one end to the other, as in the beam of a common balance, without altering the equilibrium.

Fig. 17 is a representation of a wheel in a state more advanced to completion. Here the arms A B are connected with the arms D C, both at the centre F, and by means of the circumference or rim of the wheel. By reason of this union of parts, the central axis at F becomes the common fulcrum for every portion

Fig. 17

of the wheel; therefore, from the centre to any point of the circumference is an arm of a lever, although the line of that lever be not marked or seen, as in the case of a distinct spoke.

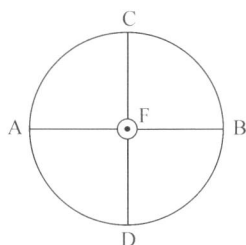

Aline through the centre from one side of the circumference of a wheel to the opposite side, is a diameter; from the centre to any part of the circumference, is the semi-diameter or radius. The arms or spokes are said to radiate from a centre. The circumference is sometimes called the periphery.

Besides wheels with axes in the centre, there are wheels with axes not in the centre, called eccentric wheels. At present, however, we are treating only of wheels having their axes in the centre.

Wheels with a central axis may be rendered available as levers in various ways, according to the placing of the weight or resistance. The plan commonly pursued consists in giving to the wheel an axle which is fixed to its arms, and placing a weight near the axle or fulcrum, to work against another weight at the circumference.

Thus a machine is formed called the Wheel and Axle, which constitutes one of the simple mechanical powers founded on the lever.

The machine termed the wheel fixed upon an axle or spindle,

which axle turns horizontally on its two ends in upright supports. See fig. 18. The fulcrum of the machine is common to both the wheel and the axle, and is the centre of the axle. A is the wheel, B is the axle, and H is a handle with which the machine may be turned. By turning the wheel, the axle is also turned, and a rope being fixed to the ax-

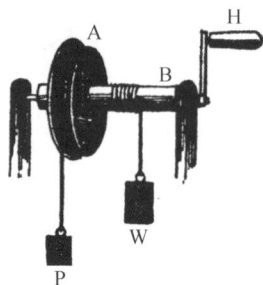

Fig. 18

le, with the weight W hanging at its extremity, the turning of the wheel causes the axle to wind up the rope, and so lift the weight. If, instead of turning the wheel with the hand, we wind a rope round the circumference of the wheel, in a contrary direction from that in which the axle rope is wound, and also hang a weight of a certain heaviness, P, to its extremity, then the draught or pulling of the wheel rope in unwinding, will turn the axle, and so wind up the axle rope with its weight. In this manner, one power works against another, exactly as in the case of the lever. By properly apportioning the two powers in correspondence with the diameters of the wheel and the axle, the one power or weight may be made to balance the other power or weight, so as to produce an equilibrium of the machine.

The wheel arid axle form what is called a *perpetual lever*. Common simple levers act only for a short space, or by reiterated efforts, so as to be adapted for lifting an object from one place to another on the ground. The perpetual lever, formed by the wheel and axle, turns round without intermission, and is therefore suitable for lifting weights attached to a rope, through a considerable space upward from the ground without stopping.

Fig. 19 is a representation of the machine endwise, and shows how the lever operates. The line going across the machine from A to B represents the line of the lever. A is the situation of the power, F is the centre or fulcrum, and B is the situation of the weight; therefore, from A to F is the long arm, and from F to B is the short arm of the lever. In other words, the long arm is half the diameter of the wheel, and the short arm is half the thickness or diameter of the axle.

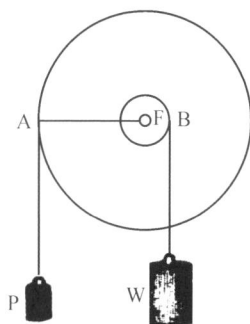

Fig. 19

By widening the wheel, and so lengthening the long arm of the lever, the smaller will be the power necessary to overcome the weight on the axle or short arm; but what is gained by this mechanical advantage is loot by the circumstance that the power must descend through a proportionally greater in order to raise the same weight through the same space in the same time.

To find what forces will balance each other, let the same rules be followed as those formerly given for the simple lever. Multiply the weight by its distance from the fulcrum (that distance is half the diameter of the axle); then multiply the power by its distance from the same point (that is, half the diameter of the wheel), and if the products be equal, the weight and the power will balance each other. Thus, a power of one pound at or depending from the circumference of a wheel of twelve inches in diameter, will balance a weight of twelve pounds at or depending from the circumference of an

Note.—No allowance is made in these calculations for the overlaying of the rope in winding, which affects the length of both the long and the short arm; but this is a matter of practical, not of theoretic import. The principle of the wheel and axle, or perpetual lever, is introduced into various mechanical contrivances which are of great use in many of the ordinary occupations of life. One of the simplest machines constructed on this principle, is the common windlass for drawing water by a rope and bucket from wells. Coal is lifted from the pits in which it is dug, by a similar contrivance, wrought by horse or steam power.

The capstan or drawing up anchors, and for other operations, is an of the wheel and axle, constructed in an upright or vertical, instead of a horizontal, position. In fig. 20, one of these capstans is represented. The axle is placed upright, with the rope winding about it, and having a head

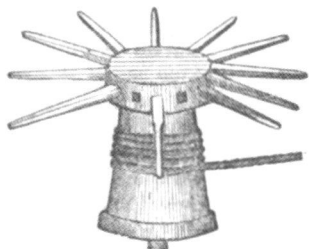

Fig. 20

pierced with holes for spokes or levers, which the men push against to cause the axle to turn. This is a powerful and convenient machine on chipboard; when not in use, the spokes are taken out and laid aside.

An illustration of the wheel and axle, in a combined form, is afterwards given in the case of the crane.

OF CORDS AND PULLETS

The pulley, or cord, is one of the primary mechanical powers. A pulley is a wheel, with a groove in its circumference, and is suspended by a central axis. In fixed pulleys, a flexible cord, which is made to pass over and hang from the upper part of the groove, has at one extremity a certain weight to be raised, and at the other extremity a power is attached for the purpose of pulling.

There are two kinds of pulleys, the fixed and movable.

The annexed cut, fig. 21, represents a fixed pulley. A is the wheel, B is the beam or roof from which the wheel is suspended. P is the power hanging at one end of the rope, and W is the weight at the other end. This kind of pulley is called a fixed pulley, because it does not shift from its position.

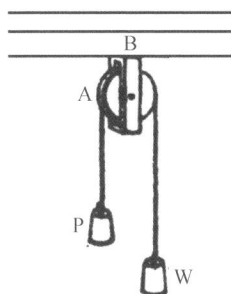

Fig. 21

The fixed pulley possesses no mechanical advantage. The wheel is merely a lever with e-qual arms, and therefore the cord which passes over these arms gains no advantage. To raise a pound weight from the ground at the one end of the cord, the power of one pound must be exerted at the other.

The object of the single fixed pulley is not to save power, but to give convenience in pulling. For instance, by pulling downwards, a weight may be made or by pulling in one direction, a load may be made to proceed in another. The same object might be gained by drawing a cord over a fixed post or pivot, but in this case the friction of the cord would chafe or injure it; the wheel or pulley is therefore a simple con-trivance to prevent friction, for it turns round along with the cord.

The movable pulley is in form the same as the fixed pulley, but in-stead of being placed in a fixed position from a beam or roof, it hangs in the cord which passes under it, and from it the weight is suspended. In fig. 22, a movable pulley is represented. A is a hook in a beam to which one end of a cord is fixed. B is the movable pulley, under which the cord passes and proceeds upwards to C, a fixed pulley, from which it depends to P, the power or the hand pulling. The fixed pulley C is of no further use than to change the direction of the power. W is the weight hanging from B.

The movable pulley possesses a mechanical advantage. The first point to be observed is, that the weight hangs in the cord; second, that the weight presses down each side of the cord equally—that is, it draws as hard at A as at C or P; third, that the consequence of this equal pressure is the halving of the weight between the two ends of the cord. The *halving of the weight* is therefore the mechanical advantage given by the movable pulley.

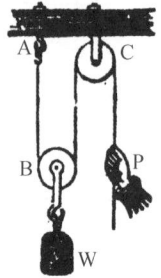

Fig. 22

Example.—If the weight W be ten pounds, five pounds is borne by A, and five pounds by P. The case is precisely the same as that of two boys carrying a basket between them. The basket is the weight, and each boy, with his hand upholding the handle, bears only half the load, whatever it may be. If, instead of holding by the handle, the boys slip a cord beneath it, and each take an end of the cord, the case is the same.

In order to save expenditure of power in lifting weights by pulleys, it is always contrived to cause some inanimate object, as for instance a beam or roof, to take a share of the weight, leaving only a portion to be borne by the person who pulls. But in this, as in all cases of mechanical advantage, the saving of power is effected only by a certain loss of time, or a longer continuation of labour. To lift a weight one foot from the ground, by the movable pulley, a man must pull up the cord two feet; therefore, to lift a weight, it will take double the exertion to draw it up a given height in a given time without the pulley, than it would require with the intervention of the pulley.

As the power which a man can exert by his hands, is able to overcome a weight greater than the weight of his own person, this circumstance may be taken advantage of in a very peculiar manner, through the agency of the fixed pulley. As represented in fig. 23, a man may seat himself in a loop or seat attached to one end of a cord, and passing the cord over a fixed pulley above, may pull himself upwards by drawing at the other end of the cord. By adding a movable pulley and another fixed pulley to the apparatus, the exertion of pulling would be diminished one half. An apparatus of this nature, having two fixed pulleys and one movable pulley, is used by house masons and other artisans, in making repairs on the fronts of buildings.

Fig. 23

The principle upon which pulleys act, is the distribution of weight throughout the different portions of the cord, so as to lessen the power necessary to be exerted by the operator. And along with this principle is the changing of the direction of the power for the sake of convenience in pulling.

According to ordinary language, the mechanical power of which we are treating is called the power of the pulley; but, in reality, as has been just shown, the pulley has no power in itself. The power of the machine is in the cord. *It is in the equal tension of the cord through its whole length, by which the weight is distributed upon intervening points, that the machine offers any mechanical advantage.*

In all cases in which cords are drawn tightly, so as to hold objects in close contact, the same species of power or mechanical advantage is exemplified. For instance, in drawing a cord in lacing, or a thread in sewing, this distribution of power is observable. If all the power which is distributed throughout the sewing of a single pair of strong shoes, were released and concentrated in one main draught, it would, in all likelihood, be a power sufficient to lift one or two tons in weight.

Technically, the wheel of a pulley is called a *sheave*; for protection and convenience this sheave is ordinarily fixed with pivots in a mass of wood called a *block*; and the ropes and cords are called a *tackle*. The whole machine, fully mounted for working, is termed a block and tackle. By causing a wheel and axle to wind up the cord of a block and tackle, the power of the lever is combined with that of the pulley in the operation.

There is no assignable limit to the power which may be exerted by means of pulleys. The machine may be constructed to raise with ease any weight which the strength of materials will bear, provided the combination is not so complex as to exhaust the power by the friction produced.

The power of pulleys is increased by a combination of wheels or sheaves in one tackle. There are different kinds of combinations or systems of pulleys. In some there is only one fixed pulley, and in others there are several.

The following are examples of different combinations of pulleys:

Fig. 24 represents a compound system of pulleys, by which the weight is distributed through four folds of the same cord, so as to leave only a fourth of the weight, whatever it may be, to be raised by the operator. In this illustration, the cord number 1 bears one-fourth of

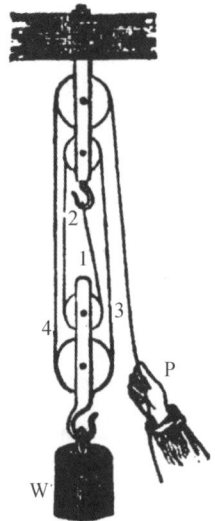

Fig. 24

the weight; the cord number 2 bears a second fourth; the cord number 3 bears a third fourth; and the cord number 4 bears a fourth fourth. Here the mechanical advantage ceases. For although the cord number 4 passes over the topmost fixed pulley down to the hand of the operator, no more distribution of power takes place; this topmost pulley being of use only to change the direction of the power. The person who pulls has thus only a quarter of the weight to draw. If the weight be one hundred pounds, he has the labour of pulling only twenty-five pounds.

Thus it is observable that the diminution of weight is proportion to the number of movable pulleys. To calculate the expenditure of power or diminution of weight, therefore, we have only to multiply the number of movable pulleys by two, and the product shows the power to be exerted. Two movable pulleys multiplied by two, gives 4; therefore a fourth of the weight is the power required, and so on. The addition of a single movable pulley to any system of pulleys, at once lessens the apparent weight one-half, or, in other words, doubles the effect of the power; but every such addition causes more time to be spent in the operation, there being at every additional fold of the cord more cord to draw cut, and also more friction to overcome.

In the annexed system of pulleys, Fig. 25, a series of movable pulleys, with different cords, are made to successively on one another, and the effect is doubled by each pulley. At the extremity of the first cord, a power of one pound depends. This cord, marked 1, by being drawn below a movable pulley, supports two pounds—that is, 1 pound on each side. The next cord, marked 2, in the same manner supports four pounds, or 2 pounds on each side. The next cord, marked 4, supports 8 pounds, or 4 pounds on each side. Thus, I pound at P supports 8 pounds at W. If another movable pulley were added, the 1 pound at P would support 16 pounds, and so on.

In working pulleys, the power must be applied in a line perpendicular to, or parallel with, the weight; that is, straight above the weight, in order to produce the full efficacy of direct force. If the power be applied obliquely—do not draw fair up—there will be a loss of power in proportion as the line of draught departs from the perpendicular.

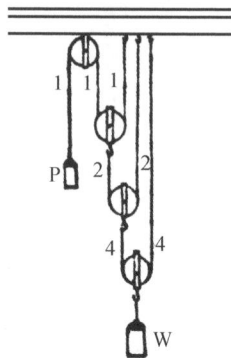

Fig. 25

Pulleys are used chiefly on board of ships, where blocks and tackle are in constant requisition for raising and lowering the sails, masts, and yards. They are likewise in considerable use by house-builders and others, in connection with the wheel and axle, for raising or lowering heavy masses of stone and other articles.

Fig. 26 is a representation of a system of pulleys, commonly used in practical operations. Three movable pulleys are enclosed in the block A, and three fixed pulleys are enclosed in the block B. Suppose, therefore, that the weight W, in this case, is six hundred pounds, the hand P pulls it up wards by exerting a force of one hundred pounds. A combination of pulleys resembling this is used in turning kitchen jacks. The weight in sinking draws off the cord from a spindle, by which motion the jack is turned. In order that a consider able weight falling slowly through a com-

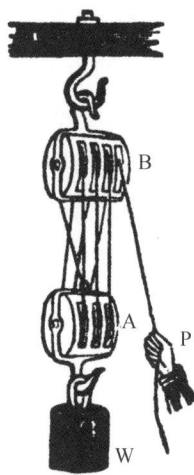

Fig. 26

paratively small height may keep the jack in motion for a long time, as many as ten or twelve movable and fixed pulleys are used.

OF THE INCLINED PLANE

A horizontal plane is a plane coinciding with that of the horizon, or parallel to it; when the plane is not level or horizontal, but lies in a sloping direction, with one end higher

Fig. 27

than the other, it is said to incline, or is called an inclined plane. Fig. 27 is an example.

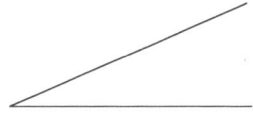

The inclined plane, as already stated, is a primary mechanical power. The object which is accomplished by it is the raising of weights to considerable elevations, or the overcoming of resistances by the application of lessor weights and resistance; or, making a small power overcome a greater.

To raise a load of a hundred pounds to an elevation of fifty feet by a direct perpendicular ascent, and without using any mechanical advantage, the power exerted must be a hundred pounds, or equal to the weights to be overcome. If, instead of raising the load directly upwards, we raise it by the gradual ascent of an inclined plane, the power required is less than a hundred pounds, and the diminution is in proportion to the smallness of rise in the inclined plane. But this saving of power, as in all other instances of mechanical advantage, is accomplished only by a corresponding loss of time.

In drawing a load, as, for instance, loaded carriage, along a horizontal plane, the resistance to be overcome is chiefly the friction of the load upon the plane. If there were no friction or impediment from inequalities of surface, and if the load were once put in motion, it would go on moving with the smallest possible expenditure of power.

In drawing a load up an inclined plane, ordinary friction has to be overcome, and also the gravity of the body, which gravity gives it a tendency to roll down to the lowest level. In this constant impulse to descend, it is not at liberty to pursue the same line of descent as bodies falling freely from heights. It falls or rolls down as much less speedily than a free falling body (omitting the loss by friction) as the length of the inclined plane is greater than its height. A freely descending body falls about 16 feet in the first second; and a body rolling down an inclined plane, rolls just as many feet the first second as the number of feet of inclination is in sixteen feet. If the inclination be one foot in sixteen, the body rolls down one foot, and so on.

Anybody in being drawn up an inclined plane, by a power parallel with the plane, presses at right angles with the plane. The common expression is, that the reaction of the plane upon the object is perpendicular to the plane. When an object, as a ball, rests upon a horizontal plane, its pressure is at right angles with the plane; or, what is the same thing, the reaction or resistance of the plane is at right angles with it. This is seen in Fig. 28, in which a ball is represented lying on a level plane, with the line of pressure A passing down to B, which line is at right angles with the plane. Suppose, then, that the end of the plane at C is elevated to D, as in Fig. 29, so as to form a slope; in this case the line of pressure of the ball on the plane is also moved, so as still to be at right angles with the inclination.

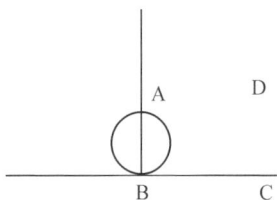

Fig. 28

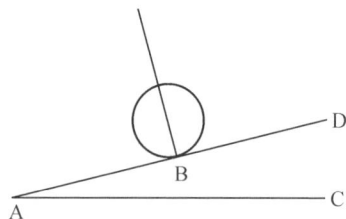

Fig. 29

The power which is required to be sustained for the purpose of o-vercoming friction or inequalities of surface on level planes, is for the purpose of drawing the load up or over the inequalities.

The amount of the power corresponding to different weights and inclinations of the plane has been correctly ascertained, and the following are the rules upon the subject:

First.—The quantity of weight is great in proportion to the inclination of the plane; consequently, so is the difficulty of raising greater, and the rate of elevation or motion slower.

Second.—To overcome the weight or resistance, and the slowness of movement, a corresponding increase of power must be given.

Third.—The smaller the inclination, so is the pressure if the weight on the plane the greater.

Fourth, *or Special Rule of Calculation*.—Whatever is the unit of inclination in a given length, the same is the [inclined] of weigh that can be lifted, and the unit of power to be exerted.

If the inclination of a road be *one* foot in ten, *one-tenth* is called the unit of inclination; hence, *one-tenth* part at the nominal weight of the load has to be lifted; and a power to draw this one-tenth part of the load has to be exerted. Or, to put the case in other words:—If the road rise one foot in ten, there is in the ten only one foot of perpendicular height to be lifted through; and the weight at any point of the ten feet is only a tenth of what it would be if it were to be lifted through a perfect perpendicular ascent of ten feet.

The reason is now perceived why a small power over comes a greater in the case of draughts upon inclined planes. The load is, as it were, lifted by instalments. Partly supported as it advances, and always supported more completely the smaller the inclination, the weight of the burden is apparently lessened by merely taking the rise gradually and slowly.

If we suppose a case of two roads, the first rising one foot in twenty, and the second rising one foot in fifty, a loaded carriage will be found to go over the filly feet of the one with precisely the same expenditure of power, that would be required to make it go over the twenty feet of the other—that is, always providing that friction and other circumstances are alike.

Fig. 30 represents a supposed case of two inclined planes of the same height, but different slopes, meeting together at the top, with a weight resting on each, P and Q, hanging by a string, H which passes over the pulley

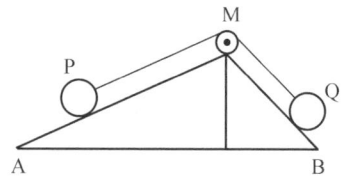

Fig. 30

M. If the length of the longest plane from A to M be two feet, and that of the shorter from B to M be one foot, then two pounds at Q, on the short side, will balance four pounds at P, on the long side; and so on in this proportion, whether the planes he longer or shorter.

In this manner, weights moving on two adjoining inclined planes may be adjusted so as to balance each other, although the inclinations be different; and they are so made to act on various sloping railways connected with public works, where one wagon descending on one plane is made to draw up another wagon on another plane.

An inattention on the part of our forefathers to these exceedingly simple principles of mechanical science, led them to form roads over steep hills, pursuing, as it was imagined, the best routes, because they were the straightest in a forward direction. In modern times, this error has been avoided by enlightened engineers, and roads are now constructed with as few risings and fallings as possible. When roads have necessarily to be carried to the summits of heights, they are very properly made either to wind round the ascent, or to describe a zig-zag line of direction.

The drivers of carts are aware of the saving of labour to their horses by causing them to wind or zig-zag up steep roads instead of leading them directly forward.

The inclined plane is resorted to for a saving of labour in many of the ordinary occupations of life. By it loaded wheelbarrows are with comparative ease wheeled to considerable elevations in house building and other works of art; hogsheads are rolled out of or into wagons, and ships are launched into or drawn from the water, the inclined plane being as useful in giving facilities for letting downloads as in drawing them up.

It is also by inclined planes that we reach the higher floors of a house from the ground, or attain other elevations. For all such purposes, the inclined plane is formed with steps to ensure our safe footing. All stairs or flights of steps are inclined planes. A ladder forms a steep inclined plane.

OF THE WEDGE

The inclined plane has been described as being fixed or stationary, as, for instance, a common ascending road, or a sloping plank, upon which the weights are moved. It has now to be viewed as a *movable plane*, in which form it suits many useful purposes.

When an inclined plane is movable, and the load or weight which it affects is at rest, it receives the name of a wedge. The wedge is, therefore, a mechanical power, founded on the principle of the inclined plane.

The wedge is an instrument or simple machine, consisting of a solid body of wood, iron, or some other hard material, and is triangular in form. See Fig. 31. Here the wedge is seen to taper from a thick end or head at B to a thin edge or point at A. This, however, is only the more common form of the wedge. It is made with sides of various angularities or degrees of slope, and, in some cases, it possesses a flat and a sloping Bide. When it slopes on both sides, it consists of two inclined planes joined together; and when one of its sides is flat, it acts as only one inclined plane. The wedge is employed as an instrument for cleaving solid masses asunder, to compress bodies more closely together, and to move great weights through small spaces. Fig. 32 is a front view of a wedge in the act of splitting asunder a piece of timber. The power employed to force the wedge forward, is either repeated blows with a mallet or hammer, or the gradual pressure of a weight. In general, the power is applied by rapid strokes, or quick applications of some kind of external pressure. The rules for calculating the pressure.

Fig. 31

Fig. 32

The rules for calculating the power of the wedge are similar to those for the inclined plane. In proportion as the inclination or angularity is great, so is the resistance greater, and the power must be greater to overcome it. Thus, if the wedge be of short dimensions and thick at its head, it will require a greater power to move it than if it be long and thin in its form.

The resistance offered to the wedge of equal sides, when the pressure is equally applied, is, as in the case of the inclined plane, at right angles with the sides. See fig. 33, in which the oblique cross lines represent the direction of the pressure passing at right angles through the sides, and meeting at the centre.

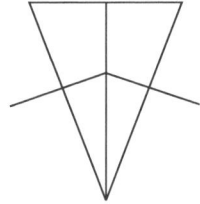

Fig. 33

It is difficult to calculate the precise power of the wedge, for much depends on the force or the number of blows which may be given to it, together with the obliquity of the sides, and the power of resistance in the object to be split. In the splitting of timber, for instance, the divided parts act as levers, and assist in opening a passage for the wedge.

The wedge is the least used of the simple machines, but the principle upon which it acts is in extensive application. Needles, awls, bodkins, and driving nails, are the most common examples. Knives, swords, razors, the axe, chisel, and other cutting instruments, also act on the principle of the wedge; so likewise does the saw, the teeth of which are small wedges, and act by being drawn along while pressed against the object operated upon.

The principle of the inclined plane, which is the basis of that of the wedge, is particularly observable in the action of the razor and the scythe, both of which cut best by being drawn along the materials against which they are applied. When the edge of a scythe or razor is examined with a microscope, it is seen to be a series of small sharp angularities of the nature of the teeth of a saw.

The principle of the wedge operates in the case of two glass tumblers, one placed within the other, as in fig. 34. A very gentle pressure applied to the uppermost tumbler would be sufficient to burst the lower. At every little advance of the uppermost tumbler, it acts more and more as a lever power on the rim of the lower, and at last overcomes the resistance, and fractures the vessel.

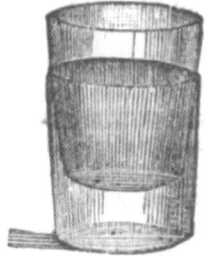

Fig. 34

OP THE SCREW

The screw is the fifth, and usually the last mentioned mechanical power. Like the wedge, it is founded on the principle of the inclined plane.

The screw consists of a projecting ridge winding in the form of an inclined plane, and in a spiral direction, round a central cylinder or spindle, similar to a spiral rod winding round a precipitous mountain. Fig. 35 is a representation of a common strong screw used in various mechanical operations. The projecting ridge on the spindle is technically called the *thread*. The thread in not always made in this square projecting form; it is frequently sharpened to a single thin edge, as in fig. 38, but does not affect the principle of the machine.

Fig. 35

One circumvolution or turn of a thread of a screw is, in scientific language, termed a *helix* (plural *helices*), from a Greek word signifying winding or wreathing. The spiral winding of the thread is called the helical line.

The helices of a screw do not necessarily require to have a central spindle. They may form a screw of themselves, and do so in the case of the common corkscrew (fig. 36). A screw of this pointed or tapering form, in penetrating a substance, possesses the advantage of the inclined plane in three ways—first, by the gradual thickening of the substance of the thread from a sharp point; second, the gradual widening; and, third, the gradual ascending, of the thread.

Fig. 36

The screw acts on the principle of the inclined plane, and this is obvious from the consideration of the nature of the threads. If we were to cut through the turns of the threads straight from top to bottom, and draw them out to their full extent, each separate and retaining its own inclination, we should find that they were so many inclined

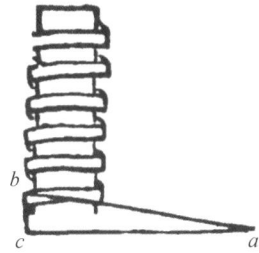

Fig. 37

planes. In the annexed cut, fig. 37, one entire turn of the thread is thus drawn out, reaching from b to a, and is seen to form an inclined plane. If not drawn out, it would wind down to c; therefore, while a weight is raised by one turn of the screw over the limits of one thread, or from c to b, it has actually been carried up the inclined plane from a to b.

The screw has no power by means of pressure against the threads of another screw which overlaps it and holds it. This exterior screw, which is technically called a *box* or a *nut*, consists of a block with a central tube cut out in spiral grooves so as to fit with perfect exactness to the screw which has to work in it. Fig. 38 represents both screws in combination. M is the box or nut through which the screw passes. L is a lever inserted into the head of the screw, for the purpose of turning it.

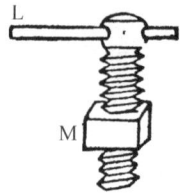

Fig. 38

The object required by the use of the screw is to apply force or pressure. To produce the intended effect, either the outer or inner screw, that is, either the nut or the screw, must be fixed. If the screw be fixed at one extremity, say at the top, to a solid body, the nut may be turned round it so as to move from the bottom to the top; and if the nut be fixed, held fast by some solid body, the screw in the same manner may be turned round till it reach its extremity. Thus, either the point of the screw, or the nut, may be forced in each a way as to squeeze or press any object presented to them.

Practically, the screw is never used as a simple machine; the power being always applied by means of a lever, passing either through the head of the screw, or through the nut. The screw, therefore, acts with the combined power of the lever and inclined plane; and, in investigating the effects, we must take into account both these simple mechanical powers, so that the screw now becomes really a compound machine.

In the inclined plane, as has been seen, the less it is inclined, the more easy is the ascent, though the slower is the process of rising to a certain elevation. In applying the same principle to the screw, it is obvious that the greater the distance is betwixt the threads, the greater or more rapid is the inclination, and consequently, the greater must be the power to turn it under a given weight. On the contrary, if the thread inclines downwards but slightly, it will describe a greater number of revolutions in a given space, so as to diminish the distance betwixt the threads, and the smaller will be the power required to turn the machine under a given weight. Therefore, the finer the screw, or the the threads to each other, the less the power will require to be for a given resistance.

Suppose a case of two screws, one having the threads one inch apart, and the other half an inch apart; then, the force which the first screw will give with the same power at the lever, will be only half that given by the second. The second screw must be turned twice as many tines round as the first, to go through the same space. At the lever of the first, two men would raise a weight to a given height, by making one revolution; while at the lever of the second, one man would raise the mire weight to the same height, by making two revolutions.

It is apparent, that the length of the inclined plane up which a body moves in one revolution, is the circumference of the screw, and its height the interval between the threads. The proportion of the power would therefore be—"as the circumference of the screw is to the distance between the threads, so is the weight to the power." By this rule, the power of the screw could alone be found, provided the action of the machine was not affected by the lever which works it. As that is the case, the circumference described by the outer end of the lever employed is taken instead of the circumference of the screw itself.

The rule by which the true force of the screw is calculated, is, by multiplying the circumference which the lever describes by the power. Thus—*The power multiplied by the circumference which it describes, is equal to the weight or resistance multiplied by the distance between the two contiguous threads*. Hence, the efficacy of the screw may be increased, by increasing the length of the lever by which it is turned, or by diminishing the distance between the threads. If, then, we know the length of the lever, the distance between the threads, and the weight to be raised, we can readily calculate the power; or, the power being given, and the distance of the threads, and the length of the lever known, we can estimate the weight which the screw will raise.

Suppose the length of the lever to be forty inches, the distance of the threads one inch, and the weight 8000; required—the power, at the end of the lever, to raise the weight. The lever being 40 inches, the diameter of the circle which the lever describes is double that, or 80 inches. Reckoning the circumference at thrice the diameter (though it is a little more), we multiply 80 by 3, which gives 240 inches for the circumference of the circle. The distance of the threads is one inch, and the weight 8000 pounds. To find the power, multiply the weight by the distance of the threads, and divide by the circumference of the circle.

$$\begin{array}{r} 8000 \text{ weight} \\ \underline{1 \text{ distance}} \\ 240 \overline{)\ 8000} \\ \hline 33\frac{1}{3} \end{array}$$

Thirty-three and a third is the product, and it would require that power or number of pounds to raise the weight. This, however, is only in theory. In practice a third of the amount of power would require to be added to overcome the friction of the machine.

In the ordinary working of the screw, velocity is incompatible with great power. This is a truth, however, which applies only to a screw with one thread. There is a way of making a screw, by which great velocity and power may be combined. This is done by forming the screw with two, three, or more threads. To understand how this is accomplished, we have only to conceive the idea of a screw with one thread, very wide betwixt its turns, and then imagine one or two other threads placed so as to fill up the intervals; thus composing a fine close screw. And as by this means all the threads descend with equal rapidity, we have a screw which will not only descend with great velocity but which will apply a very great degree of pressure. A screw of this nature is used in the printing press, by which a pressure of a ton weight is applied instantaneously by a single pull of a lever.

The most common purpose for which the screw is applied in mechanical operations, is to produce great pressure accompanied with constancy of action, or retention of the pressure; and this quality of constancy is always procurable from the great friction which takes place in the pressure of the threads on the nut, or on any substance, such as wood, through which the screw penetrates.

The common standing-press used by bookbinders for pressing their books, affords one of the best examples of the application of the screw to produce great pressure (fig. 39). The screw A has a thick round lower extremity B, into holes in which the lever is inserted. This extremity B is attached by a socket joint, to the pressing-table C, so that when the screw is turned in one

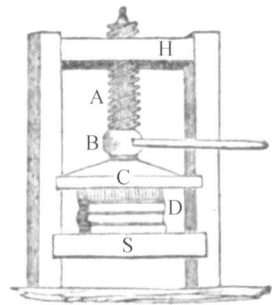

Fig. 39

direction, the table sinks, and when turned in another, the table rises. The books D lie upon a fixed sole S, and are thus between the table and the sole. H is a cross beam above, in which is the box or overlapping screw to give the necessary resistance.

MECHANICAL COMBINATION AND STRUCTURE

Mechanical action is applied to the action of forces that produce no change in the constitution of bodies, and is therefore distinguished from chemical or any other species of action, in which change of constitution is less or more effected.

Great changes are continually taking place in nature and art by mechanical action. Mechanical action generally implies movement or change of place, and is most cases alteration of external features and circumstances. The whole of the planetary movements are mechanical; the motions of water and winds are mechanical; and the new appearances produced in art by placing different objects together, are mechanical.

The action of forces upon solids, or mechanical action, is taken advantage of by mankind for the production of numerous useful results in the arts. And success in attaining these results depends in a great measure upon the knowledge we have of the principles of mechanics, and the skill and care we use in applying them.

When skill, care, and ingenuity, are brought fully into operation for these results, very great wonders are in many instances achieved. But where there is ignorance or negligence, the object in view may not only be defeated, but very mischievous consequences may take place.

Example first.—If a tall mast or beam break through at two-thirds of its height, and the two fractured ends be simply placed together and tied with a rope, the upper piece will, by the action of a small force, again fall. It will act like *the arm of power of a lever* against the rope, which is the *weight*; and as this weight is inconsiderable, the arm of power will preponderate. But if we take the two pieces nod saw each of them lengthwise, so as to make four pieces, and then, as represented in fig. 40, lay a short piece alongside of a long piece, and another long piece on the top of the first short piece, with the second short piece opposite to this second long piece, the whole will he effec-

Fig. 40

tually *spliced* together; in such a case, with the aid of an overlapping rope, the beam will in all likelihood be stronger than it was before it was fractured. The cause of its being stronger, at least of its remaining firm, is, that the weaker part at one side is supported by a stronger part on the other side. Thus by skilfully taking advantage of certain forces acting in connection with solids, we are able to rear a structure of the utmost possible strength.

Example second.—If a man, in making repairs upon the outside of a building, project a plank from a window for the purpose of standing upon it, and if he proceed to place himself near the outer extremity of the plank, without having placed a sufficient counterbalancing weight at its inner extremity, he will assuredly be precipitated to the ground, and perhaps killed; because the *gravity* of his body acted like a *power* on the arm of a lever, while the lever was without a sufficient *weight* to preserve the apparatus in equilibrium. From such neglects of the operation of forces in nature, dreadful consequences frequently ensue.

The study of the operation of mechanical forces, along with experience, teaches that there are certain bulks, positions, and forms of bodies, which produce the greatest strength for purposes of art.

The strength of beams or masses of the same kind and bulk, and fixed in the same manner, in resisting a transverse force which tends to break them, is simply as their breadth, as the square of their depth, and inversely as their length—that is, the thicker and shorter they are, they are the stronger. Thus, if a beam be twice as broad as another, it will also be twice as strong; for the increase of breadth doubles the number of the resisting particles. By making the beam double the depth, the strength is four times as great; because the number of fibres is doubled and the lever by which they act is also increased.

But this increase of strength, by increasing bulk, has a practical limit. It is found that in increasing the dimensions of a body, or combination of bodies, preserving all proportions the same, *the weight increases more rapidly than the increase of strength, or power of endurance*. This is one of the most important principles in mechanical science, and ought to prevent undue extension in structural arrangements.

Take a block of stone, and fix one end of it into a wall, leaving its other end projecting. By this arrangement of position, each particle of matter in the block acts as a weight pulling downwards as with a lever, the fulcrum of the lever being at the point of support, and the particles of matter in the mass forming at once the arm of power and the weight Hence, every particle we add to the length of the block beyond a certain length (whatever may be its constitutional strength), we shall certainly cause the mass to break, and fall, from the effect of gravity, upon the outer extremity.

A similar lever action takes effect in the case of blocks or beams supported on both ends, the only difference being, that, in extending them to an undue length, they will break in the middle, or at the weakest point between the two supports.

The strength of a beam supported at both ends is twice as great as that of a beam of half the length, which is fixed only at one end; and the strength of the whole beam is again increased if both ends or fulcra be firmly fixed, as into a wall.

In the case of fibrous or grained materials, as, for instance, wood, the body sustains the greatest pressure when weight is applied to the grain endwise, or to the beam longitudinally. The nearer that the pressure can be applied to any beam endwise the better. Thus, a beam supports most weight on its upper end, the other end being fixed to the ground, and its strength is next greatest when the pressure is applied to it leaning at top against another beam. This is exemplified in the angular roofs of houses, in which two beams lean against each other like the two sides of the letter A. In arranging beams to support great weights, as in building bridges, each beam is made to push obliquely upward with one end, while it pushes obliquely downward with the other, and thus an extensive combination of beams is firmly supported.

In rearing structures consisting of beams, it is an important point to convert, as far as possible, by mode of erection, cross or transverse strains into longitudinal strains, or into forces acting on the ends of beams, in the direction of their length.

Nature appears to have designed that strength of structure should be accomplished with the least expenditure of material. It is obvious, that, if trees and animals were made many times larger than we now find them, and of the same kinds of substance, they would be borne down by their own weight Small animals endure greater comparative violence, and perform greater feats of strength, in proportion to their size, than large ones. The largest bulk which a human being can possess in his person, at the same time retaining activity of motion, is not more than is usually seen in well-grown men. Thus, from a simple natural cause, men of very gigantic figure never could have existed on our earth. Men must always have been about the size which they are at present; or, if they were considerably larger, they must have been constituted of much stronger materials, without a corresponding increase of weight.

The same principles relative to mechanical strength apply to contrivances in the arts. As already stated, the strength or power of endurance in a material does not increase in proportion as the weight increases. Hence there is a practical limitation of the magnitude of machines and other structures. For example, a bridge or roof of beams may be very strong when of small or moderate size, but if the dimensions be extended beyond a certain limit, the structure will fall, by not being able to support its own weight.

The strength or power of endurance of pressure upon a fixed body, is greatly increased by giving the body a certain form. The strongest form in nature or art is that of an *arch*.

An arch is a skilful disposition of parts, forming convex and concave side, the convex side being that upon which the pressure is applied. The arch, which takes its name from *arcus*, a Latin word, signifying a *bow*, may be either a portion of a circle or ellipse, or entirely rounded is form. Whether shaped like a bridge, or round tube, or the shell of an egg. The principle which causes the power of endurance of pressure is the same.

The principle of endurance consists in the particles of the arched body hearing upon each other like a series of wedges, thus causing a compression of particles on the concave side of the circle, which enables the mass to bear in enormous pressure on the convex side. Indeed, the greater the pressure is (to a certain extent), perpendicular to the convexity, so also the compression and power of resistance become the greater.

附:《重学浅说》译名对照表

王韬译名	可能对应的外文词语	今译
总论	General Definitions	总论
重学	mechanics	力学
杆	the lever	杠杆
滑车	the pulley, or cord	滑轮
斜面	the inclined plane	斜面
轮轴	wheel and axle	轮轴
劈	wedge	楔子
螺旋	screw	螺杆
力点	the power（the force applied）	动力
重点	the fulcrum（the prop or support）	支点
倚点	the weight（the resistance or burden to be lifted）	阻力
直杆	straight bar	直杆
速率力	virtual velocities	虚速度
天平	scale beam	秤杆
秤	steelyard	杆秤
车牀	turning-lathe	车床
踏板	footboard	踏板
打麦杖	flail	连枷
叠杆	compound lever	复式杠杆
曲杆	bent lever	曲臂杠杆

重學淺說

光緒庚寅仲春淞北逸民校刊

倚距八寸一端有重八斤重倚距一百一寸則二重必相連蓋八
乘一百得八百一百乘八亦得八百二數相等故也假如重與
重倚距已知亦知力倚距約之所得即力數也如重十斤重倚距十寸
重倚距以力倚距求加若干力令力相定法以重乘
相乘得一百以力倚距二十寸約之得力五斤此力之能率若

一與二重倍
于力也 凡
木工用木桿
移木石工用
鐵桿移石皆
是理也 凡
器有二股之
公倚點也
臑關中所用
天平亦合此
皆合此種桿

理日用所恒
需者為剪刀
所剪之物即
重指力即力
銷即二股之

重學淺說

重學原始

英國　偉烈亞力　原譯
長洲　王韜崇詮　筆述

重學之由來古矣製物造器無不出於重學不知重學則不明
夷險之理當中國秦政之世希臘亞奇默德創立重學法於適
當其中之處立杆懸物輕重適均遠近如一視其倚點而悟其
理重學且可施之於戰陣爲時西西里國濱海建都與鄰國構
怨交兵鄰國駕艨艟直逼城下城人洶懼王命造備禦之具亞
奇乃製大鐵鈎鈎取敵船舉而覆之城賴以全其法胥出於重
學由是亞奇重學之名著於一時凡考重學之理者於物由高
墜下之時可知地面吸力大小而明其速率前明意大利人仰
離暑始得此理至於考獲兩物相撞之理者爲英人瓦利斯考

《重学浅说》光绪庚寅仲春淞北逸民校刊版

六

普法战纪(节选)
(1873年)

编者按:

校自王韬编译、张宗良口译《普法战纪》(遁叟手校本)。现由哈佛大学汉和图书馆珍藏。该版于1895年出版,为1873年《普法战纪》修订本。该版《普法战纪》共20卷(原14卷),篇幅巨长,又无卷目,部分内容亦非译文,故先选校卷一。

卷 一

欧罗巴洲(Europe,今译欧洲)在五大洲中幅员为最狭,旷野居其二山岭,居其一海隅之地。湾港殊多,故其国多长于航海,善驾驶,习水攻。田土膄瘠各异,气候凉燠不同。人物英,持学,艺精巧,甲于他洲。其间诸国林立,或则控弦百万,或则带甲数十万,互为雄长,争相并吞。弱小则唇齿相依,强大则睚眦必报。故兵革之事必十余年、数十年而一见。于中有千余年以来之疆国,曰法兰西(即法国),于近数十年勃兴者,曰普鲁士。

法处欧洲西境,以甲兵雄海外。其疆宇之恢扩,土壤之膄美,屹然为西欧大国。其境东界日耳曼、瑞士,西统比斯加湾(Bay of Biscay,今译比斯开湾),北接比利时,与英吉利仅隔一海峡,南至地中海、西班牙。自西北至东南长一千九百八十里,由东北至西南长一千八百四十五里,总计六十一万五千方里。

就海滨,形势湾环,计之约长三千六百里。近海处为比斯加海口——都华河(Dordogne,今译多尔多涅河),地中海里潴。时境中,至大之河为森马罗(Seine,今译塞纳河),直流贯注遍境。国民灌溉,取资焉。其在西北海滨,由鲁瓦河(Loire,今译卢瓦尔河)至加利士(Challans,今译沙郎)濒海地。地势高耸,有一处突入作凹形,若半环,被海水所冲激,聚沙成围,风又从而震荡之,时有变迁。海长四百五十里,皆有沙为障,捍蔽如围基。然每岁涨地六十尺,近都华河旁,有地斜伸入海,状若人身之特伸一臂,名奇尼士里斯(Guyenne,今译吉耶讷,为法国旧省),又曰拉合其他(La Rochelle,今译拉罗谢尔),曰必多拉士海岛①(Biscarrosse,今译比斯卡罗斯),曰亚珊卑里挨儿(Belle-île-en-Mer,今译贝勒岛),曰畲(île d'Yeu,今译耶乌岛),曰里极亚拉龙(île d'Oléron,今译奥雷龙岛),皆沿海新地云。

其国号曰法兰西者,固日耳曼语也。始一千三百八十年前,其意即言以自主之民,为自主之国也。国中境土,自北方外,西东南三方皆负山岭而阻河海,最为巩固。周拉山(Jura,今译汝拉山)在法瑞交境。西温尼山②,其高五百尺。比里牛斯山(Pyrénées,今译比利牛斯山),其高五千尺。阿温山(Auvergne,今译奥弗涅山),其高六千尺。疴士周斯山(Vosges,今译孚日山脉),其高约四千尺。境中平原坦旷,多可种植。

国内诸山林立,自海而度之,皆不过六千尺。其间至高者,亚尔卑斯山(les Alps,今译阿尔卑斯山),高一万三千尺。性布朗山(Monte Blanc,今译勃朗峰),高一万五千尺。比里牛斯山,自西班牙入法国境,其高一万尺。境中之河,曰仙河(音亦近星通法京)。鲁依牙河(l'Allier,今译阿列河)、加仑尼河(Garonne,今译加龙河)、陇河(Rhône,今译罗讷河),水道纷歧,达于四境。

---

① 比斯卡罗斯(Biscarrosse)并非岛屿,而是法国西海岸重要海滨城市。但许多情形中,凡带"岛"字的地名实则为法语单词île,音译为"里"。

② 此处"西温尼山"高度为500尺,即170米左右,但全文提述的山脉多高于1000米以上,故"西温尼山"似误。

山地、平原气候不同,因之寒暑针,高低亦异。初测针度,知其悬殊者。其人名巴士谷(Bassin parisien,今译巴黎盆地)。试较之于阿温山,方验其理。国中时序淑和,风景清嘉,四时天气朗霁开豁,甚为宜人。原泽肥美,田土膏腴,山中各兽无不备,兼有异种殊形者。耕时雨泽均和,是以林树丛茂,约居七分之一。

山矿多产,五金、煤铁、盐盬毕具,山石亦有数种。惟煤不及英国之佳,且多仅能及十二分之一。近比利时境多煤、盐,因是法西南境最称富饶。石盐产于摩塞稀河(Moselle,今译摩泽尔河),至为充足。

农民多耕植五谷、萄葡、烟、麻、桑,其农多勤敏,为他国所不及。居乡者,率务田业。土著约五百万,所植以萄为最盛,约居二十六分之一。因其多植葡萄,故南方之米贵于北方。

其所制造各物,皆与欧洲列国通商,利市三倍,如丝斤、棉纱、呢布、磁器、金银器皿。列国出口之货,英居其最,而其次即当及法。其所织呢布,坚密、精致,尤甲于欧洲。其购贩于他处者,如木棉、蚕丝、羊毛、铜靛、煤、木料,此即入口数也。每岁入口货银,约金钱八十兆磅(每磅抵吕宋,银四圆有八)。出口货银,约金钱七十五兆磅。

所与贸易往来之国,则以英美为大宗。国中诸海口,马塞里(Marseille,今译马赛)尤为富盛。估舶货舰,鳞萃羽集。其他则希瓦布多(Strasbourg,今译斯特拉斯堡)、士南士鲁(Saint-Nazaire,今译圣纳泽尔)、西耳士敦(Dunkerque,今译敦刻尔克)、各结波龙(Grenoble,今译格勒诺布尔),皆商贾辐辏处也。

生民户籍之数,计三十六兆,每方里约居五十八人。军额三十万,其兵素号精锐,惟英国可与并驾齐驱,然不及其众也。俄奥之兵多于法,特临陈无其猛鸷,统兵官弁亦逊其智勇。前王拿破仑第一(即拿破仑一世),训练精甲,几六十万,非英之水师与搏,则举欧洲之兵皆不足以当之,而列国必为其所挟制。其水师战舰,居欧洲之次,以有英为之雄也。所有驻泊兵,舶海湾如皁里士(Brest,今译布雷斯特)、都龙(Toulon,今译土伦)、路蕤佛(Le Havre,今译勒阿弗尔)、沙波(Cherbourg,今译瑟堡)、亚灵

(Amiens,今译亚眠)诸处,皆冲要所也。卑里士在压蓝的洋(即大西洋),都龙在地中海。岁糜饷项无算。沙波所筑炮台,雄固非常,难以施攻,敌不能入。国债三百五十兆磅,每岁国用约七十兆磅。

一千八百六十二年,今法王拿破仑第三(即拿破仑三世)为全权之主,称恩伯腊(empereur,即皇帝)。国位循世及之例,设立上下二议院。上议院爵臣由王自简,下议院绅士,由民间推举。

英法国例不同,王有权得以更张律例,变革制度,所奉为天主教,而别教亦得行布。传教之士俸糈给自公家,国中奉耶稣教者,仅十之一。朝廷设有六部,而另以一部,大臣专司学校,故其学艺闻于列邦。惟东北境,民俗稍偷于读书,乐道之法有缺焉。

通国分三十三部,后改为八十六郡。迩年得以大利所割地,增置三郡,于是为郡八十有九。

至于国位相传,率以子继嗣统,绝则选于宗族。历代以来,鲜女主。始开国者为哥罗昧(Clovis I,466—511,今译克洛维一世,法兰克王国奠基人),大略雄才,国人所推服,以次驱除北狄,疆土日开。时在耶稣降生后四百八十一年,当中国齐高帝建元三年也。自是国势日尊,传三百余年。

嗣王北尔给里哥(Chlothar I,555—561,今译克洛塔尔一世)无道,国人废之,立相臣北比诺(Pepin,714—768,今译丕平)为王。其子甲利曼(Charlemagne,748—841,今译查理曼)继位,并有贤声,长于用兵,威行各国。传世数叶,中[终]衰。国人立公爵武额加颁多为王,不数传而统系绝,更立瓦罗义斯。迨后路易嗣位,增修国政,号为中兴。

明万历时,显理第四(Henri IV,1553—1610,今译亨利四世)以旁支嗣统,至路易第十四(Louis XVI,1638—1715),好大喜功,战争不绝,诸国怨叛。路易第十六嗣,内宠擅权,民不堪命,遂弑杀王。国大乱,推拿破仑般拿拍(Napoléon Bonaparte,1769—1821,今译拿破仑·波拿巴,即拿破仑一世)为首领,事时一千七百九十九年也。

一千八百四年十二月二日,建号称恩伯腊。

一千八百十四年四月十一日,逊位出奔,为列国幽之易北河台上。国人迎故王裔,路易第十八(Louis XVIII,1755—1824,今译路易十八)回法为王,逾年三月出避于外。

拿破仑复入法国为王,是年六月二十二日兵败,身禽为英人流之三厄里那岛(Saint Helena,今译圣赫勒拿岛)。

七月,国人迎路易第十八复辟,在位十年而薨。其弟查鲁士第十(Charles X,1757—1836,今译查理十世)即位,立六年而出亡。

是年八月,奉路易非立(Louis-Philippe I,1773—1850,今译路易-菲利普一世)为王。

一千八百四十八年,国人逐之遁于英,乃推戴拿破仑第三(Napoléon III,1808—1873,今译拿破仑三世)主国事,期以四年。

一千八百五十二年十一月二十一日,遂即真,即其今在位之法王也。

普鲁士乃日耳曼列国之一地,居欧罗巴之中,近时欧洲之雄国也。其境东至俄罗斯,北界波罗的海。日耳曼南及墺地里。日耳曼西接法兰西、荷兰,长一千二百里,广二千里,总计之三十六方里。

自伐啳(丹麦王国旧译名)攻墺(奥地利旧译名)后,拓土开疆,约得四十一万一千二百九十八方里。民籍生齿之数,二十二兆七十六万九千四百三十六人。通国分东西两土,并不毗连。设立部落,凡八区,置郡二十。有五东土广于西,土地势平衍,惟正南及则极高耸。其由渐而低者为坡,乃趋入波罗的海。

海滨东土共建六部。一曰巴郎丁堡(Brandenburg,今译勃兰登堡),湖荡薮泽殊多。沿海有大湖①三曰波迷里士(德语 Putziger Wiek,英语 Bay of Puck,今译普茨克湾),曰佛里士(德语 Frisches Haff,英语 Vistula Lagoon,旧译"弗里舍湖",今译维斯图拉潟湖),曰加里士(德语 Kurisches Haff,英语 Curonian Lagoon,今译库尔斯潟湖)。都城曰伯灵(Berlin,今

---

① "沿海大湖"可能多指海湾或潟湖。普鲁士有三处大型海湾及泻湖临近波罗的海,即普茨克湾、维斯图拉潟湖与库尔斯潟湖。

译柏林),即普京(即普鲁士京城)也。建于塞孛里河(Spree river,今译施普雷河)岸,城中户口四十五万八千六百三十七人,城四周约广三十里许。城门丨有六壮丽峻整,著名于欧洲园囿,广敞颇足以供游览。其学校黉序,肄习艺文者,尤为欧洲冠。凡属城一百三十八,公会部城二十七。

二曰波美拉尼(Pomerania,今译波美拉尼亚,神圣罗马帝国解体后曾为普鲁士王国的一部分),境中亦多湖。水泽汇流,脉络联贯。其北近海会城曰士得丁(波兰语 Szczecin,德语 Stettin,今译什切青),在阿河(Oder,今译奥得河)左滨。城垣坚固,为普国冲要之地。有轮车、铁路以达伯灵。近城河流深广,故商舶云屯,贾帆雨集,贸易之盛甲于国中。城中户口五万八千七十三人,凡属城七十二,公会部城七。

三曰细勒西(拉丁语 Silesia,德语 Schlesien,今译西里西亚)。其地多高冈峻岭,所产山石尤饶。会城曰北勒斯劳(德语 Breslau,波兰语 Wroclaw,今译布雷斯劳,现为波兰城市),在阿得岸奥澜(英语 Stara Odra,波兰语 Stara Odra,今译斯塔拉奥得河)河口。有轮车、铁路达于四处。城广而固,规制一准古昔。惟街冲狭迫未壮,观瞻贸易,以毡、麻两项为大宗。百工居肆,制造日盛。庠序广雅文,儒所萃城中,户口十万五千六百六十人。凡属城一百四十一,公会部城五十四。

四曰萨索尼(德语 Sachsen,英语 Saxony,今译萨克森),与日耳曼境壤相接。阡陌交通,境中冈峦起伏,亦多崇山绝巘,多产灰石。会城曰马丁堡(Magdeburg,今译马格德堡),在抑耳比河(德语 Elbe,捷克语 Labe,波兰语 Laba,今译易北河或拉贝河)左滨,距京都伯灵二百二十里许。有轮车、铁路相通,最为国中巩固之所。高垒深沟,倚之若金城汤池,在欧洲中亦当屈一指焉。故虽大敌屡侵,卒赖以捍蔽。城中户口六万五千二百四十七人,别有一城曰威丁堡(Wittenberge,今译维滕贝尔格)。昔本为天主教所统辖,明时路德崛起于此,特创耶稣正教,而天主教之权遂衰。凡属城一百四十,公会部城三十。

五曰普鲁士(Preußen),境中亦多巨湖。会城曰哥宁堡(Königsberg,现为俄罗斯的加里宁格勒,该地名旧译柯尼斯堡),界处孛里格(德语

Pregel,英语 Pregolya,今译普列戈利亚河,位于俄罗斯加里宁格勒州)、佛里士(即库尔斯泻湖)两河之间①,距孛里格河仅十五里。其城空阔,不能守御。城中户口八万七千二百六十七人。海口曰但泽(德语 Danzig,波兰语 Gdańsk,今译格但斯克),建近维士都拉河(Vistula,今译维斯杜拉河)左滨。城系古筑,向属波兰。至一千七百九十五年,乃隶普国版图,商舶往来贸易极为繁旺。凡属城一百二十一,公会部城三十九。

六曰波森(Posen,在 1846 年至 1918 年是普鲁士王国的一个省,在 1919—1939 年间是波兰第二共和国的一个叫"波兹南"的省),本波兰旧壤,与俄奥瓜分得之。会城同名建于瓦他罗拿(Warta,今译瓦尔塔河)两河之间。士得丁轮车、铁路至此,而竟四周城垣极其巩固。市衢宽广,车马辐辏。城中户口四万七千五百四十三人。昔年侵割之时,居民咸怀旧思,不乐新政,今则已由渐化。凡属城一四十五,公会部城三。

天气南北不同,然寒热均不过甚,极南极北之地,终岁寒暑表之准率不逾五十二分。西土分为南北二部,境中亦有大山,然不若东土之攒聚一处。河之大者曰来尼南(德语 Rhein,英语 Rhine,今译莱茵河②),曰惟士发里(Weser,今译威悉河,长度仅次于莱茵河)。田土膏腴,林木慈郁。

居民以织布为业,贩售各方。会城曰闵士得(Münster,今译明斯特,现为德国北莱茵-威斯特伐利亚州北部的主要城市),建于抑阿河(Ems,今译埃姆斯河)滨。城基峻整,亦为商贾之所集。城中户口二万六千三百三十二人,通部凡属城九十八,公会部城六十四。北曰勒纳(Rheine,今译赖内,现为德国北莱茵-威斯特伐利亚州的一个市镇),又分为上下来尼(Haut-Rhin,Bas-Rhin,即上莱茵与下莱茵,现为法国省份),盖以来尼河而得名。

上来尼沿河傍山,形势甚壮。会城曰哥罗尼(Colmar,今译科尔马,是

---

① 从地图上看,柯尼斯堡(今加里宁格勒)地处维斯图拉潟湖和库尔斯潟湖之间,而维斯图拉潟湖的上游是普列戈利亚河(即"孛里格")。因此,王韬可能将普列戈利亚和维斯图拉潟湖视为同一条河流。

② 本文中,"莱茵河"的译名并不统一,包括"来尼南""来因河""吴河"。

上莱茵省的省会），建于来尼河左滨。基址广斥，创筑已久，周约三十一里许。特街衢迫狭，纡曲殊不便于车马。城中户口十一万四千四百七十一人，善造铁器，所织缎布殊佳，又工制香水，驰名遐迩。舟楫往来有如梭织。

下来尼，山水清秀，远地游人多往眺览。会城曰下来尼，建于山谷之中。峰峦环其四周，巩固异常。地有温泉可浴，民勤织纴，故多饶足。距哥罗尼一百十六里许。城中户口五万三千四百七十四人，通部凡属城一百二十四，公会部城一百十八。

溯普立国之初，盖非久远，古时北狄据其疆土。南宋初，日耳曼人征服北狄，遂备藩封。有阿兰分种之民居，于波罗的沿海东土曰普鲁士国，由此得其名。其酋目扶烈达力疏伦（Friedrich I, Count of Zollern, 1125—1142/1145，今译腓特烈二世，绰号"铁人"、"铁牙"，勃兰登堡选帝侯），仕于北日耳曼朝浒升伯爵，雄才伟绩，振烁一时。朝廷甚见宠任，娶一伯爵女为室。伯爵无子，疏伦遂承其遗业，世袭公爵。其食邑甚当冲要，以此日强。疏伦既受王室重畀，当屏藩之寄。人皆称之浩轩疏伦（Hohenzollern，今译霍亨索伦王朝，为勃兰登堡-普鲁士及德意志帝国的主要统治家族），迨后日耳曼欲使其统辖罗马事，以益其封，未果。继至一千四百七十一年，封布兰顿壁侯（即"勃兰登堡选帝侯"），是为今普鲁士立国之始。

一千五百十一年嗣君（即 Albrecht von Preußen，1490—1568，今译普鲁士的阿尔布雷希特，1490—1568，条顿骑士团的第 37 任大团长，霍亨索伦家族的第一位普鲁士公爵），与日耳曼之鲁他人（英语 Jutes，德语 Jüten，今译朱特人）往还甚密。见其气宇不凡，仪观伟如隐，劝其乘时崛起，暂为普鲁士一方主，而密与波兰相结。嗣君从之，阴遣使与波兰王言，苟得君普鲁士者，愿以其地永为藩属。波兰国王许焉，于是其地复入于波兰。嗣君后娶嗹国公主（即 Dorothea of Prussia/Dorothea of Denmark/Dorothea of Hohenzollern，1504—1547，今译普鲁士公爵夫人多萝西娅）为后，威权日盛，远近归之。一千五六十八年薨，传位其子，是为新君（即

Albrecht Friedrich，1553—1618，今译阿尔布雷希特·弗里德里希）。

一千六百十八年，新君殁，无嗣，乃召巴郎丁堡统领威廉（George William，1585—1640，今译格奥尔格·威廉），入继其位。因此，普鲁士与巴郎丁堡合而为一国，益强。遂自附于日耳曼，归其统辖。别本或作明万历年间，日耳曼复取其地，建国置君，成为一邦，其实非也。普鲁士君殁，无嗣，与巴郎丁堡合并，而遂自归于日耳曼，以备一邦，非日耳曼为之建国也。

威廉克慎厥职，忠谨可嘉，日主悦之，屡益以地。一千六百四十年，威廉薨，子扶烈达力威廉（Friedrich Wilhelm，1620—1688，今译弗里德里希·威廉）嗣。在位四十八年，拓地开疆几倍于昔。一千百八十八年薨，传位其子扶勒达力第三（Friedrich III，今译弗里德里希三世，1657—1713），国益昌，炽因有席卷囊括意。

一千七百一年正月十一日，自立为王，建王宫于哥宁堡，定国号为普鲁士。初犹以固藩篱，扩疆围为词。王甚材武，长于韬略，菲食恶衣，躬为节俭。晚年帑藏丰盈，国用充裕。

一千七百十三年王薨，其子扶勒达力第一（Friedrich Wilhelm I，1688—1740，今译弗里德里希·威廉一世，绰号"士兵王"）嗣，增拓规模，设立法制，于是列于欧洲诸大国中。王在位颇有政声，强邻慑伏，疆宇宴然，称贤主焉。尝与兵攻，细勒西（Schlesien，今译西里西亚，是中欧的一个历史地域名称）胜之，遂取其地，与波兰分析，自为一国，不复归其辖治。从此舆图日扩，生齿益繁，地广于前几二倍。初年，民籍二百五十万，季年至六百余万。

一千七百八十六年，王殁，无子，乃传侄威廉第二（Friedrich Wilhelm II，1744—1797，今译弗里德里希·威廉二世）。初政颇善，攻伐波兰，割其地几半。迨后嗜酒耽色，怠于政事，国势渐衰。普之西南境，固与法接壤，犬牙交错。法时怀图并之，念向特惮普王英明，不敢发耳。时法人已举拿破仑为君，其人雄猜[才]，有大略，善用兵，几于战无不胜，攻无不取。时已帝制，自娱妄欲，混一区宇，继迹罗马，以普有衅可乘，遂于一千八百五年(即嘉庆十一年)帅师伐普。

是时,王扶勒达力威廉第三(Friedrich Wilhelm III,1770—1840,今译弗里德里希·威廉二世)(按:威廉弟第二薨十一于七百九十七年,是年子扶勒达力威廉第三嗣位),秉国素无储备,各郡邑望风解体,势不能支。其地半为法有,普于是遂弱。或谓普自开国以来,未有如此之危蹙者也。

越六年,普民患苦,法政之不善,咸怀怨咨,而思其故主。普王因民之怨也,纠合诸国攻法。法师溃,委地而去。普尽复故土,惟南方之罗来内(Lorraine,今译洛林,现为法国大区名)、里疴内(法语 Alsace,德语 Elsaß,今译阿尔萨斯,现在法国东部地区名)二省,仍为法所割据。盖此二省乃一千六百八十一年,法先王侵普所得,非拿破仑近时所吞并者。特于墺京威也纳(Vienna,今译维也纳)议正各国疆界时,此二省仍为法属耳。

一千八百三十九年,王非的利(Friedrich Wilhelm IV,1795—1861,今译腓特烈·威廉四世)即位,勤政爱民,设学校,课农桑,惠商旅,恤鳏寡,修文讲武,百废俱举。由是远近归心,百姓亲附,邻国之民无不喁喁然,向风慕义,遂为西土之显国。

一千八百四十九年,取荷恒梭兰地(Holstein,今译荷尔斯泰因)。

一千八百五十三年,灭荷耳颠白邦公爵(Duke of Oldenburg,今译奥尔登堡公爵)之属地,曰查特国(英语 Jade 或 Jade Bight,德语 Jadebusen,今译亚德湾 ①),益大,兵益强。普自得此地,遂有北海口。其制民及岁者,工入肆,秀入学,因材施教,否则罚其父母。年二十以上男丁皆入伍学艺,三年放归,每岁秋大阅,施赏罚。故其国兵多而精,国中驻防军额约五十七万,仓卒有事即可调集。

一千八百六十一年,王威廉第一(Wilhelm I,1793—1888,今译威廉一世)继祚,即今在位之普王也。按普王生于一千七百九十七年三月二十二日,至今七十有三岁矣。一十三年至十五年,曾随征德卑顿邦。

---

① 亚德湾占地约 180 平方千米,普鲁士于 1853 年自奥尔登堡购买此处的西海岸,以建造海军基地,即今威廉港(Wilhelmshaven)。

一千八百四十九年六月,立为统兵大师[帅]。

一千八百五十八年十月,因兄(即威廉四世)①病摄位。

一千八百六十一年正月元日,践祚为王。此普法两国之所由来也。

普弱法强,欧洲诸国无不人人知之。然普之得以勃焉,以兴者其一在伐墺,其一在伐嗹。一千八百六十四年,帅师伐嗹(即丹国),大败之师,旋命立石于疆周,而书其事于碑以纪功,如古之勒石燕然者。然未过功,而有伐墺之役。

一千八百六十六年,普与墺地里(即奥地利)战,克之。墺人成盟于哿士北地(Habsburgs,今译哈布斯堡),盟言曰:南北日耳曼自为邻邦,无预墺事。墺惟谨守一隅而已。北以普为长,南以巴华利亚(Bavaria,今译巴伐利亚)为长,悉听其便,或南附于北亦无不可。北日耳曼共得地四十七万九千二百八十方里,户口二千九百二十万八百六十二人。南北日耳曼(即上下日耳曼)以缅河(Main,今译美因河)为之界。于是,墺弱普强,日耳曼列国咸奉普为盟主,执牛耳焉,而墺之权替矣。

普王以伐墺之功,不在伐嗹,下爰命史官,此事属辞缀之碑,后用彰厥勋。先是普国伐墺之时,法欲兴师助墺,以为法墺合力,攻普势在必胜。既胜,则割普来因河(德语 Rhein,英语 Rhine,今译莱茵河)上之地易若反掌耳。

普相俾思麦(Otto von Bismarck,1815—1898,今译俾斯麦)闻法王之谋,知法志在得地,因谓法若不为墺之外援,则普愿割来因河上之地,以馈法用酬和好。法王大悦,罢兵不出,以为是役也。无论普墺胜负,地在必得,胜则法乘机进去,墺必无不许,以其地即为法国所取,无伤于墺也。普胜,则彼固许我以地矣,遂束手作局外观。事平,法遣一介之,使索赂于普,请以来因河以西未普法交界地。

---

① 1857年,威廉四世中风,身体局部瘫痪,无法料理国事。1858年,威廉亲王摄政,1859年10月执掌政权(即位后称威廉一世)。

普报书于法云,其地具在大国,能取即自取之,敝邦弗敢闻命。法得书知所索不遂其谋,以寝然阴甚衔之时有责言。

逸史氏王韬曰:从来两国相持,皆以为师不厌诈,或以为兵行诡道。此所其在战阵之时耳,未有方当交好,而即挟诈谖者。方普之用兵于墺,法乘机请割来因河地,以益其封,并许出兵力助夹击墺境,潜相立约,否则将移助普之师以援墺。撒攻墺之兵,以伐普。

斯时,普相倬思麦恐法之无所得利,必将反助墺也,乃与法商曰:若尔不助墺,吾将以地畀汝。法人以普之有此言也,思普若为墺所败,则其势蹙弱,来因之地,吾以重兵往取,必无不得。普胜,则彼固然已许我矣。胜负有利焉,是以于普墺大举之役,按兵旁观。普既胜,法人往索割地,普以君可自取对。法虽憾甚,然无如之何。此盖普相谋公之胜算也噫。法国狡矣,而普亦不为谲也。法人卒不知备,终蹶于普。宜哉。

一千八百七十年,西班牙国乱,顽民倡叛,揭竿竞起,振臂一呼,云集响应,国后因是出奔,方图乞师进讨,然卒无助之者。是时,国中无主,人心震动,国人群思,拥立贤君,以资治理。惟是简之王族,选之爵绅,未有堪膺是任者,乃暂以布廉(Juan Prim y Prats,1814—1870,今译胡安·普里姆)为将军,权摄国政。

久之,环顾列邦,为民心所归,往向服者,卒未有其人。最后,群举普国郡王子夙,著贤声,有人君度,可抚。有西土王子,名理乌佛(Leopold Ludwig Philipp Maria Viktor,1835—1909,今译利奥波德二世),世袭浩轩疏伦王爵,加厘安郭郡王(Leopold Georg Christian Friedrich,利奥波德一世)之第二子也(普国咸奉耶稣教,惟此部则信天主,与西班牙同教)。

一千八百七十年六月,布将军亲莅议院,宣言于众,曰:我国无君,民心涣散,内患未宁,外忧将至,非择贤而立,不足以安宗社。普王子品超贵胄,行冠宗潢,必能胜此大任,予欲奉以为君,愿让斯位,爰命议院各员参酌可否。众议金同,乃遣人致书普王子,曰:敝国不幸,猝遘闵凶民乱君,逐朝廷无主所赖,贤智之俦收拾人心,裁平祸难。环顾我邦,德薄才鲜,俱不足以堪巨任。王子才冠时流,学迈群彦,实可履大宝,晋尊号以抚我社稷,安辑我民人。惟祈降敕国,即日临御,万毋固逊,以慰臣民之望,不胜幸甚。王子答书不辞。(按:浩轩疏伦虽属普王宗派,然谱牒疏远,传位例所不及。)

王子年三十有五,立行端谨,储才宏富,得书后以普王为一族弁冕,乃往请命。普王意不以为可,因谓之曰:此无异于昔者,墨克迷仁(Maximilian I of Mexico,1832—1867,今译马西米连诺一世,墨西哥皇帝)往,君于巴拉利司(Benito Juárez,1806—1872,今译贝尼托·胡亚雷斯,墨西哥政治人物及民族英雄),国事也。墨克迷仁本为墺国王子,巴拉利司招之为王,后卒被弑①。汝若为之,恐异日蹈杀身之祸,其勿往理乌佛。弗从。

七月四日,布将军行文于驻法京西班牙公使谓,理乌佛王子已允为,西班牙王议院,亦无议。法国闻是消息,上下大骇奋然,曰:普西无亲焉,得妄预其国事,且是举意将大不利于我也。普西相合,其势益强。倘其比而攻我,法将弗堪。法京所刊日报劝王必止是事,毋许其成。于是,法通国臣民无不深憾于普,痛诋狂詈,众口一词。

七月五日,普国驻法公使,几欲旋斾,以与王商。

七月六日,强请法王移书劝止。法王颁谕于驻普公使边尼德体(Vincent Benedetti,1817—1900,今译樊尚·贝内代蒂),令谒普王,请王子逊位,勿行嗣后,永不得为西班牙王。法京外部大臣加拉文公爵(Antoine Alfred Agénor, Duc de Gramont,1819—1880,今译格拉蒙公爵,于1870年被任命为法国外交部长)集论议院,谓是事于法堕国势,陨

---

① 马西米连诺曾是奥地利哈布斯堡王朝成员(即奥地利王子),1864年4月10日在法国皇帝拿破仑三世的怂恿下,接受了墨西哥皇位,成为墨西哥皇帝。1866年,墨西哥军事法庭以颠覆墨西哥共和国罪判处其枪决。欧洲各国君主致信胡亚雷斯,要求不执行枪决,但遭到胡亚雷斯反对。1867年6月19日,马西米连诺被执行死刑。

国体,所系非轻,宜请于普王,命王子勿君西国,庶免后日虞时。普王避暑于奄士(Ems,今译埃姆斯)行宫,法公使边尼德体自普都前往谒见。

七月九日,法使进谒普王,以法王赐书上呈,陈说利害,且请收回成命。王子勿行,毋伤普法两国辑睦。普王曰:浩轩疏伦,寡人之同宗也。以分言,则族党;以义言,则助君臣也。西人选择及之欲立为君,是一国之公事,非一家之私事也。今事始终由其自主,我既未许其受位,又焉能命其退位。祈复于王,敢告不敏。

十一日,法使又请见普王,旋命召入,仍以是事请。普王曰:是事进退系于王子,寡人弗欲预。闻且王子游旌所指,我未及知。或传其税驾鸭岭,马首所瞻,行踪靡定,将从何处告之乎。普王始终持是说,而普法之衅由此起矣。

七月十二日,乌理佛王子致书法国朝廷曰:不佞已辞王位,不特我两君志在二国,辑和共享昇平之福,即予小子,亦不敢。以是一端。俾彼此怀疑抱憾,是以再三,固逊愿授他人。谨以上告。英使谓法之廷臣曰:王子辞位,启衅之端可自此息矣。后闻王子辞位,盖出自普王所命。顾法人以为犹未慊志,法相加拉文位:英使曰法国骚然,人心不靖,其奈之何。法廷臣集,论于议院,并不以是事之寝,宣示众民,以期安辑,故众之抢攘尤甚。

普国驻法公使,拟请普王致书任过。是言一发,而普国亦为震动,谓如是殆将挟制我普国,卑屈我君臣也,共何能堪。普相俾思麦谓英之驻普公使曰:法至今日要,宜直任厥咎,不再凌侮我朝廷,然后我国民心乃能克靖。

是时,普法两国已有两不相下之势。七月十三日,普王驾幸庵士,别墅其地之名园也。花木崇绮,景物清幽,銮跸所至,侍从如云。法使适至,普王延之入见,甚加优礼,示以哥伦日报(即《科伦日报》)中载王子逊位一事。

法使庄阅既竟对曰:是事臣已知之矣,敝国朝廷已于昨夕檄谕四境,咸使闻知普王曰此事如已涣然冰释,不致乖和。如天之福,敝国臣民无不利赖法使。复前而致词曰:虽然以臣度之,是事仍未有止境,嗣后理乌佛王子当永不为西国君,即有他王子入继西统者,大王亦必止之,庶不徼怨于后日。王其许之。普王弗从。法使再三渎请,亦不许。前日之言既已阅,闻命业有成约,他非所知。法使既出,阅数时复诣行宫请见。普王遣近侍谕之曰:顷已有言,何弗闻也,今而后勿复见汝矣。遂以是事刊列邮报宣示,遐迩布告列邦,俾知法使之无礼也。于是,法使束装返国。

普法构兵。由此遂成时,欧洲诸国于局外者,皆欲为之排解,而英为尤力。恐一旦兵连祸结,靡所底止,因请于普西两国勿立王子为君。法外部大臣加拉文亦求英国居间调停,毋启二国纷争。及边尼德体既旋法都,则普法各执一词。法以为辱我使,普以为侮我君。普相俾思麦谓英使臣曰:我王接见法使原极礼貌,优崇彼民,不知谓辱其使,愤怒无端。今我朝必欲法任过而后已,普外部大臣宣示欧洲列国自此告绝于法。法之首相加拉文所英使曰:伯灵日报(即《柏林日报》)所载普延告绝之文大抵欲顺民心耳,非出普王本意也。

法王于是发号施令,声罪致讨,分兵两队,预备出征。立帅二:一为巴彦(François Bazaine,1811—1888,今译弗郎索瓦·巴赞),一为李布爱(Edmond Le Boeuf,1809—1888,今译埃德蒙·勒伯夫,法兰西第二帝国元帅,普法战争初期的陆军大臣),统率兵士启程。十二日离法都,向摩塞里(Moselle,今译摩泽尔)前进。十四日,法军机大臣集议于条拉利甸(Palais des Tuileries,今译杜伊勒里宫)[①],升帐誓师,定与普战。传令国中即募余勇同伸义愤。

翌日再会,廷臣几拉棣厘(Jules Ferry,1832—1893,今译朱尔·茹费理)问于李布爱曰:臣奉命出师,军实已齐乎。曰:备矣。曰:能昌言之于畴人广众中乎。尚慎旃哉。苟有一事之未备,必至贻误军机,损伤国体。廷臣沙纳(Jules Simon,1814—1896,今译朱尔·西蒙)曰:亦知备之一字

---

① 经查,1870 年 7 月 14 日,当埃姆斯密电抵达法国,法国各部长和拿破仑三世于杜伊勒里宫商议战事。此处地名似为"杜伊勒里",有待进一步考证。

作何解与。李布发奋然曰:我所谓备者,即普法交兵积日矿时,虽一物之微,无庸取之于外。有备不虞又何足患。

十五日,法廷下战书于普,谓启衅有三端:一、普王在奄士显辱法使,而普臣不闻有谏阻;二、普王不谕理乌佛王子逊位而去。三、不惟不言,且阴以后日难知拒我。此三事,法所据以责普者也。议院中群论愈同,惟爹亚(Adolphe Thiers, 1797—1877,今译阿道夫·梯也尔)发孚以为不然。

当议院之酌下战书也,廷臣对众言曰:我朝廷惟望臣民协力赞襄,共申保疆御敌之谋,咸奋敌忾同仇之志。七月六日,我已授意于邻邦,使为排解。列国人心,无不以我为是。无奈普王悍然不许,绝使臣弃旧好。今日我国先事预备者,实处于万不获已。诸将士既奉朝廷重命,各有专司,所望竭忠尽智,协力一心,克敌伐雠,共伸义愤,毋负此大任可也,汝众其各勉旃。法国廷臣既行,交于普,刻期示战,复集议于议院。

法都之民闻是消息,无不跃然,以起誓欲灭此。而朝食畿外之众,边徼之氓,同声愤激,一倡百和。国中所刊日报,无不以讨普之举,于理甚公。其措词最激切者,莫如调那顺日报[*L'Opinion Nationale*,今译《民论报》,1859—1914,是一份波拿巴左翼的政治日报,由阿道夫·乔治·盖鲁(Adolphe Georges Guéroult,1810—1872)于 1859 年在拿破仑三世的领导下创办,一直刊印至第一次世界大战],咸谓法廷张挞伐之师,奋遏防之力,洵足以振国威,伸国体,且曰:普人辱我亦太甚矣。请渡来因河,我兵已早备矣。

有英人旅居普国者,知普法兵衅将启,因于十五日夕间,巡行国中,审察其民情向背若何,则民间咸怀愤。皆曰:吾王受侮,吾国之耻也。我侪小人,尚敢安食甘寝于家乎。必报仇,有死无二。

街衢间或有悬灯树帜者,顷之有自灭其灯者曰:此非喜乐时也。曲巷中,酒垆家,男妇老壮聚谈喁喁,听之悉为后日出征计。居者、行者,皆作抚慰劝勉词。有妇别其夫,子别其父,幼别其长者,无不流涕相告。语亦有慷慨赴敌,踊跃思战者。有缅述起衅之由,谓折之于理,普直法曲。

有逆料后日之胜负者,有大声呼吁寐中者曰:善妒哉,法人也。彼常妒俄、妒英、妒美,以其国势强盛也,今又嫉普矣。彼既怀此忮心,何不于各国之语言、文字究习稍多。于一千八百六十七年以前,我军时称其行阵之整、演练之精,谓之为能兵。由今观之,殊不然。设在今日与之絜长较短,彼不逮我矣。我军之所以异于彼者,彼师剽疾而多轻,我军持重而能久当大敌而不惊,遇甚败而弗避,勇前而耻后,知进而难退。此其所以胜也。今日者,我国士庶无不怀忿切齿,敌忾同仇,不灭拿破仑朝,誓不息兵罢战,必使减兵额,削国权,割地求和为我藩属而后已。民间之私论如此,亦壮矣哉。

普相俾思麦告戒日耳曼各船舶须避入港内停泊,免遭敌国俘虏。荷兰国招集民壮以防两国之兵,越境肆扰。墺地里(即奥地利)声明为两不偏助之国,若有别国助此,则墺国助彼,以均其势。斯时南北日耳曼各调集兵勇,下令八遄征。普国京师,伯灵居民约有十万。是夕在衢市间言论者,数约八分之一。近郡邑无不同心响应。

是夕亥刻,普王自奄士返,乘车回宫,马行甚驶,行经名人石坊——先王扶烈达力第二坊下,时已抵王宫外。民间犹未知其为王也。睹车饰之异,而后知之。各趋前免冠瞻觐,齐声呼贺。有傍銮舆疾走言事者,王车乃缓辔徐行。于是,民间始知法国将战消息,无不扼腕切齿,作忿恨状。

南北日耳曼民志齐心,固如出于一通衢。广众中淡论纷纭,皆普构兵事。普王将抵伯灵,普太子已偕首相俾思麦、军师毛奇(Helmuth von Moltke, 1800—1891)、兵部尚书乐将军(Albrecht von Roon, 1803—1879,今译罗恩将军,曾是普鲁士陆军部长)沴嘉,暨各廷臣已在轮车驿馆敬迓。

顷之,外部大臣携法国战书呈于王前,盖从电报所译。递者俾思麦为之朗声宣读。王聆既毕,容色甚和,词气温豫,即召军机大臣共议。出师招募民兵,刻期团练。普太子即将法国所下战书,颁告臣民。先营员而及国人,瞬息间,如电之速。其传殆遍,通国无不勇气百倍,愿赴行阵。

七月十五日,两国战事始矣。

先是七月十四日,法国十部大臣集议于朝,持论久不决。自辰达午,未有成说。忽传普公使文移,自普至书,以普文约若干余言。乃召部员译,以国书俾众传观。初意为公使边尼德体书,继乃知为各不偏助之国劝和之函。英驻法公使亦请法王急收成命,母[毋]乖两国之欢心。如必强邀其一,言激忿,失和必由此起。况今者两不偏助之国,已为之委曲挑调停。西班牙王位自不为普王子所居,是则何不可之有。朝臣闻英公使言韪之重,集参议甫集时,忽闻普王已与法驻普公使绝和,于是战议遂决,而辞英国劝止之约。

先是于一千八百五十六年,英法两国立约,嗣后遇有军国重事,彼此宜相筹劝排解。今法人言是事不在约中,英又劝普勿启兵端、乖邻谊,普亦弗听。普首相俾思麦言于众曰:欲息干戈,修玉帛,岂一国所能独为乎。

十五日午正,法王于京外胜克流宫(Château de Saint-Cloud,今译圣克卢宫,建在巴黎以西5公里处德上塞纳圣克卢的塞纳河上,俯瞰塞纳河),召集群臣筹议战事。爵臣绅士遝迱云集。法国公爵首相加拉文莅上议院,宣读法王战论于众前。其略曰:七月二十日,朕颁诏书告尔有众,尔众无不咸怀一心,愿竭赞襄,忠勤为国。朕实深嘉赖焉。凡我友邦无不悦我国所行之公。是事与西班牙无预,毋庸往问,亦与普王子不相涉。我惟向普王言可己。盖所以主持保卫此王子者,固普王也。普王为一国君,亦为一家主纲。

维[惟]是事非,普王其谁属。普王乃谓:是事无预于已[己],告彼臣谓当以家事理之,毋以国事治之。朕闻斯言殊失所望。当朕与普王往复筹商之际,西班牙国已有书至言普郡王子今已辞位,弗居。朕以为此仅弗为于一时,未能逆料于后日。况王子而外普王子弟,可以入继西班牙王位者,当不乏人,难保无再酿事端,以致不利于我国。是以,朕请命于普王,至再至三更谕驻普使臣,廷谒普王,求其俯纳,务期面许,一言为信。朕非好为多事也,实冀将来彼此共享绥安耳。讵意不蒙,见谅于普王,以不欲预闻斯事为辞,相臣读至是。闻者咸色变,怒气勃郁不可遏,久之始定。

相臣又曰:以是今日布告,尔众咸使闻,知更可异者,普王罔念旧好,绝我使臣,命其侍臣谓之曰:今而后不复见汝矣。昨获是耗,殊骇听闻。

非特此也。普又移文于欧洲列国,将摈我使臣于其都以示绝,则其蔑辱我国体也甚矣。

众闻怒益甚,有叱咤于坐者。相臣旋又曰:我闻普王、普相授甲兴戎,厉兵秣马,调师出境,将与我国决一战。如是我国虽欲仍敦辑睦,亦不可得,其势不免于用兵。夫兵凶战危,我国岂乐出于此。特是我之委曲周旋于其间者,原以冀睦邻弭衅耳。今日者,权自彼操,难非我发。彼方欲为祸首,我岂能受之而甘心。惟当整防兵,选余勇备战,攻严守御,藉以保疆而克敌,以求一洗此耻。咨尔有众左右,翼辅以保卫我国家,勤劳于王室。众闻至此,同声称颂,读竟众退。

法国廷臣传檄约战曰:敬告普王左右。贵国欲立王子为西班牙君,此举也敝国断不能置之局外。有碍敝国土疆,所关殊钜,必上请于贵国,务使其说永废不行。陈词渎冒,至再至三,不意大王弗图,且谓敝国使臣曰:后事如何,要难逆料。大王专制一国,凡所举动悉由大王裁夺,王子逊位系于大王一言耳。此犹不蒙应许,于此可觇大王之志矣。此实有害于敝国升平之局,欧洲均一之权。伏闻大王邮示各国不肯延见,敝国使臣与之筹商,其蔑忽我使臣,凌辱我国体也甚矣。敝国今者,亟自整顿,务在保疆御敌。此非敝国所乐,迫之以不得不然耳。从此敝国与贵邦乖辑睦之欢心,失和同之雅谊,各兴战伐,视若仇雠。贵国自取,于我无尤。法廷臣咸签名于下方。

同日,大臣但部阿厘华宜(Auguste de Talhouët-Roy,1819—1884,今译奥古斯特·德·塔尔豪埃特-罗伊,在普法战争开战伊始任立法会议副主席)读是书于下议院,请筹措饷五十兆佛狼(即法郎)(每佛狼约吕宋银一圆五分之一)以充军实。于是,使众各取黑白珠,以决可否。可者,取白珠,否者取黑珠。众中取黑珠仅一人而已,乃爹亚也。起而言曰:是役也,师出无名,于理为曲。我所请者,普已许之,又何求焉。因请于大臣求观普王,告绝法国使臣之书,宜示于众。大臣不许,绅士中有言宜观者,百六十有四人。有言不必观者,有三人,其议以寝。或曰:法臣中不许宣示者,乃相臣柯利威亚(Émile Ollivier,1825—1913,今译埃米勒·奥利维耶,于

1870年1月2日至8月10日任法兰西第二帝国的内阁总理)也。

普国闻是消息,宣言于欧洲诸国,谓邮示各国之书,普并无之。或系电报一则,寄往普国廷臣并普使臣之出驻他国者,盖欲其稔知普法目下情形耳。此书竟为日报所知,互相钞录。日报所刊电报,所传其词相同,无一差异,则普无此书,邮示各国可知矣,法相臣所以不能呈之于众前也。于时兵部大臣李布殳将军以调集师旅,请许之。西基利(Alexi Segris,1811—1880,今译阿莱克西·塞格里斯,时任法国财政大臣)请拨十六兆佛狼为水师需,整治战舰,取道于波罗的海,攻普。亦许之。

是夕,法京人民闻将战之,信举欣欣然有喜色,趾高气杨[扬],迥异恒态①。操艺术者,讴战歌以助工作,旁有和以笙笛者。衢市中,灯火辉耀,球②彩深鲜明。酒肆中,三五群聚,酣饮高歌,旁若无人。或有在街结队游行者,唱诗长扬市中者,或有凑乐跳舞手指普京,而言曰:汝京计日亡矣。几于举国若狂,行人为阻。

顷之,巡丁前来弹压,告之曰:将临大事,宜静无哗。普驻法公使森士(Karl von Werther,1809—1894,今译卡尔·冯·维特)拟于七月十九日离法京,求领文凭,启程归国。先是前数日间,小民夜叩其门,掷以瓦砾;或有谋毁其公廨之外墉者。适邻有致仕之老者,出而劝阻,折以正理。曰:奈何无礼于邻国之大臣乎。众始散,或有唱麦须儿之诗(La Marseillaise,即法国国歌《马赛曲》)而退者。

王韬按语:

法国所传麦须儿诗,每歌于世乱时危之际,人或多有未之知也。是诗盖作于一千七百九十二年。是时,法自立为民主之国,有武士之娴于文墨者,曰鲁实棣厘士(Claude Joseph Rouget de Lisle,1760—1836,今译鲁热·德·利尔),从戎于外,特作是诗。俾军中壮士歌之,以寄意焉。诗之

---

① 原为"態"。
② 原为"毬"。

大旨谓国弊民愁,由于暴君御下严酷,当除独夫,更新主,共睹夫升平。向时讴此诗者,有厉禁,苟有歌于衢间者,巡丁必立执之,目为叛人。今略译其诗于下。诗云:

法国荣光自民著,爰举义旗宏建树,母号妻啼家不完,泪尽词穷何处诉。吁!王虐政猛于虎,乌合爪牙广招募,岂能复睹太平年,四出搜罗因[困]①奸蠹。奋勇兴师一世豪,报仇宝剑已离鞘,进兵须结同心誓,不胜捐躯义并高。

维今暴风已四播,屏王相继民悲咤,荒郊犬吠战声哀,四野苍凉城阙破。恶物安能著眼中,募兵来往同相佐,祸流远近恶贯盈,罪参在上何从赦。奋勇兴师一世豪,报仇宝剑已离鞘,进兵须结同心誓,不胜捐躯义并高。

维王泰侈弗可说,贪婪不足为残贼,揽权怙势溪壑张,如纳象躯入鼠穴。驱使我民若马牛,瞻仰我王逾日月,维人含灵齿发俦,讵可鞭笞日摧缺。奋勇兴师一世豪,报仇宝剑已离鞘,进兵须结同心誓,不胜捐躯义并高。

我民秉政贵自主,相联肢体结心膂,脱身束缚在斯时,奋发英灵振威武。天下久已厌乱离,诈伪相承徒自苦,自主刀锋正犀利,安得智驱而术取。奋勇兴师一世豪,报仇宝剑已离鞘,进兵须结同心誓,不胜捐躯义并高。

逸史氏王韬曰:中土诗歌,肇自虞廷,喜起赓飏,君臣并咏,千载而下,遂有三百篇之作。诗教于以大昌,若在西国,其于殷周之际乎。古贤王辟

①　查同治十二年版(1873)《普法战纪》,该字为"困"。

百五篇,载于西古史,彰彰可考。所罗门雅歌亦其流亚也。厥后推叙利亚为极盛,以文章雄于西土。自是以来,代有诗人。诸国文士以诗歌名者,指不胜屈。或以陶写其性情,或以颂美。大造化率皆朝脱于稿,而夕播其诸弦。其音韵之短长,节奏之高下,虽不与中土同,而宛转悠扬。以出之,激昂顿挫;以谐之,则无弗同也。中土音有七,而西国之所以抚琴唱诗者,其调所编之字,亦以七殆天籁欤。余尝过苏格兰旧京一丁字(Edinburg,今译爱丁堡),往游兰娱士园(Prince Street gardens,今译王子大街花园 ①),见巍然一亭中,坐衣冠者一人,须眉奇古,问之,则其地诗人也。殁后,立像于此,以志人怀思。噫!以一技之长而为人景仰,如此则西国之传名亦殊易矣。不禁为之徘徊其下,而不能去。纪中有法国《麦须儿诗》,普鲁士《爱国诗》(Was ist des Deutschen Vaterland,即《祖国歌》,原名《何为德国人的祖国》,作者是恩斯特·莫里茨(Ernst Moritz Arndt,1769—1860)类,皆著自名流,传播人口。特为译录二诗,以见其凡。

法京中之刊示邮传日报者,深惜下议院许战之,非太息不置。最后言曰:今既许之,乌能挽回,无已,则尽力与之战耳。

于是,法王传檄各国,言将兴师伐普。普王乘车至行宫,召集群臣等筹议军事。国民十万见普王来,无不免冠祝贺,群歌爱国之诗。

王韬按语:

爱国之诗,其来久矣。冀为张大普国之疆宇而作,盖有强兵辟土之思焉。其诗曰:

谁是普国(Preußenland,英 Prussia,今译普鲁士)之土疆兮?

---

① 王子大街花园英文名与"兰娱士园"似有出入,但后文所述亭子及亭中坐像,推测为王子大街花园中建于 19 世纪中叶的司各特纪念塔(Scott Monument),塔中建有苏格兰著名作家沃尔特·司各特(Walter Scott,1771—1832)的坐像。

将东顾士畏比明（Schwabenland，英 Swabia，今译施瓦本）分？

抑西瞻礼吴河（Rhine，今译莱茵河）旁，

将礼吴河红葡悬纠结分？

抑波的海（the Belt，指贝尔特海峡）白鸥飞翔翔分？

我知其非分，

我宗邦必增广而无极分，

斥远而靡疆。

谁为日耳曼之祖国分？

将士底利赢（Steierland，英 Styria，今译施蒂利亚）之腴壤分，抑巴华里亚（Bayerland，英 Bavaria，今译巴伐利亚）之崇岗？

将摩辰（Marsen，英 Marsi，今译马尔西）牛羊游牧分？

抑麦介物产蕃康①（Ist's，wo des Marsen Rind sich streckt）？

我知其非分，

我宗邦必增广而无极分，

斥远而靡疆。

谁为日耳曼之祖国分？

将威士非邻（Westfalenland，英 Westphalia，今译威斯特伐利亚）之界址分，抑巴买兰尼（Pommerland，英 Pomerania，今译波美拉尼亚）之版章？

将岸边之沙随流而入海分？

抑旦纽（Donau，英 Danube，今译多瑙河）之水波溶漪而荡漾？

我知其非分，

我宗邦必增广而无极分，

斥远而靡疆。

---

① 原文为：Ist's，wo der Märker Eisen reckt？中文译为：是否为马克伯国居民铸铁之地？

谁为日耳曼之祖国兮？

将济济盈庭者权能倜傥兮，

干略雄强而告我以綦详？

将在呵发（Schweizer，英 Swiss，今瑞士）之境外兮，抑于兜耳（Tirol，英 Tyrol，今译蒂罗尔）之域旁？

彼两地之人民，

余中心爱慕而弗忘。

我知其非兮，

我宗邦必增广而无极兮，

斥远而靡疆。

谁为日耳曼之祖国兮？

我今将告尔以何方。

我方言必远而弗届，

流行四极兮而散播八方。

将与我同奉一主兮，

讴歌于会堂。

其隶属于日耳曼之版图者，

试观此幅员之孔长。

此乃日耳曼列祖之所启疆，

翦枭猰兮驱虎狼，

挞傲慢兮伐矜张。

必仇敌之骨泯兮，

而憎妒之全降。

不见夫我之友朋，

无非荣显与轩昂。

惟日耳曼之全土兮，

开辟非常。

此为日耳曼奄有之土疆，
长邀鉴顾于穹苍。
俾我侪心志雄兮膂力强，
尽心爱此宗邦兮，
志之衷藏。
此乃日耳曼之祖国兮，
渺渺兮，余怀望。①

声韵悠扬，众口如一。国民皆环立宫门，静俟王命。王时出宫外，以温语拊循之。民咸感悦，悉愿为王致死。

七月十八日，普国绅士献颂于普王曰：克敌致果，正在斯时。愿作士气，无损国威。强邻肇衅，弃好崇仇。折冲行伍，无贻王羞。我岂欲战，惟求辑洽。彼不愿和，乃怀残贼。彼击我攻，兵刃既接，甲仗器械，失罔所惜。王赫斯怒，戎首是求。我民咸愤敌，忾同仇。

王览之称善，因谓之曰：此衅之启非由于我，惟我之心，上帝克知。我昨答法王书，无卑无亢，不激不随，此日耳曼诸邦所传观。旅于远地之日，民咸日所乐闻也。前日，朕甫回车而来，众民之踊跃迎迓者，无不欢然相庆。然兵端一开，伤民命，耗物力，当不知凡几。前者伐哵、伐墺二役，速于奏捷，会不浃旬。此词之战，当必不同。军饷浩繁，所关甚巨。但此桓桓之猛士，赳赳之武夫，余可恃之以无恐。况乎兵甲之雄壮、器械之精锐，何往而不克。至于操成败胜负之数，则在彼苍而已。朕知戮力于疆场者，无非忠君爱国之士，朕甚嘉之言。竟众民威呼万岁。

十九日，普王开门告众曰：我国家南北一体，联若同气。前者集议已

① 此即德国爱国诗人恩斯特·莫里茨·阿恩特（Ernst Moritz Arndt，1769—1860）的《祖国歌》（"Was ist Des Deutschen Vaterland"）。

申此旨。志一心齐，欣悦靡暨。昊苍眷顾，国步斯亨。凡百作为，协于众心。宣扬教化，训我齐氓。寻盟守约，辑睦四邻。若此而犹不免出战争，则非我国家，实职其咎。此尔有众所共见，共知者也。我已预备，我甲兵善保我疆土，彼来我斯应之而已。夫西班牙之迎我世子入缵王祚，或舍、或立，我国皆不及知，乃法王遽以启衅之端，执词致讨。稽诸前史，实所未闻。

昔者法之先王，穷兵黩武，俶扰邻邦。罔顾人民和乐之休，不念家国升平之福。喜功好大，日寻干戈。我日耳曼诸邦挫败之辱至今未洒。何则？势分而形涣，则御侮难。地隔而情疎，则受制易。今日者，惩兹覆辙，誓作联邦，内外同心，遐迩一德，罔分畛域，实共兴衰。一或见侮，众共击之，并力合进，务雪深仇。

顾余之言，此非有意欲攻之也。

胜负由天，讵能自主。好胜多敌，佳兵不祥。毋为戎首，不亦善乎。兵端一启，不可猝弭。先发难者，必受其殃。余岂不愿普法民生，涵濡于圣泽之中，胥跻乎仁寿之域。咸赴乐易，不遘艰危。无如法国执政者，贪功肆志，乐祸居心。惑于人言，罔修邻好。恃战攻为已利，藉兵革以洩[泄]忿。愚弄其民，使之好战，而忘生。

惟我国家以含忍为先，不争为宝，必不肯无故兴戎，致欧洲复睹流离，猝多变乱。乃彼敌人刃既接，虽欲不战，亦不可得。凡我南北日耳曼列邦，其辅翼予勇而忘身，忠以爱国。彼攻，我拒；彼退，我进。武卫振励，国威庶可长享，康宁于欧士[土]矣。呜呼！惟我列祖列宗夙承天宠，今无异昔，必袭休祥。

普王在朝宣谕如此。当诏书未读之先，议院长铎德禅臣（Eduard von Simson，1810—1899，今译爱德华·冯·希姆森，1867—1871 年任北日耳曼联邦议院长）（铎德，西国儒者。尊称若中国翰林院学士），起立众中朗声称颂。普王宣诏书时，容貌肃毅，言词严厉，听者无不魄然动容。普王每数十言，旷然若有所思，恻然如欲下泪。读未及半，同声叹美者，如出一口。读为之少止。

是日申刻诸部大臣,筹度军机者咸集,列邦群有司自远毕至。普国首相告众曰:今日法国已兵临我境矣。众皆起立,额手曰:美哉,敬为相国贺。

七月十五日,法王传檄布告各国,言将兴师伐普。爰命六军刻期出境,羽林次①飞之俦,咸束装以待,令下即行。

普法之战于是乎成矣。

普法战纪第一卷终。

乌程钱征昕伯②校字

---

① 原为"伙"。
② 钱征(字昕伯)为王韬长女王婉(字苕仙)的丈夫。

普法戰紀

光緒乙未重鐫　弢園王氏藏版

同治九年庚午秋法因爭立西班牙王位
先興師伐之懸軍深入所向皆捷法
軍進圍其都城一百四十二日糧絕援窮法人不得已願如
約議和同治十年辛未春盟成釋兵弭怨計兩國相持七閱
月法坐是地削國蹙幾於一蹶不振而普愈稱雄於歐土余
撫拾其前後戰事彙爲一書凡十有四卷大抵取資於日報
者十之四五爲張芝軒所口譯者十之四網羅總括於此
他處者十之二三既成將付剞劂而爲述其大略曰嗚呼余
之志普法戰事豈獨志普法哉歐洲全局之樞機括於此
矣普強法弱此其由來也普中歐洲而立國西
有法而東有俄皆鄰也最者爲法所制戳於一步不可復

西日耳曼南北列邦勢漸而不聚雖推壞爲盟主亦僅擁虛
名而已以春秋列國之大勢例之歐洲普僅等宋衛爲耳英
法俄壞則晉楚齊秦也近十餘年閒普國勢日骎自恃伐壞此
坐成強大而法方晏然於其際狻復自恃雄盛啟釁端此
法之所以幾覆也昔普興而壞衰論者乃舉英普俄爲四
大今普強而法弱論者乃舉英普俄爲三雄然而法國之興
衰強弱實爲歐洲變局一大關鍵何則以地當衝要也若英
雖強弱其地辭懸海外無繫於大局故以法輔英則英益強
以英輔法則法不賸昔之英法常相攻以其時歐洲諸勢
均力敵皆不足以制英法也今之英法常相合以俄驥興於
東方以制土強普幅起於西境以制壞強皆足與英法抗衡

《普法战纪》光绪乙未重镌版

七

西学图说

编者按：

　　王韬与艾约瑟、伟烈亚力合译著作的同时，也根据其所见、所学，另外辑撰了《西学图说》、《西学原始考》（为《格致新学提纲》之扩充）、《泰西著述考》等书，后一同编入《西学辑存六种》中。《西学图说》介绍西方主要学说，配图三十一幅，计有太阳说、地球赤道图说、行星绕日图说、岁差图说、行星说、五星说、空气说、光动图说、声学浅说等。

太阳说

　　日月星辰皆丽于天，自人观之，虽见其时起时落，而不知所处，实有一定。其中有互为转移者，论其体，日大而月小，星则有大有小，其动者为行星。吾人观定星，而行星之经道始明。即如月亦行星之一，昼夜行于天，周流无定。今见其近于此，度明；又见其近于彼。度其行也，不特与星同旋，并能直经于天。然月之行与诸星之行，道相反。人见月较诸星之行稍迟，今见与此星并行，忽又见其在后。假使人每夜细观月之行法至一月，而知其历遍诸星矣，故晦朔月之位，向无殊（因此故名为一月）。其法一定，初无错乱。至于日之行，不特与星同旋，亦与星相反。吾人不能细见其行法者，因日之光炽，周天之星皆隐而不见，故人不能如月之见其转移，须以别法推之。

　　吾人常谓星之一周，昼夜约十二时，实则止十一时四刻五十六分；日则历昼夜十二时为一周星之行,故每日较日少四分。假如今夜见此星没于子正,至明夜则少四分,后夜则少八分矣(以此推之,可以积算)。若使日与星相并而行,可以同出而同没,因日之历时较星为长,故即星而观,知日之退行与月同。

且常考星之出没也有一定。假如出于东者,吾人不易所居,常见其自东而升,虽时有四季,而其出没之方未常少异。日则不然。其出与没及行至天心时,有变迁,惟变迁之中恒有定向。中国在赤道之北,吾人所谓夏者,因日在赤道,北昼则不止六时,且行于天顶,阳光正射,故热。至冬,则行于赤道之南,自出至没不及六时,行亦不至于天顶,其光斜照,故短而冷。

地球赤道图说

赤道分地球为南北,南北为时不同,彼昼短则此长,彼寒则此热。此如春分时,日出于丙没于丁,行于地之赤道。是时,昼夜平分,后则渐出于东北,没于西北。至夏至,则出于乙,没于甲(自丙至乙,计时为一季。乙至甲为度远,故昼长)。后又渐退至丙,没于丁,是为秋分(计时亦一季)。

盖春分至秋分,自丙至乙,复自乙至丙,适时半年。此半年中,日常在赤道北,渐觉昼长而热。秋分后,渐见其出于丙之南,没于丁之南。至冬至,则出于戊,没于巳(计时亦一季),行亦于赤道之南,其相去赤道与丙至乙同。后又渐退至丙(计时亦一季),复为春分。

其周行之有度,所以定四时,别寒暑而一岁,乃成日之运旋,非环行于列星之上,不过其体自为转移,计二十五日七时为一周。何以知其故,因日中有黑斑,见其绕至原处,即知为一周,其黑斑在日中时,或见多时,或见少,究未知为何物。昔侯失勒(Wilhelm Herschel,1738—1822,今译威廉·赫歇尔)曾用大千里镜观之云：日之明也，其周围之光，气为之光，气下有云一层，受此光，返照于地。球有时二层，俱裂则见黑斑中之深黑者，日体也；四边淡黑者，云也。使地球上无日之光，人不能生；果谷草木，亦不长；海中之水，亦不能变质。盖海为咸水，日可吸取其咸者成雨而为淡，且无日之热，风亦不生。

行星环绕太阳图说

太阳者，诸行星之心也。曷谓诸行星之心？太阳居中，不动其外，辰星绕之。又其外，太白(即金星)绕之；又其外，地球绕之；又其外，荧惑(即火星)绕之；又其外，谷女、武女、天后、火女等十四小星绕之；又其外，岁星绕之；又其外，填星(即土星)绕之；又其外，天王绕之；又其外，海王绕之。故曰：太阳为诸行星之心，地球亦绕太阳乎。曰然。

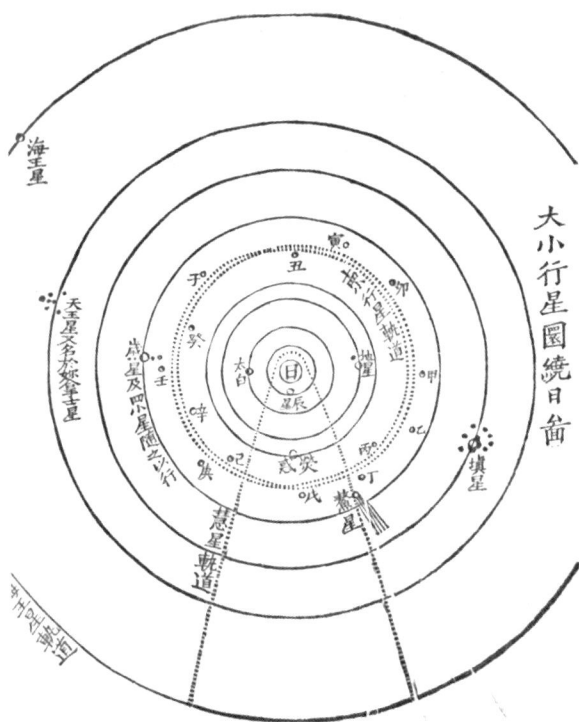

然则太阳及周天之星,每日东出西没者何也? 曰此地球本体之动也。地球有之动,所以成昼夜。有证乎? 曰:有古人谓荧惑、岁星、填星皆有岁轮,岁轮之大小与日天等。所谓日天者,即地球绕日之轨道也,而岁轮则地球离星远近之迹也,使早知地球绕日,则无岁轮之说矣。

今之历家以远镜测外行星,春夜窥之略大而速者,秋夜窥之必略小而迟。秋夜窥之略大者,春夜窥之必略小。此第一证也。以远镜测内行二星,有晦朔弦望,且近地球则大,远地球则小。此又一证也。以远镜窥恒星,因地球行速而成视差,此第二证也。

诸行星有本体之动乎? 曰有。西国以远镜测诸行星,见其有高低形迹,因得见其有转动也。此理自哥白尼发之三百年来,泰西诸国信而不疑,盖至真至确之故,久而益明也。中土未明历法之士,闻之或有惊且骇者,亦未深思之耳。

行星续说

星之繁不可穷,而自恒星外,其周太阳之各行星,则有可计焉。

居中为日。

周日第一道曰水星,其广大较地八分之一,凡八十八日限周日一转。

第二道曰金星,其广大约与地均,凡二百二十五日限周日一转。

第三道曰地球,即人所居者。是凡三百六十五日二时七刻零周日一转。南北极枢纽,不离其处,而东西则每一昼也一易转。有一太阴旋绕,即月也。因是而有月道,朔望晦明,上下弦望焉。

第四道曰火星,较地略小,凡六百八十七日限周日一转。

第五道曰花女星,凡一千一百九十三日限周日一转。

第六道曰火女,即陆星,凡一千三百二十五日限周日一转。

第七道曰虹女星,凡一千三百四十二日限周日一转。

第八道曰海女星,凡一千三百四十六日限周日一转。

第九道曰酒女星,凡一千三百八十日限周日一转。

第十道曰义女星,凡一千五百十一日限周日一转。

第十一道曰天后,即巧星,凡一千五百九十四日限周日一转。

第十二道曰谷女,即威星,凡一千六百八十二日限周日一转。

第十三道曰武女,即焰星,凡一千六百八十七日限周日一转。

自五道至此,凡九星较水星更小,古人未尝寻见。今西国天文士用大千里镜,窥其形多,棱角虽各异,其道而有相交之际,或曩为一星而分裂之,未可知也。

第十四道曰木星,广大百倍于地,凡四千三百三日限周日一转。有四太阴旋绕。

第十五道曰土星,即铅星,较金星略小。其象与众星殊,外有长圆光圈如带然。凡一万零七百五十九日限周日一转,有八太阴旋绕。

第十六道曰天星,又较小于土星,凡三万零六百八十七日限周日一转。有六太阴旋绕。

第十七道曰海王星,亦是近时测得者,较天星略小,而大于地数十倍。凡六万零一百二十七日限周日一转,曾于初次测见之时,已见一太阴旋转。然细思此星离日已远,又大于地球,必非一太阴所能偏照,必再以大远镜谛观,然后悉其底蕴也。

若彗星,圈道长圆竟天,其邈远难以厘定。有时见其光下垂者,人谓之尾云。夫诸行星皆随日旋转,或迟或速,而日亦二十五昼夜零为之一转。果谁系之,而谁运之者哉,盖必有主宰纲维之者在也。仰以观于天文,能不憬然以深思哉。

五星说

行星有七,曰:水星、金星、地球、火星、木星、土星、天王星。行于地球之内层者,为水星与金星,其余五星在地球圈线之外,远近不一。吾人细观行星,知其非常。在旧处时,有变迁,吾人定不能见。

行星与日相对,比如早上日在东,则不能见其在西;晚时日在西,则不能见其在东。考诸图即可知行星之环行于日上,犹月之常从于地球也。

圖日繞星五

水 星

水星在行星中与日最近,其体之直径长九千里,其行于地球也,离日有一万万里,八十七日为一周。

其自为旋转也,一周为十二时。其体上有空气与否,则无所证据。受日之热较地球多七倍,倘使造物主布置水星时,与地球同法,则水星中之水必尽变为气,其热必较地球为更甚,乃造物主实有全能之法,使之不变。譬诸人至海底则不生,而海中实有千万生物在焉,岂非位置使然哉。

水星近于日,其光面有时不与地球对,故地球上人不多见,时或见者于日未出之前与日既没之后而已。日没后见者,其光摇动而色白,此时有晦色朦胧光,故似乎幽暗。有时经过日与地球之间,人见之似有黑点在日上也。

金 星

金星直径有二万三千一百里,其行于日上,二百二十四日为一周,离日之远约二万二里。其自为旋转也,约十一时半。星上之日稍短于地球上之日,吾人见此星在行星中,除月外惟此为最明,故虽于昼时,日光甚炽,而有时亦能见之为此。星四周有光,故知有空中气在焉,以千里镜观之，遥见星体有痕迹，其面时有黑点。

星上之山，较地球上之山高数倍，有高三十里者，有高六十里者。金星之经于日与地球之间不多见，前在西国纪元一千七百六十九年后，此则在纪元一千八百七十四年。知天文者常细勘经过之行度，即知诸行星及地球离日之路若干。吾人见此星，似在日之西，比日先出，即名旦星；或在日之东，较日稍后，即名黄昏星，非地球之年，亦非金星之半年。因轮转二百九十日为星，亦轮转二百九十日为黄昏星，何也？金星之行与地球同路也。吾人在地球因与彼同路，故不见其行之速，若地球静而不动，则此金星半日为旦星，半日为黄昏星矣。

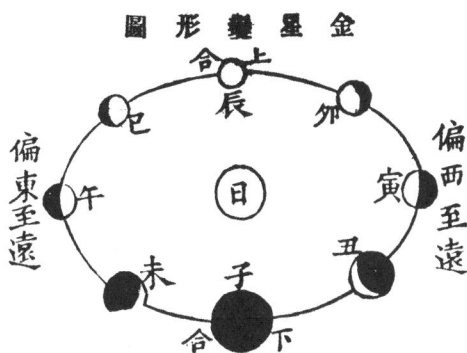

金星又名太白星，以千里镜窥之，其形与月之朔望、上下弦相同。盖金星绕日而行，在黄道之内线，有时见其面，有时见其侧与背，故亦如月之有晦望焉。因其亦借光于日，故其体半明半暗，从图之下面斜观之，其形随时如此。

火　星

在地球轨道之外，其体之直径一万二千里，较地球之直径约仅一半。其环行于日，近于六百八十七日为一周，于地球上计时将近二年。其自体之旋转一周得十二时四十分，离日之远有四万五千万里，故半时中能行一百余万里。此星上之昼夜与地球上相似，因其离日如此之远，故所受光与热，较地球止有半耳。

此星上无月，金星与水星上亦无月，即有之，吾人亦无从测见也。此星之光似红而色蒙，故见之即知为火星。以千里镜观之，甚奇。面上有无数黑点，有空中气至大、至厚，何以知之。假使吾人见一定星不甚光明者，因火星经过于定星之前时,有空中气蔽之,故不能了了。如行与定星正对,则定星不见矣。此行星时见为大,时见为小者,何也?因有时近于地球一万五千里,有时远地球七万万里,故也。火星上人见地球之轮转,与地球上人见金星之轮转,或为早星或黄昏星,亦如是耳。

木 星

木星乃行星最大者,星体直径有二十七万里,较地球大一千二百倍。其行于日外十二年始一周,离日十五万万里。除金星外,最明亮者,莫如此星。日之光与热至彼,较地球小二十五倍。星面有环带,或大或小,时不一定,时有八九。带经过其面时为平直。然侯失勒曾以远镜观之,带不常为平直,而时有湾[弯]曲。知天文者,亦不一其说,或云为云裂,或云星上有火,时为迁变。此中定非无故,惟世人不能细知耳。

此星上有四月,吾人可亲见者惟二。此四月常从木星行,犹月与地球然。四月之行亦不一,或一日九时为一周,或三日六时半为一周,或七日零一时半为一周,或十六日零八时为一周。行至星之影上,即为月蚀。

博学者见木星上之月蚀,可细论其光行之速为何如也。倘吾人于木星至近之时见月蚀,较诸至远时速十六分,以是知此光经于地球四围之直径。适时为十六分,因日在直径之中,光至地球适得其时八分。盖日远地球二万八千五百万里,日光一秒能行六十万里,故计时八分即至地球也。

土 星

土星行于日外三十年为一周,远日二十七万一千八百万里,其体直径长二十三万里,其自为旋转,约六时十三分为一周,较地球大九百倍,因离日远,故其光与热小地球九十倍。星上有八月,其行也至速者,一日一周,迟者约八十日。

土星与他星异,星外有圈以千里,镜观之亦至大至光者,圈系实物,犹星然。圈有二层,内色昏黑,星与圈约远九万里。二圈之相去,约六万里,内亦有黑色。圈与星常行于日上,其圈之厚,据侯失勒云约有六百里至八百里者。此圈于星上一周约五时二十五分,不但自为旋转,亦从此星同行其圈。

如此之大,究何所用?议者论说纷纭,莫衷一是。天文者,想此圈得日之光,可回照于星。故此星虽离日甚远,得此回光之照,亦不甚冷。此星之行于日上,半为日照,其半则日不及也,故三十年一周,十五年为昏暗,十五年为光明,犹地球之南北极处,六阅月为夜,六阅月为昼也。

天王星

木星与土星之行于日上时稍有差,昔人见之即知其外之有星摄动也。侯失勒于纪元一千七百八十一年三月十三日夜间得见此星。其星较土星又远于日五百五十万万里。其自为旋转,约八十四年为一周。其上有六月,随之以俱行星。体之直径约十一万里,大于地球八十倍。日之光与热至此较地球小三百七十倍。然博学者推算此星之光约可抵望日之月二百四十八倍,齐放光明,遍烛大千世界。由此观之,日光之大能普照万方也。固如是哉。

星气说

太虚无尽界,无尽界中有无尽星气,何谓星气?聚万万星于一处,远望之蓬蓬勃勃如一点白气。中法星图中,传说积尸气之类皆是也。而万万星即万万太阳,每一太阳想亦有数地球环绕之。

天河亦星气,本地球上所见太阳及诸恒星,皆天河中之星也。太阳为本地球所环绕之最近,故视之最大;诸恒星皆太阳四面相近之星,故之历历可数,渐远则诸星相去,渐狭亦渐糢[模]糊,而成天河白气一道。若在他星气中,望之则太阳及诸恒星,皆在天河中而成一点白气矣。天河形长而有两歧,太阳在近分歧处。

行星图二说

西国天文士分诸行星为三类:曰内类、曰中类、曰外类。内类者,水金地火四星,其体在大小之间,其质甚重,其形扁圆。地面赤道线与绕日相离,度分不小,惟地有一月,余俱无。

中类,十四小行星,即图上甲、乙、丙十干,及子、丑、寅、卯是也。其体甚小,其质甚轻。其轨道十四,互相交错。相距角不小,与黄道所成之角亦甚大,俱无月。

外类,木、土、天王、海王四星。其体甚大,其质较内类略粗疏,较中类略坚致,其形更扁。南北径较内类更短于赤道径。俱有多月绕之。其本体之赤道与各月之轨道平行,复有光带,形迹亦平行于赤道。其赤道、黄道距角甚小。

岁差图说

岁差之故,中法谓黄道西移。古西法谓恒星东行,而皆非也。康熙时,英国天文士奈端(即牛顿)始明其理。盖岁差之源,生于地动。

地动之理有七。

一岁绕日一周,其轨道即黄道也。动一。

一日自转一周,其腰带即赤道也。动二。

赤极带动,赤道绕行于黄极二万五千八百六十八年而一周。动三。

绕黄极之圈上,又有小椭圆,赤极又行于小椭圆之边,十九年而一周。动四。

太阳挈地球及诸行星以绕行于昴宿之大星,一千八百二十万年而一周。动五。

太阳吸引地球半年之间,日日有差,至最高、最卑,而复名曰半年差。动六。

太阴吸引地球半月之间,日有微差至朔望,而复名曰半月差。动七。

合七动观之,其赤极绕行于黄极,平岁差所由生也。其又绕行于小椭圆,则定岁差也。至半年半月,二差虽于岁差无关,然而测算之际,必加减此二差,始得真岁差也。此岁差之理也。

以中土书证之。道光时,所测恒星表较之康熙时所测,冬至后至夏至半周,其星去极之度,皆小于前。盖赤道半圈,自南而北,南纬增而北纬减,故去极之度渐小也。夏至后至冬至半周,其星去极之度,皆大于前。盖赤道半圈,自北而南,南纬减而北纬增,故去极之度渐多也。此一证也。

古测极星即不动处,齐梁间祖暅(祖冲之之子,480—525)测,离不动处一度强。宋熙宁时,沈括(1031—1095)所测,离三度。元至元中郭守敬(1231—1316)所测,离三度半,使赤道不动,何以赤极易地乎。此二证也。

二十八宿离赤道度,古今六测皆不同,史册彰彰。此三证也。

然安知非恒星循黄道东行而必为赤道西行乎?曰:凡行星东行必与太阳平面。今恒星皆不与太阳为平面,凡行星高卑不同,速亦异。今恒星高卑各不同,而迟速则一。据此二者,可定为赤道西行,而非恒星东行矣(韬按:日居于中,地球环日而行,月又绕地球而一周,每年自正月朔至十二月晦,所行之轨道稍有不及。是生岁差,积差一月,则必置闰。此古说之至浅,而不可易者)。

岁差一图

东春西秋为赤道面,甲春乙秋为黄道面,甲春东为黄赤交角,太阴、太阳吸引之力加于地球腰带高处(地球正圆腰带半径大于南北半径二百余里)。今东点渐近于甲点,东春西面渐近于甲春乙面,故春秋二点每岁退行五十秒四一。

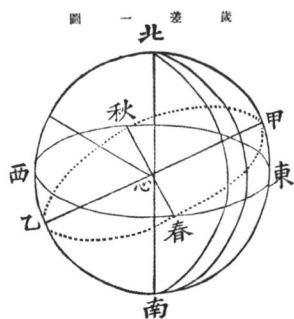

又诸行星太阳与地球皆相吸引,故黄道亦动。春秋二点每年东行一百分秒之三十一,是为岁差减分。

岁差二图

未为黄极辰为北,极北极行于小椭圆。辰寅巳卯十九年一周,而小椭圆心午点,行于距等圈。申丑子午二万五千八百六十八年一周。椭圆高半径九秒二五,卑半径六秒八七。

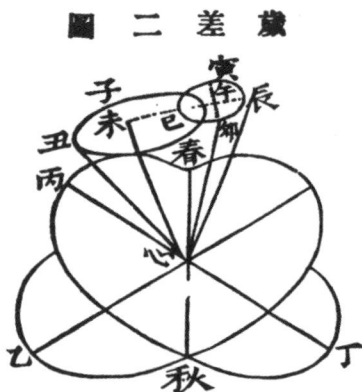

空气说

空气合养气(即氧气)、淡气(即氮气)、轻气(即氢气)、炭气(即二氧化碳)而成。试以百分论,淡气约归七十五分半,养气约归二十三分二毫半,炭气、轻气约归一分二毫半,故淡气之重而大,较诸气为甚。

然其气亦有时变坏,因其中或有秽气杂之;而人吸空中之气于内,亦常有变化者,因所吸之养气或入于血,或出而变为炭气。盖人吸入者为清气,出者即为浊气。假如多人处于一室中,其呼出之气充满于中,人易疾病,炭气多而养气少也。

人于半时中,能吸气约二百四丈立方尺,及气之出,则尽变为坏气,空中气亦因此而坏,若使无法以处之,恐人多受病而死。幸赖海中之风,将炭气散尽,并有日光及草木中常出之养气,以生人命。

空气之环绕于地球外也,如蛋白之包裹其黄。即至高之山顶计之,其相去犹高一百五十里,其气能滋长百物,化生万类人。离此气,则不生物,离此气,则不长其流,行于诸空处,如水之流下,遇隙即入。

其气不独在诸生物中,凡湿物中亦俱有之气,近地球其力更厚而大,犹海底之水,较海面为厚耳。试至于山顶渐高,则气渐薄;至忙宇浪山之巅(高九里),其气之薄,几至人难吸取。虽然气离山之最高者一百五十里,此犹约而言之。人在气球中,业经试验,极高可升至六十丈。吾人见上之青气为天不知,人若上升,青气渐无;若至山顶一百五十里外,则天为昏暗,其气能常引湿气于中。湿气过多,则为雨。

博学者业经推算,若空中之湿气齐降于地球,为雨不过八寸,其气之收摄湿气,热时较寒时更多。然时热,湿气虽多,不为雨;时寒,则不然。盖寒风至,则气亦寒。湿气蒸为云,云即为雨。

以寒暑针测之,地球之面较山顶为热,因愈高则愈冷,故云行至山下,则渐消热故也;行至顶则成雨,顶处冷也。

气之围绕于地球,其用甚大(气有二层,外层气薄,内层气厚),如无,即无云、无雨、无虹，且不能使日光转射而入。如日在天心，其光始能射，乃日在天之偏侧，其气能使日光斜折而入，始入则少斜，继进则更折，因第二层之气，较初层之气为厚耳。

人接其光而所见，一若无所偏侧者，故知在天之物，比本体之所在恒高。假如人在地球之己上，日在甲，人何以见之，如在乙然。因其光斜折，故自在己之人，若见为直射者，其实即此斜折之理。其光之斜折也，亦非一定。日在朝暮，其光更斜，因近于天地交接之处，其气厚，故在未出已没之时，亦能见者，是其气能引日光转折而入也。

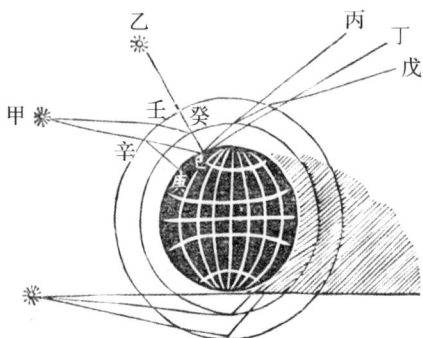

考诸图自可细知其理。比如，人在己，日在戊，业已没山不能见也。因有转照，故与在丙同。至初层气渐折，而进至二层，则更折，在己之人犹能见之。故日之出，更见其早，其没更觉其晚，且其气不特可使日光之斜折，并能散日光为返照，如无返照之理，人仅能直视其物，而横侧处犹不及见。今乃上下偏正，无数诸星瞭如指掌者，岂非返照之故欤？

声学浅说

大凡有声之器悬诸空中，以物击之，其体若见，为战动而耳中，已闻其声。其声何自而至？盖战动时，有空中之气为之引导耳。若无空中气，其声定无所闻。设有一物，形似小钟，其内机键似表，以匙开之，其舌自为击动。置诸抽风器内，虽远亦闻其声，如以器中之气渐为洩出，则舌虽击，而钟若无声。后复鼓之以气，其声复得而闻。如空中气较平时为厚，则其声更亮，器内之气较外为厚，则声亦更亮。

比如入水，钟沉于水内，下面之水将气上逼，人虽轻语于中，闻者不觉其细，若同于寻常之语，则觉其声之喧阗矣，气厚故也。假使人放枪于山顶,而下若无听闻,或两人于山顶叙语,稍离则其语难闻。因山顶之气较地为薄,以是知东击而西应者,空中气之围绕于人也。虽然有响斯应者,空中气能引之,而实体之物为尤甚。

试以大木论。两端相去十丈,我立于此端之前,使人轻击其彼端,而寂然无闻。若以耳按于木,则彼端之击虽轻,而其声无不觉者。有如声出于地中,地虽深而自能使之上达,故火山欲裂之。前其中先有声响,人尚未闻,而犬马之类先知,以其耳近于地故也。有美洲西境人以耳向地于人,马未至时,先能预知,乃地为之引其声也。

博学者推之,知声之行也,一秒[秒]时能行六千二百三十七尺,故闻其声,即能知其路之远近。譬之于雷,自电闪时至,雷发声计几秒,即知雷之相去几何。如电闪后一秒,雷声即起,知雷远一千二百三十七尺;二秒,则倍之。且实体物之引声也,较空中气更远。

设有中空之筒,约长三千五百丈,贴一铁圈于其口,圈口悬一小钟,人于一时中,擎其钟并擎其圈,使一人于彼口听之。钟之声不若铁圈之声为速,因钟悬于空圈,则实于筒也。盖实体物之引声,较空中气速十倍有半。且声之行也直,如光然,凡遇物之坚而光者,声即回,犹谷声之相应也。或所遇之物,峻嶒而不平;或柔软而小者,其声即不能回。人欲其声之回也,必直对之,而其声乃闻。

第 一 圖

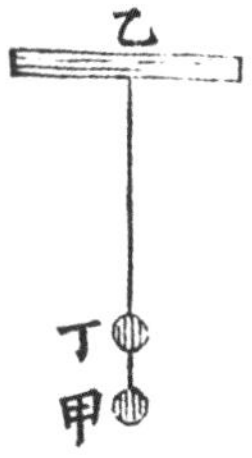

比如人在甲,其声至乙之光面,及其声之回,丁与甲者俱闻之。或其声横出者,则可见第二图。此如人在丙,声至甲,因非径直,故声不回,其声由甲而回至丁。盖声之所处与声之所回,其斜折之路同也。以故声之直至者,其回也亦直;声之斜出者,其声必斜至彼面也。

第 二 圖

假使声出于光面,所至者亦光面,其声之应也不一。有如声自甲出,至丁而复,回于甲;或声由甲而至丙,其回声则至于戊。乙与己亦同。如人在圆圈内,声自丁出,四面之回声俱集于中,故声最响。

 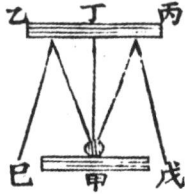

第 三 圖　　第 四 圖

或有房如椭式,声出于甲,或至丁,或至戊。遇光面,声俱回至乙。比如,甲上出三声,人在丙、丁、戊,闻者仅各一声。如在乙,则三声俱闻。因声之回俱集于乙也。面之光者,回声自远。如人立于两岸,其声隔河可闻。倘易以地,同此远近,则无闻矣,因水之面光也故。砲[炮]发于海,远处俱闻。

如有浪起,则声不远传,即如欧罗巴(即欧洲)与阿非利加(即非洲)交界处,中间以海约三十里,如风顺而浪平,则彼此之声可闻。洋枪之声,可闻二十里。如数枪举发,则声较远。

纪元一千六百七十二年,荷兰在海角战之时(即 1672 年法荷战争),英国虽相距六百里,其炮声亦常闻之。

光动图说

新法论光,自出光之处至受光之处,自远及近有行分,名曰光动。以木星证之。如图,辛为木星,丁甲子为木星月道,巳壬庚戌为地球道。木星之月绕木星行至巳,则木星上见日食;至甲乙,则月入木星之影无光,而为月食;至丑,则地球上见木星中有黑点;至丙,则地球上见木星掩月。地球在巳壬庚,半周恒见木星之月出,影在庚戌巳半周,恒见入影。

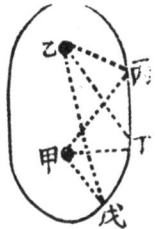

第 五 圖

两出两入之间,为木星月一周时刻。最近木星第一月，一周恒为二十一时一刻十三分三十五秒，而地球在庚时，见出入影及有黑点与掩食，恒迟十六分二十六秒。在巳时，恒早见十六分十六秒；在壬戌时，较在庚早八分十三秒，较在巳巳迟八分十三秒，岂非木星之光。自巳至庚，须行十六分二十六秒乎。

以此例推之，日光至地球行八分十三秒，至土星行五刻三分二十秒，至水星行三分十秒，至海王星行四时，强最近定位。星光行至地球，最少三年四十五日。铅子疾飞一年，与一秒中光行其路恰等也。窃思光行之理，与质体行之理不同，而与声行之理同。质体之行可测量者，水星最速一秒中行九十里，光行速于水星约六千倍。

第一图说

凡气、水、玻璃等物，俱为透光之质，亦曰空质。空质有厚薄，水厚于气，玻璃等物厚于水。光之出薄入厚，或出厚入薄，俱成斜线。如甲乙为厚薄界线，与子丑成十字线。丙光过戊点，当至丁；若出薄入厚，则成戊。辛近于子丑线，若出厚入薄，则成戊。庚远于子丑线，戊辛、戊庚俱为光差。子丙为子戊丙角正弦，辛癸为辛戊癸角正弦，此两正弦恒有此例，庚壬与丙子亦然。

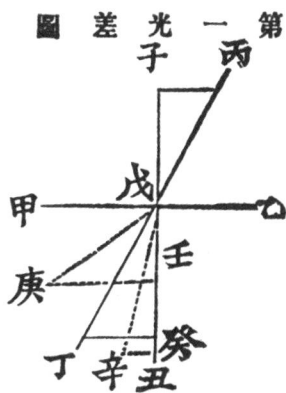

第二图说

凡有平面如金水等物，其面能照物生影者，谓明面光之射于明面也，必成反照。如甲乙为明面，丙光射于戊点，反照在丁子丑，与甲乙成十字，丙戊子、丁戊子二角必等。

第三图说

凡光由薄质而出入于厚质，厚质之两面平行，则出入之线，亦必平行。

如甲乙丙丁为厚质,子光由戊入,复由己点出至丑。甲乙、丙丁为平行面,故戊子、己丑成平行线。

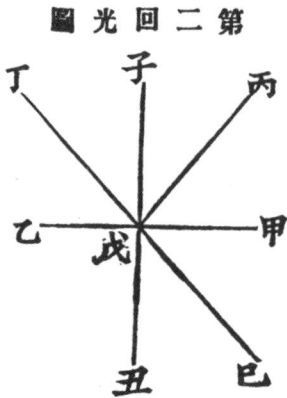

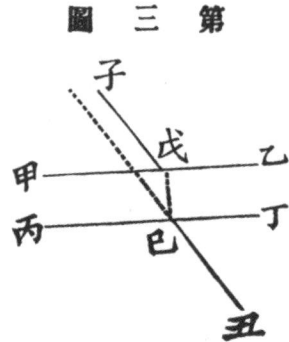

第四图说

凡光出入于厚质,厚质之两面不平行,则出入之线亦不平行,而与面所成之角必等。如甲乙丙为三角体厚质,甲乙、甲丙两面不不行,则子光由戊入,必由巳出至丑,子戊、巳丑亦不平行,而子戊乙、丑巳丙两角必等。

第五图说

以空质作透光镜,有凹镜、有凸镜。光之透凹镜也,则能变小为大,如甲丙、戊巳、乙丁三平行线过凹镜。惟巳辰中线与戊巳平行,丙子、丁丑俱向外,不与甲丙、乙丁平行,而甲乙变为子丑所成之象,大于本物也。

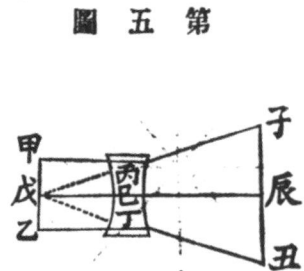

第六图说

光之透凸镜也，最小之处成一点，曰聚光点，亦曰光点。如甲丙、戊巳、乙丁三平行线过凸镜，惟巳子中线仍与戊巳平行，丙子、丁子俱斜向内，不与甲丙、乙丁平行，而成聚光点于子。若平行线为庚丙、壬巳、辛丁，则惟巳寅中线仍与壬巳平行。丙寅、丁寅俱不平行，而成聚光点于寅。若平行线为乙丙、戊巳、亥丁，则惟丑巳中线仍与戊巳平行。丁丑、丙丑俱不平行，而成聚光点于丑。

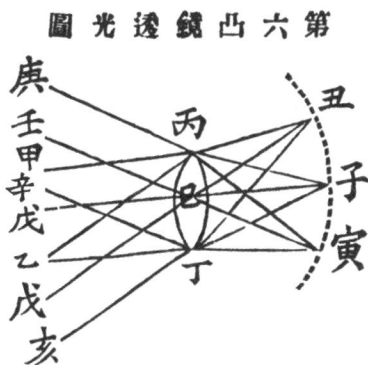

第七图说

人目视物近，则见大，远则见小。其大小生于视角。如心为人目，物在甲乙，其视角为甲心乙。移物于丙丁，则其视角为丙心丁。甲心乙角大，故见物亦大。丙心丁角小，故见物亦小也。甲心乙角正切与丙心丁角正切之比，同于视大与视小之比。

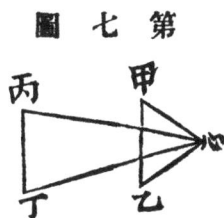

第八图说

凡凸镜照物，在聚光点必有物之反像，物近则反像大，物远则反像小。人目窥镜见像，不见物。物远像近，视角变大，故所见亦大。如甲乙为镜，戊巳为物，丙丁为像，子为人目。丙子甲角大于戊子巳角，故能变小为大也。聚光

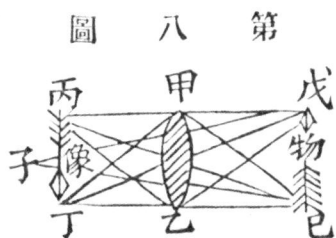

点离镜,为镜点距,造千里镜,以凸镜置窥筒之外端,筒之长短较镜点距,令多五寸,光点上有物之反像,人目离五寸,视之最分明也。

第九图远镜说

如图,戊巳为物,甲乙镜映大十倍,人目不免离开像六寸。人若又欲映大,置于像目之间点距一寸之镜,又以六倍相乘之得六十倍。光平行入目,无不明矣。若物近像,则远于前镜。如是镜上之小筒,宜退出些须[许],故作可进可退之镜。

另有回照远镜,以铜与玻璃为之。近年英国三品官员名老师,作极大回照镜,能见星中之白气,仍于诸星之体,历历分明。

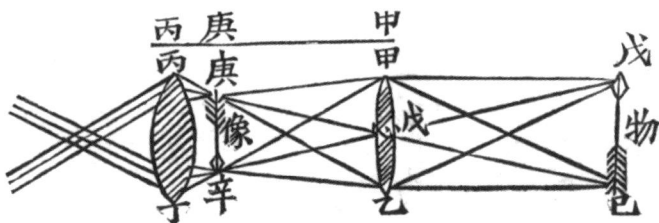

第九圖觀星遠鏡

第十图说

显微镜之理,欲视小成大,必使物像之光平行入目为最要理。盖物像之位甚近于目,视之甚大而模[模]糊,必使光平行入目,则大而且明。凡光自聚光点起,再过一凸镜,则变平行,乃以聚光点最近之镜置于目前甚近,以光点切于物像,则物像之光平行入目,视之必明矣。

如甲乙为前镜,亦曰映大镜。戊巳为物,庚辛为物像,在前镜光点上,丙丁为后镜,其光点切庚辛。人目自壬观之,物像甚大而甚明也。后镜置之离映大远之镜为千里镜,离映大近之镜为显微镜。物近,则像离前镜远;物远,则像离前镜近。故前后二镜,必置大小二筒,可进退窥之。

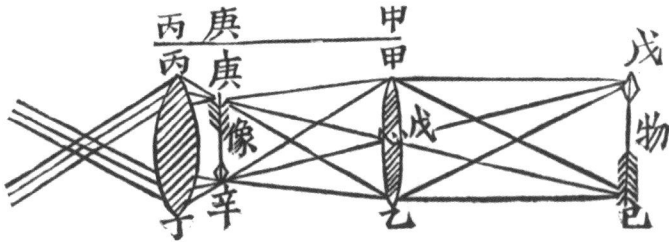

第九图 观星远镜

附光差表

空一　油一四六

气一〇〇〇二九　厚玻璃二五一四

水一三三六　绿玻璃一五七

水晶一五六二　金刚二四三九

空明之质俱有光差，质愈厚差亦愈大，表数与差角恒有反比例。

曲线图说

第一图如直线乙丙直线之外有戊点为定点，丁为动点，乙丁、戊丁恒等，乙丁恒与丙戊平行，则丁点动时，必成单曲线。此线亦名为抛石线，即抛石空中所行之线也。彗星亦有行此线者也。

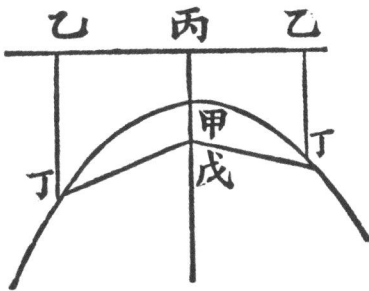

第一图 抛石线

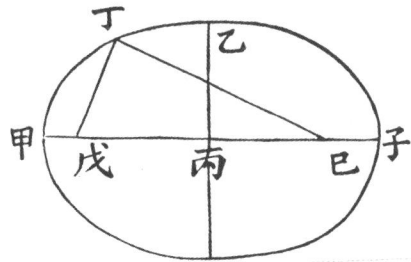

第二图 撱圆线

第二图戊巳为二定点，丁为动点。丁戊、丁巳之和恒等，则丁点动时，

必成椭圆,即名椭圆线,诸行星绕日,皆行此线(椭小员[圆]狭长也,谓长
而去四角也。见尔雅注)

　　第三图戊巳二定点不在一箇曲线内,庚丁为二动点,丁巳、丁戊之较,
或庚巳、庚戊之较恒等,则庚丁二点动时,必成双曲线。试作午未、寅卯二
切线,取巳戊之中丙点作壬癸线,与切线平行;取巳丙之度作子乙子线,自
乙丑二点作寅午未卯线,成长方形,乃作午卯寅未对角线,对角线引长之,
至于无穷,与双曲线永不相遇,而对角线与曲线中间所容之面积,即对数
面积也。彗星亦有行双曲线者。

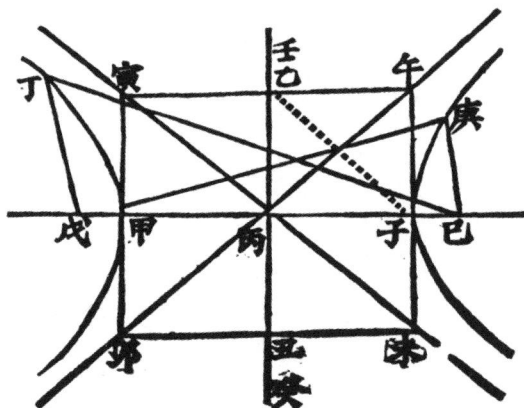

第三圖　雙　曲　線

　　第四五六图,平圆甲乙丁顶为定点,顶甲为动线,行于甲丁乙周,成
圆尖体形。若甲戊顶线引长之,则上面必成一倒圆尖锥。此体剖分之,
有五面,一过顶点,剖之成三角形。如顶甲丁一平行于底,剖之成平圆,
如戊巳庚一平行于顶,甲线剖之成抛石线面。五图,子壬丁一下交于顶
甲线,剖之成圆面,如寅卯;上交于顶甲线,如未点;剖之成双曲线之面,
如辰午巳。

線曲二第一第錐圓　　　　線曲三第錐圓

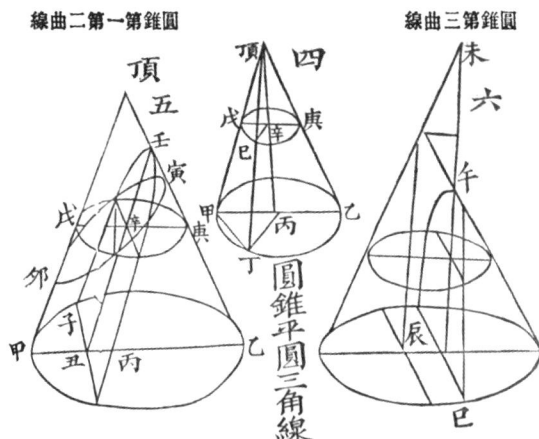

圜目测也,远镜始于光学,汤若望(Johann Adam Schall von Bell,1591—1666)远镜说已开其端,至侯失勒,而其制乃精。嗣是而后,既先之以推算,复佐之以侧验,两者皆符。始笔于书,始知行星之道为椭圆。世上一切物皆有藉于日光,始能长养生育。

英人爱理(George Biddel Airy,1801—1892,今译乔治·比德尔·艾里)始知日月之光,激动空气。月体本无光亮,人所见之光,乃日之光照于月面,而返照于地。此皆非远镜不能明,亦非从算学中出,则不能知。既以算学为根柢,而后格致之理,乃扩之而愈广。由此而气学、声学、化学、电学相继而兴。悉心究察,穷极精微。

余于西学,粗涉其藩篱,入之未深,然性所好焉,常于西儒之说,而求其故,偶有所得,辄志不忘。西学图说,不过追纪所闻之绪余耳,恐其久而浸失,聊复存之而已。如欲辑成一书,尚俟异日。

西学图说终。

门人吴县叶耀元子成①校字

---

① 叶耀元,字子成,别署味道馆主、水镜天仙,是当时著名的算学家,著有《中西算学大成》等书。

西學圖說

榮祿拜題

天南遯叟手校刊行

西學圖說

長洲 王韜 紫詮輯撰

太陽說

日月星辰皆麗於天自人觀之雖見其時起時落而不知所處
實有一定其中有互爲轉移者論其體日大而月小星則有大
有小其動者爲行星吾人觀定星而行星之經道始明即如月
亦行星之一晝夜行於天周流無定今見其近於此度明又見
其近於彼度其行也不特與星同旋并能直經於天然月之行
與諸星之行道相反人見月較諸星之行稍遲今見與此星並
行忽又見其在後假使人每夜細觀月之行法至一月而知其
歷遍諸星矣故晦與朔月之位向無殊〔此故名〕其法一定初
無錯亂至於日之行不特與星同旋亦與星相反吾人不能細
見其行法者因日之光熾周天之星皆隱而不見故人不能如

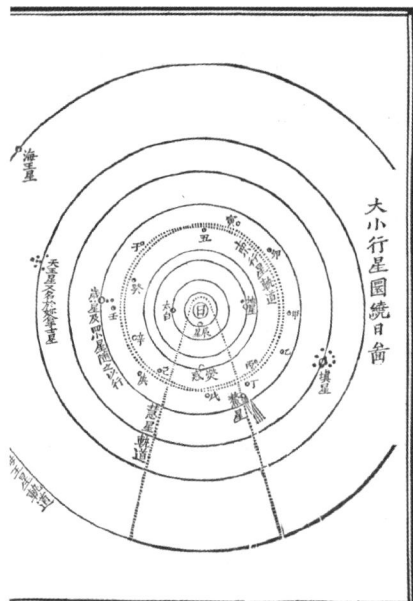

大小行星圖號日命

海王

《西学图说》天南遯叟手校印行版

第二编

中学西传

书经(节选)
(1865 年)

理雅各　译

王　韬　佐译

编者按语：

　　王韬协助理雅各译出《书经》(即《尚书》，*The Shoo King* or *The Book of Historical Documents*，1865)、《诗经》(*The She King* or *The Book of Poetry*，1871)及《春秋左传》(*The Ch'un Ts'ew；With The Tso Chuen*，1872)等典籍著作，以上三种分别属于《中国经典》(*The Chinese Classics*)的第 3、4、5 卷。

　　《中国经典》的前 2 卷，即"四书"的翻译，王韬并未参与。王韬与理雅各曾合作二十余年，其对理氏的评价，主要见《送西儒理雅各回国序》，特抄录点校其中部分文字如下：

　　嘉庆年间，始有名望之儒至粤，曰马礼逊(Robert Morrison，1782—1834)，继之者曰米怜维琳(William Milne，1785—1822)。而理君雅各先生，亦偕麦都思(Walter Henry Medhurst，1796—1857)诸名宿，橐笔东游。先生于诸西儒中年最少，学识品诣，卓然异人。

　　和约既定，货琛云集，中西合好，光气大开。泰西各儒，无不延揽名流，留心典籍。如慕维廉(William Muirhead，1822—1900)、禆治文(Elijah Coleman Bridgman，1801—1861)之地志，艾约瑟(Joseph

Edkins，1823—1905)之重学，伟烈亚力(Alexander Wylie，1815—1887)之天算，合信氏(Benjamin Hobson，1816—1873)之医学，玛高温(Daniel Jerome Macgowan，1815—1893)之电气学，丁韪良(William Alexander Parsons Martin，1827—1916)之律学，后先并出，竞美一时。

然此特通西学于中国，而未及以中国经籍之精微通之于西国也。先生独不惮其难，注全力于《十三经》，贯串考核，讨流溯源，别具见解，不随凡俗……译有《四子书》《尚书》两种。书出，西儒见之，咸叹其详明该洽，奉为南针……

其持己也廉，其待人也惠，周旋晋接，恂恂如也。骤见之顷，俨然道貌，若甚难亲，而久与之处，觉谦冲和蔼之气，浸淫大宅间。即其爱育人才，培养士类，务持大体，弗尚小仁，二十余年如一日也。粤中士民，无论识与不识，闻先生之名，辄盛口不置。

本节保留原译本的大小写、斜体等格式。限于篇幅，这里只誊录《书经》中《书序》《尧典》《大禹谟》及《旅獒》等四篇，且未包括原译文下方的长篇注解。①

___

① 王韬. 弢园文录外编卷八. 癸未仲春弢园老民刊于香海，1883：3-4.

书 序①

PREFACE TO THE SHOO KING, ATTRIBUTED TO CONFUCIUS.

一节　昔在帝尧,聪明文思,光宅天下。将逊于位,让于虞舜,作《尧典》。

1　Anciently there was the emperor Yaou, all-informed, intelligent, accomplished, and thoughtful. His glory filled the empire. He wished to retire from the throne, and resign it to Shun of Yu. *Descriptive of all this*, there was made THE CANON of YAOU.

二节　虞舜侧微,尧闻之聪明,将使嗣位,历试诸难,作《舜典》。

2　Shun of Yu was in a low and undistinguished position, when Yaou heard of his comprehensive intelligence, and wishing to make him successor to his throne, made proof of him in many situations of difficulty. *With reference to this*, there was made THE CANON of SHUN.

三节　帝釐下土,方设居方,别生分类。作《汨作》、《九共》九篇、《槀

---

①　Legge, J. *The Chinese Classics*, *Vol*. 3. Hong Kong: The London Missionary Society's Printing Office, 1865: 1-14.

饫》(亦作《槁饫》)。

3　The emperor regulated the territories, appointing *nobles* to every quarter to reside in them, giving them surnames of distinction, and defining the constituents of each. *Descriptive of this*, there were made the KWUN TSŎ, the KEW KUNG, in nine Books, and the KAOU YU.

四节　皋陶矢厥谟,禹成厥功,帝舜申之。作《大禹》《皋陶谟》《益稷》。

4　Kaou Yaou unfolded his counsels; Yu completed his work; the emperor Shun made him go on to further statements. *With reference to these things*, there were made THE COUNSELS OF THE GREAT YU, and OF KAOU YAOU, and the YIH AND TSEIH.

五节　禹别九州,随山濬川,任土作贡。禹敷土,随山刊木,奠高山大川。

5　Yu marked out the nine provinces; followed the course of the hills, and deepened the rivers; defined the imposts on the land, and the articles of tribute.

六节　启与有扈战于甘之野,作《甘誓》。

6　K'e fought with the prince of Hoo in the wilderness of Kan, when he made THE SPEECH AT KAN.

七节　太康失邦,昆弟五人须于洛汭,作《五子之歌》。

7　T'ae-k'ang lost his kingdom; and his five brothers waited for him on the north of the Lǒ, and made THE SONGS OF THE FIVE SONS.

八节　羲和湎淫，废时乱日，胤往征之，作《胤征》。

8　He and Ho, sunk in wine and excess, neglected the ordering of the seasons, and allowed the days to get into confusion. *The prince of Yin went to punish them. Descriptive of this*, there was made THE PUNITIVE EXPEDITION OF YIN.

九节　自契至于成汤八迁，汤始居亳，从先王居。作《帝告》《釐沃》。

9　From Sëĕ to T'ang the Successful, there were eight changes *of the capital*. T'ang at first dwelt in Pŏ, choosing the residence of the first sovereign of his House. *Then* were made the TE KUH, and the LE YUH.

十节　汤征诸侯，葛伯不祀，汤始征之，作《汤征》。

10　When T'ang chastised the various princes, the chief of Kŏ was not offering the *appointed* sacrifices. T'ang began his work by chastising him, and *then* was made the T'ANG CHING.

十一节　伊尹去亳适夏，既丑有夏，复归于亳。入自北门，乃遇汝鸠、汝方。作《汝鸠》《汝方》。

11　E Yin went from Pŏ to Hea. Indignant with the sovereign of Hea, he returned to Pŏ; and as he entered by the north gate, met with Joo Kew and Joo Fang. *With reference to this* were made the JOO KEW, and the JOO FANG.

十二节　伊尹相汤伐桀，升自陑，遂与桀战于鸣条之野，作《汤誓》。

12　E Yin acted as minister to T'ang, and *advised* him to attack Këĕ. They went up from E, and fought with him in the wilderness of

Ming-t'eaou. *Then* was made THE SPEECH OF T'ANG.

十三节　汤既胜夏,欲迁其社,不可。作《夏社》《疑至》《臣扈》。

13　When T'ang had vanquished Hea, he wished to change its sacrifices to the Spirit of the land, but concluded not to do so. *With reference to this* there were made the HEA SHAY, the E-CHE, and the CHIN-HOO.

十四节　夏师败绩,汤遂从之,遂伐三朡,俘厥宝玉。谊伯、仲伯作《典宝》。

14　The army of Hea being entirely defeated, T'ang followed it and smote San-tung, where he captured the precious relics and gems. *Then* E-pih and Chung-pih made the TEEN PAOU.

十五节　汤归自夏,至于大坰,仲虺作诰。

15　When T'ang was returning from *the conquest* of Hea, he came to Ta-këung, where Chung Hway made his ANNOUNCEMENT.

十六节　汤既黜夏命,复归于亳,作《汤诰》。

16　T'ang having made an end of the sovereignty of Hea, returned to Pǒ, and made the ANNOUNCEMENT OF T'ANG.

十七节　咎单作《明居》。

17　Kaou Shen made the MING KEU.

十八节　成汤既没,太甲元年,伊尹作《伊训》《肆命》《徂后》。

18　After the death of T'ang, in the first year of T'ae-kĕǎ, E Yin made THE INSTRUCTIONS OF E, the SZE MING, and THE

TSOO HOW.

十九节　太甲既立,不明,伊尹放诸桐。三年复归于亳,思庸,伊尹作《太甲》三篇。

19　When T'ae-kĕǎ was declared emperor, he proved unintelligent, and E Yin placed him in T'ung. After three years he returned with him to Pǒ, when he had applied his thoughts to the course of duty. *Then* E Yin made the T'AE-KEA in three Books.

廿节　伊尹作《咸有一德》。

20　E Yin made the BOTH POSSESSED PURE VIRTUE.

廿一节　沃丁既葬伊尹于亳,咎单遂训伊尹事,作《沃丁》。

21　When Yuh-ting had buried E Yin in Pǒ, Kaou Shen then set forth as lessons the doings of E Yin, and there was made the YUH-TING.

廿二节　伊陟相大戊,亳有祥桑谷共生于朝。伊陟赞于巫咸,作《咸乂》四篇。

22　E Chih was prime minister to T'ae-mow, when ominous appearances showed themselves in Pǒ. A mulberry tree and a stalk of grain grew up in the court. E Chih told Woo Heen, who made the HEEN E in four Books.

廿三节　太戊赞于伊陟,作《伊陟》《原命》。

23　T'e-mow spoke on the subject with E Chih, and there were made the E CHIH and the YUEN MING.

廿四节　仲丁迁于嚣,作《仲丁》。

24　Chung-ting removed to Heaou, and there was made the CHUNG-TING.

廿五节　河亶甲居相,作《河亶甲》。

25　Ho-tan-kĕă lived in Sëang, and there was made THE HO-TAN-KEA.

廿六节　祖乙圯于耿,作《祖乙》。

26　Tsoo-yih met with calamity in Kǎng, and there was made the TSOO-YIH.

廿七节　盘庚五迁,将治亳殷,民咨胥怨。作《盘庚》三篇。

27　Pwan-kang made the fifth change *of capital*, and was about to repair Pǒ, *as the cradle of the* Yin. The people murmured, and expressed themselves resentfully to one another. *With reference to this* there was made the PWAN-KANG, in the three Books.

廿八节　高宗梦得说,使百工营求诸野,得诸傅岩,作《说命》三篇。

28　Kaou-tsung dreamed that he got Yuě, and made all his officers institute a search for him in the wilds. He was found in Foo-yen; and THE CHARGE TO YUE was made in three Books.

廿九节　高宗祭成汤,有飞雉升鼎耳而雊,祖己训诸王,作《高宗肜日》《高宗之训》。

29　Kaou-tsung was sacrificing to T'ang the Successful, when a pheasant flew up, and lighted on the ear of a tripod, and *there* crowed. Tsoo Ke lessoned the king *on the subject*, and made THE

DAY OF THE SUPPLEMENTARY SACRIFICE OF KAOU TSUNG, and THE INSTRUCTIONS TO KAOU-TSUNG.

卅节　殷始咎周,周人乘黎。祖伊恐,奔告于受,作《西伯戡黎》。

30　Yin's first hatred of Chow was occasioned by its conquest of Le. Tsoo E, full of dread, hurried off to inform Show. *With reference to this* there was made THE CHIEF OF THE WEST'S CONQUEST OF LE.

卅一节　殷既错天命,微子作诰父师、小师。

31　Yin having cast away the sovereignty conferred on it by Heaven, the count of Wei made his announcement to the Grand Tutor and to the Junior Tutor.

卅二节　惟十有一年,武王伐殷。一月戊午,师渡孟津,作《泰誓》三篇。

32　In the eleventh year king Woo smote *the power of* Yin. On the mow-woo day of the first month, his army crossed *the Ho* at Măng-tsin. *Descriptive of this* there was made the great speech, in three Books.

卅三节　武王戎车三百两,虎贲三百人,与受战于牧野,作《牧誓》。

33　King Woo, with three hundred chariots of war and three hundred tiger-like officers, fought with Show in the wilderness of Muh. *Then* was made THE SPEECH AT MUH.

卅四节　武王伐殷。往伐归兽,识其政事,作《武成》。

34　King Woo smote Yin; and the narrative of his proceeding to the attack, and of his return and sending his animals back to their pastures, with his governmental measures, form THE COMPLETION OF THE WAR.

卅五节　武王胜殷,杀受,立武庚,以箕子归,作《洪范》。

35　When king Woo conquered Yin, he slew Show, and appointed Woo-kǎng *over the original principality of his Home*. He got the count of Ke to return to him, and THE GREAT PLAN was made.

卅六节　武王既胜殷,邦诸侯,班宗彝,作《分器》。

36　When king Woo had conquered Yin, he appointed the princes of the various States, and distributed among them the vessels of the ancestral temple. *With reference to this* there was made the FUN K'E.

卅七节　西旅献獒,太保作《旅獒》。

37　The western people of Le made an offering of some of their hounds; and the Grand Guardian made the HOUNDS OF LE.

卅八节　巢伯来朝,芮伯作《旅巢命》。

38　The chief of Ch'aou having come to court, the chief of Juy made and impressed on him the CH'AOU MING.

卅九节　武王有疾,周公作《金縢》。

39　King Woo was sick, which gave occasion to the Book about the duke of Chows making THE METAL-BOUND CASKET.

四十节　武王崩,三监及淮夷叛,周公相成王,将黜殷,作《大诰》。

40　When king Woo had deceased, the three overseers and the

wild tribes of the Hwae rebelled. The duke of Chow acted as prime minister to king Ching; and having purposed to make an end of *the House of* Yin, he made THE GREAT ANNOUNCEMENT.

四十一节　成王既黜殷命,杀武庚,命微子启代殷后,作《微子之命》。

41　King Ching having made an end of the appointment *in favour of the House* of Yin, and put Woo-kǎng to death, he appointed K'e, the count of Wei, to take the place of the descendants of Yin. *Descriptive of this*, there was made THE CHANGE TO THE COUNT OF WEI.

四十二节　唐叔得禾,异亩同颖,献诸天子。王命唐叔归周公于东,作《归禾》。

42　The *king's* uncle, the prince of T'ang, found a head of grain, *two stalks* in different plats of ground growing into one ear, and presented it to the king. The king ordered him to send, it to the duke of Chow in the east. *Upon this* was made the KWEI HO.

四十三节　周公既得命禾,旅天子之命,作《嘉禾》。

43　The duke of Chow having got the *king's* charge and the head of grain, set forth the charge of the sovereign, and made the KEA HO.

四十四节　成王既伐管叔、蔡叔,以殷余民封康叔,作《康诰》《酒诰》《梓材》。

44　The king Ching having smitten his uncles, the prince of Kwan and the prince of Ts'ae, invested his uncle K'ang with the rule of the remnant of Yin. *With reference to this*, there were made the

ANNOUNCEMENT TO K'ANG, THE ANNOUNCEMENT ABOUT WINE, and THE GOOD MATERIALS.

四十五节　成王在丰,欲宅洛邑,使召公先相宅,作《召诰》。

45　King Clung being in Fung, and wishing to fix his residence at Lǒ, sent the duke of Shaou in the first place to survey the localities. *Then* was made THE ANNOUNCEMENT OF SHAOU.

四十六节　召公既相宅,周公往营成周,使来告卜,作《洛诰》。

46　The duke of Shaou having surveyed the localities, the duke of Chow went to build *this capital*, *called* Ching Chow, and sent a messenger to announce the divinations. *With reference to this*[,] THE ANNOUNCEMENT ABOUT LO was made.

四十七节　成周既成,迁殷顽民,周公以王命诰,作《多士》。

47　When Ching Chow was completed, the obstinate people of Yin were removed to it. The duke of Chow announced to them the royal will, and THE NUMEROUS OF OFFICERS was made.

四十八节　周公作《无逸》。

48　The duke of Chow made the BOOK AGAINST LUXURIOUS EASE.

四十九节　召公为保,周公为师,相成王为左右。召公不说,周公作《君奭》。

49　The duke of Shaou acted as guardian and the duke of Chow as tutor, the chief ministers of king Ching, his left and right-hand men. The duke of Shaou was not pleased, and the duke of Chow made the

PRINCE SHIH.

五十节　蔡叔既没,王命蔡仲,践诸侯位,作《蔡仲之命》。

50　After the death of the king's uncle, the prince of Ts'ae, the king appointed his son Chung to take his place as a prince *of the empire*. Then was made the CHARGE TO CHANG OF TS'AE.

五十一节　成王东伐淮夷,遂践奄,作《成王政》。

51　King Ching having smitten the wild tribes of the Hwae on the east, at the same time extinguished the State of Yen. Then was made the CHING WANG CHING.

五十二节　成王既践奄,将迁其君于蒲姑,周公告召公,作《将蒲姑》。

52　King Ching having extinguished Yen, and wishing to remove its ruler to P'oo-koo, the duke of Chow announced the thing to the duke of Shaou. *Then* there was made the TSEANG P'OO-KOO.

五十三节　成王归自奄,在宗周,诰庶邦,作《多方》。

53　King Ching returned from Yen, and in the honoured city of Chow made an announcement to all the States. *Then* was made THE NUMEROUS REGIONS.

五十四节　周公作《立政》。

54　The duke of Chow made THE ESTABLISHMENT OF GOVERNMENT.

五十五节　成王既黜殷命,灭淮夷,还归在丰,作《周官》。

55　When king Ching had made an end of the House of Yin, and

extinguished the wild tribes of the Hwae, he returned to Fung; and there was made THE OFFICERS OF CHOW.

五十六节　成王既伐东夷,肃慎来贺。王俾荣伯作《贿肃慎之命》。

56　When king Ching had smitten the wild tribes of the east, Suhshin came to congratulate him. The king made the chief of Yung make the CHARGE TO SUII-SHIN, and gave him presents also.

五十七节　周公在丰,将没,欲葬成周。公薨,成王葬于毕,告周公,作《亳姑》。

57　The duke of Chow was in Fung and about to die. He wished to be buried in Ching chow; but on his decease king Ching buried him in Peih, making an announcement at his bier. Then was made the PO-KOO.

五十八节　周公既没,命君陈分正东郊成周,作《君陈》。

58　After the death of the duke of Chow, Keun-ch'in was commissioned with the separate charge of regulating Ching Chow in the eastern border, and there was made the KEUN-CH'IN.

五十九节　成王将崩,命召公、毕公率诸侯相康王,作《顾命》。

59　When king Ching was about to die, he ordered the duke of Shaou and the duke of Peih to take the lead of all the princes to support king K'ang. *With reference to this*, there was made THE TESTAMENTARY DECREE.

六十节　康王既尸天子,遂诰诸侯,作《康王之诰》。

60　When king K'ang occupied the sovereign place, he made an

announcement to all the princes, and there was made THE ANNOUNCEMENT OF KING K'ANG.

六十一节　康王命作册毕,分居里,成周郊,作《毕命》。

61　King K'ang ordered that a document of appointment should be made for the duke of Peih, severally defining the localities in the borders of Ching chow. There was then made the charge to the DUKE OF PEIH.

六十二节　穆王命君牙,为周大司徒,作《君牙》。

62　King Muh appointed Keun-ya to be the minister of instruction of Chow and there was made the KEUN-YA.

六十三节　穆王命伯冏,为周太仆正,作《冏命》。

63　King Muh appointed Pih-keung to be the master of his household and there was made the CHARGE TO KEUNG.

六十四节　吕命穆王训夏赎刑,作《吕刑》。

64　*The prince of* LEU was charged by king Muh to set forth the lessons of Hea on the redemption of punishments; and there was made LEU ON PUNISHMENTS.

六十五节　平王锡晋文侯秬鬯、圭瓒,作《文侯之命》。

65　King P'ing gave to prince Wǎn of Tsin spirits of the black millet mixed with odoriferous herbs. *With reference to this*, there was made the CHARGE TO PRINCE WAN.

六十六节　鲁侯伯禽宅曲阜,徐、夷并兴,东郊不开,作《费誓》。

66 When Pih-k'in, prince of Loo, first dwelt in K'euh-fow, the Seu and other wild tribes rose together in insurrection. The gates on the eastern frontier were kept shut, and there was made THE SPEECH AT PE.

六十七节 秦穆公伐郑,晋襄公帅师败诸崤,还归,作《秦誓》。

67 When duke Muh of Ts'in was invading Ch'ing, the duke Sëang of Tsin led an army, and defeated his forces in Heaou. When they returned, he made THE SPEECH OF THE DUKE OF TS'IN.

唐　书[①]

THE BOOK OF T'ANG

尧　典

THE CANON OF YAOU

一节　曰若稽古,帝尧曰放勋,钦、明、文、思、安安,允恭克让,光被四表,格于上下。

1　Examining into antiquity, *we find that* the emperor Yaou was called Fang-heun. He was reverential, intelligent, accomplished, and thoughtful,—naturally and without effort. He was sincerely courteous, and capable of *all* complaisance. The display of *these qualities* reached to the four extremities *of the empire* and extended from earth to heaven.

二节　克明俊德,以亲九族。九族既睦,平章百姓。百姓昭明,协和万邦。黎民于变时雍。

2　He was able to make the able and virtuous distinguished, and

---

① Legge, J. *The Chinese Classics*, *Vol*. *3*. Hong Kong: The London Missionary Society's Printing Office, 1865:15-27.

thence proceeded to the love of the nine classes of his kindred, who all became harmonious. He *also* regulated and polished the people of *his domain*, who all became brightly intelligent. *Finally*, he united and harmonized the myriad States *of the empire*; and lo! the black-haired people were transformed. The result was *universal* concord.

三节　乃命羲和,钦若昊天,历象日月星辰,敬授人时。

3　Thereupon *Yaou* commanded He and Ho, in reverent accordance with *their observation* of the wide heavens, to calculate and delineate *the movements and appearances of* the sun, the moon, the stars, and the zodiacal spaces; and so to deliver respectfully the seasons to the people.

四节　分命羲仲,宅嵎夷,曰旸谷。寅宾出日,平秩东作。日中,星鸟,以殷仲春。厥民析,鸟兽孳尾。

4　He separately commanded the second brother He to reside at Yu-e, in what was called the Bright Valley, and there respectfully to receive as a guest the rising sun, and to adjust and arrange the labours of the spring. "The day," he said, "is of the medium length, and the star is in *Neaou*; you may thus exactly determine mid-spring. The people begin to disperse; and birds and beasts breed and copulate."

五节　申命羲叔,宅南交。平秩南讹,敬致。日永,星火,以正仲夏。厥民因,鸟兽希革。

5　He further commanded the third brother He to reside at Nan-keaou, and arrange the transformations of the summer, and respectfully to observe the extreme limit *of the shadow*. "The day," *said he*, "is at its longest, and the star is *Ho*; you may thus exactly determine mid-summer. The people are more dispersed; and birds and beasts have their feathers and hair thin, and change their coats. "

六节　分命和仲,宅西,曰昧谷。寅饯纳日,平秩西成。宵中,星虚,以殷仲秋。厥民夷,鸟兽毛毨。

6　He separately commanded the second brother Ho to reside at the west, in what was culled the Dark Valley, and *there* respectfully to convoy the setting sun, and to adjust and arrange the completing labours of the autumn. "The night," *he said*, "is of the medium length, and the star is *Heu*; you may thus exactly determine mid-autumn. The people begin to feel at ease; and birds and beasts have their coats in good condition. "

七节　申命和叔,宅朔方,曰幽都。平在朔易。日短,星昴,以正仲冬。厥民隩,鸟兽氄毛。

7　He further commanded third brother Ho to reside in the northern region, in what was called the Sombre Capital, and there to adjust and examine the changes of the winter. "The day," *said he*, "is at its shortest, and the star is *Maou*; thus you may exactly determine mid-winter. The people keep their *cosy* corners; and the coats of birds and beasts are downy and thick. "

八节　帝曰:"咨! 汝羲暨和。期三百有六旬有六日,以闰月定四时,成岁。允厘百工,庶绩咸熙。"

8　The emperor said, "Ah! you, He and Ho, a round year consists of three hundred, sixty, and six days. By means of an intercalary month do you fix the four seasons, and complete the *determination of* the year. *Thereafter*, in exact accordance with this, regulating the various officers, all the works *of the year* will be fully performed."

九节　帝曰:"畴咨,若时登庸?"放齐曰:"胤子朱,启明。"帝曰:"吁!嚚讼可乎?"

9　The emperor said, "Who will search out for me a man according to the times whom I may raise and employ?" Fang-ts'e said, "There is your heir-son Choo, who is highly intelligent." The emperor said, "Alas! lie is insincere and quarrelsome:—can he do."

十节　帝曰:"畴咨,若予采?"驩兜曰:"都! 共工方鸠僝功。"帝曰:"吁! 静言庸违,象恭滔天。"

10　The emperor said, "Who will search out for me a man equal to the exigency of my affairs?" Hwan-tow said, "Oh! there is the minister of Works, whose merits have just been displayed in various ways." The emperor said, "Alas! when unemployed, he can talk; but when employed, his actions turn out differently. He is respectful *only* in appearance. See! the floods assail the heavens."

十一节　帝曰:"咨! 四岳,汤汤洪水方割,荡荡怀山襄陵,浩浩滔天。下民其咨,有能俾乂?"佥曰:"於! 鲧哉。"帝曰:"吁! 咈哉,方命圮族。"岳曰:"异哉! 试可乃已。"帝曰,"往,钦哉!"九载,绩用弗成。

11　The emperor said, "Oh! *chief of* the four mountains, destructive in their overflow are the waters of the inundation. In their vast extent they embrace the mountains and overtop the hills, threatening the heavens with their floods, so that the inferior people groan and murmur. Is there a capable man, to whom I can assign the correction *of this calamity*?" All *in the court* said, "Oh! there is K 'wǎn." The emperor said, "Alas! no, by no means! He is disobedient to orders, and tries to injure his peers." His Eminence said, "Well but——. Try him, and then you can have done with him." The emperor said to K'wǎn, "Go; and be reverent!" For nine years he laboured, but the work was unaccomplished.

十二节　帝曰:"咨! 四岳。朕在位七十载,汝能庸命,巽朕位?"岳曰:"否德,忝帝位。"曰:"明明扬侧陋。"师锡帝曰:"有鳏在下,曰虞舜。"帝曰:"俞? 予闻,如何?"岳曰:"瞽子,父顽,母嚚,象傲;克谐以孝,烝烝乂,不格奸。"帝曰:"我其试哉!"女于时,观厥刑于二女。厘降二女于妫汭,嫔于虞。帝曰:"钦哉!"

12　The emperor said, "Oh! you *chief of the* four mountains, I have been on the throne for seventy years. You can carry out my appointments;—I will resign my throne to you." His Eminence said, "I have not the virtue; I should *only* disgrace the imperial seat." The *emperor* said, "Point out some one among the illustrious, or set forth one from among the poor and mean." All *in the court* said to the emperor, "There is an unmarried man among the lower people, called Slum of Yu." The emperor said, "Yes, I have heard of him. What is his character?" His Eminence said, "He is the son of a blind man. His father was obstinately unprincipled; his *step*-mother was insincere; his *half brother* Seang was arrogant. He has been able, however, by his filial piety to live in harmony with them, and to lead them gradually to sell-government, so that they no longer proceed to great wickedness." The emperor said, "I will try him! I will wive him, and then see his behaviour with my two daughters." On this he gave orders, and sent down his two daughters to the north of the Kwei, to be wives in the family of Yu. The emperor said *to them*, "Be reverent!"

大禹谟[①]
THE BOOKS OF YU
THE COUNSELS OF THE GREAT YU

一节　曰若稽古大禹,曰文命敷于四海,祗承于帝。

1　On examining into antiquity, we find that the great Yu was called Wǎn-ming. Having arranged and divided *the empire*, all to the four seas, in reverent response to the *inquiries of the former* emperor,

二节　曰:"后克艰厥后,臣克艰厥臣,政乃乂,黎民敏德。"

2　He said, "If the sovereign can realize the difficulty of his sovereignship, and the minister can realize the difficulty of his ministry, government will be well ordered, and the people will sedulously seek to be virtuous."

三节　帝曰:"俞! 允若兹,嘉言罔攸伏,野无遗贤,万邦咸宁。稽于众,舍己从人,不虐无告,不废困穷,惟帝时克。"

3　The emperor said, "Yes; let this really be the case, and good words will nowhere lie hidden; no men of virtue and talents will be

① Legge, J. *The Chinese Classics*, *Vol*. *3*. Hong Kong: The London Missionary Society's Printing Office, 1865:52-67.

neglected away from court; and the myriad States will all enjoy repose. *But* to ascertain the views of all to give up one's own opinion and follow that of others; to refrain from oppressing the helpless; and not to neglect the straitened and poor: —it was only the emperor *Yaou* who could attain to this."

四节　益曰:"都,帝德广运,乃圣乃神,乃武乃文。皇天眷命,奄有四海为天下君。"

4　Yih said, "Oh! your virtue, O emperor, is vast and incessant. It is sagely, spiritual, awe-inspiring, and adorned with all accomplishments. Great Heaven regarded you with its favouring decree, and suddenly you obtained all within the four seas, and became sovereign of the empire."

五节　禹曰:"惠迪吉,从逆凶,惟影响。"

5　Yu said, "Accordance with the right is good fortune; the following of evil is bad:—the shadow and the echo."

六节　益曰:"吁! 戒哉! 儆戒无虞,罔失法度。罔游于逸,罔淫于乐。任贤勿贰,去邪勿疑。疑谋勿成,百志惟熙。罔违道以干百姓之誉,罔咈百姓以从己之欲。无怠无荒,四夷来王。"

6　Yih said, "Alas! be cautious! Admonish yourself to caution, when there seems to be no reason for anxiety. Do not fail in due attention to the laws and ordinances. Do not find your enjoyment in indulgent ease. Do not go to excess in pleasure. In your enjoyment of men of worth, let none come between you and them. Put away evil without hesitation. Do not try to carry out doubtful plans. Study that all your purposes may be with the light of reason. Do not go against what is right to get the praise of the people. Do not oppose the people to follow your own desires. *Attend to these things* without idleness or omission, and from the four quarters the barbarous tribes will come and acknowledge your sovereignty."

七节　禹曰:"於! 帝念哉! 德惟善政,政在养民。水、火、金、木、土、谷,惟修;正德、利用、厚生、惟和。九功惟叙,九叙惟歌。戒之用休,董之用威,劝之以九歌俾勿坏。"

7　Yu said, "Oh! think *of these things*, O emperor. Virtue is seen in the goodness of the government, and the government is tested by its nourishing of the people. There are water, fire, metal, wood, earth, and grain,—these must be duly regulated; there are the rectification of *the people's* virtue, the conveniences of life, and the securing abundant means of sustentation,—these must be harmoniously attended to. When the nine services *thus indicated* have been orderly accomplished, let that accomplishment be celebrated by songs. Caution the people with gentle words; correct them with the majesty of *law*; stimulate them with the songs on those nine subjects,—in order that your success may never suffer diminution."

八节　帝曰:"俞! 地平天成,六府三事允治,万世永赖,时乃功。"

8　The emperor said, "Yes. The earth is *now* reduced to order, and *the influences of* heaven operate with effect; those six magazines and three businesses are all truly regulated, so that a myriad generations may perpetually depend on them:—this is your merit."

九节　帝曰:"格,汝禹! 朕宅帝位三十有三载,耄期倦于勤。汝惟不怠,总朕师。"

9　The emperor said, "Come, you, Yu. I have occupied the imperial throne for thirty and three years. I am between ninety and a hundred years old, and the laborious duties weary me. Do you, eschewing all indolence, take the leadership of my people."

十节　禹曰:"朕德罔克,民不依。皋陶迈种德,德乃降,黎民怀之。帝念哉! 念兹在兹,释兹在兹,名言兹在兹,允出兹在兹,惟帝念功。"

10　Yu said, "My virtue is not equal *to the position*; the people will not repose in me. *But there is* Kaou-yaou, with vigorous activity sowing abroad his virtue, which has descended on the black-haired people, till they cherish him in their hearts. O emperor, think of him! When I think of him, my mind rests on him, *as the man for this office*; When I would put him out of my thoughts, they still rest on him; when I name and speak of him, my mind rests on him *for this*; the sincere outgoing of my thoughts about him is that he is the man. O emperor, think of his merits!"

十一节　帝曰:"皋陶,惟兹臣庶,罔或干予正。汝作士,明于五刑,以弼五教。期于予治,刑期于无刑,民协于中,时乃功,懋哉。"

11　The emperor said, "Kaou-yaou, that of these my ministers and people, hardly one is found to offend against the regulations of my government, is owing to your being the minister of Crime, and intelligent in the use of the five punishments to assist the *inculcation of the* five duties, with a view to the perfection of my government, and that through punishment there may come to be no punishments, but the people accord with the *path of the* mean. *Continue to* be strenuous."

十二节　皋陶曰:"帝德罔愆,临下以简,御众以宽;罚弗及嗣,赏延于世。宥过无大,刑故无小;罪疑惟轻,功疑惟重;与其杀不辜,宁失不经;好生之德,洽于民心,兹用不犯于有司。"

12　Kaou-yaou said, "Your virtue, O emperor, is faultless. You condescend to your ministers with a liberal ease; you preside over the multitude with a generous forbearance. Punishments do not extend to the criminal's heirs; while rewards reach to after generations. You pardon inadvertent faults, however great; and punish purposed crimes, however small. In cases of doubtful crimes, you deal with them lightly; in cases of doubtful merit, you prefer the high estimation. Rather than put to death an innocent person, you will run the risk of irregularity and error. This life-loving virtue has penetrated the minds of the people, and this is why they do not render themselves liable to be punished by your officers."

十三节　帝曰:"俾予从欲以治,四方风动,惟乃之休。"

13　The emperor said, "To enable me to follow after and obtain what I desire in my government, the people everywhere responding as if moved by the wind;—this is your excellence."

十四节　帝曰:"来,禹! 降水儆予,成允成功,惟汝贤。克勤于邦,克俭于家,不自满假,惟汝贤。汝惟不矜,天下莫与汝争能。汝惟不伐,天下莫与汝争功。予懋乃德,嘉乃丕绩,天之历数在汝躬,汝终陟元后。

14　The emperor said, "Come, Yu. The inundating waters filled me with dread, when you realized all that you represented, and accomplished your task,—thus showing your superiority to other men. Full of toilsome earnestness in the service of the State, and sparing in your expenditure on your family; and this without being full of yourself or elated; you *again* show your superiority to other men. Without any prideful presumption, there is no one in the empire to contest with you the palm of ability; without any boasting, there is no one in the empire to contest with you the claim of merit. I see how great is your virtue, how admirable your vast achievements. This determinate appointment of Heaven rests on your person yon must, eventually ascend *the throne of* the great sovereign."

十五节　人心惟危,道心惟微,惟精惟一,允执厥中。

15　The mind of man is restless,—prone *to err* its affinity for the *right* way is small. Be discriminating, be undivided, that you may sincerely hold fast the Mean.

十六节　无稽之言勿听,弗询之谋勿庸。

16　Do not listen to unsubstantiated words; do not follow undeliberated plans.

十七节　可爱非君? 可畏非民? 众非元后,何戴? 后非众,罔与守邦? 钦哉! 慎乃有位,敬修其可愿,四海困穷,天禄永终。惟口出好兴戎,朕言不再。"

17　Of all who are to be loved, is not the sovereign the chief? Of all who are to be feared, are not the people the chief? If the multitude were *without* the sovereign, whom should they sustain aloft? If the sovereign had not the multitude, there would be none to guard the country for him. Be reverent. Carefully demean yourself on the throne which you will occupy, respectfully cultivating *the virtues* which are to be desired in you. If within the four seas there be distress and poverty, your Heaven-conferred revenues will come to a perpetual end. It is the mouth which sends forth what is good, and gives rise to war. My words

I will not repeat."

十八节　禹曰:"枚卜功臣,惟吉之从。"帝曰:"禹! 官占惟先蔽志,昆命于元龟。朕志先定,询谋金同,鬼神其依,龟筮协从,卜不习吉。"禹拜稽首,固辞。帝曰:"毋! 惟汝谐。"

18　Yu said, "Submit the meritorious ministers one by one to the trial of divination, and let the fortunate indication be followed. The emperor said, "Yu, the officer of divination, when the mind has been made up on a subject, then refers it to the great tortoise. *Now*, *in this matter*, my mind was determined in the first place. I consulted and deliberated with all *my ministers and people*, and they were of one accord with me. The spirits signified their assent, the tortoise and grass having both concurred. Divination, when fortunate, may not be repeated." Yu did obeisance, with his head to the ground, and firmly declined the throne. The emperor said, "Do not do so. It is you who can suitably *occupy my place*."

十九节　正月朔旦,受命于神宗,率百官若帝之初。

19　On the first morning of the first month, *Yu* received the appointment in the *temple of the* spiritual Ancestor, and took the leading of all the officers, as had been done at the commencement of the emperor's *government*.

二十节　帝曰:"咨,禹! 惟时有苗弗率,汝徂征。"禹乃会群后,誓于师曰;"济济有众,咸听朕命。蠢兹有苗,昏迷不恭,侮慢自贤,反道败德,君子在野,小人在位,民弃不保,天降之咎,肆予以尔众士,奉辞伐罪。尔尚一乃心力,其克有勋。"

20　The emperor said, "Alas! O Yu, there is only the prince of the Meaou, who refuses obedience;—do you go and correct him." Yu on this assembled all the princes, and made a speech to the host, saying, "Ye multitudes, listen all to my orders. Stupid is this prince of Meaou, ignorant, erring, and disrespectful. Despiteful and insolent to others, he thinks that all ability and virtue are with himself. A rebel to the right, he destroys *all the obligations of* virtue. Superior men are kept by him in obscurity, and mean men fill all the offices. The people reject and will not protect him. Heaven is sending calamities down upon him. On this account I have assembled you, my multitude of gallant men, and bear the instructions *of the emperor* to punish his crimes. Do you proceed with united heart and strength, so shall our enterprize be crowned with success."

二十一节　三旬,苗民逆命。益赞于禹曰:"惟德动天,无远弗届。满招损,谦受益,时乃天道。帝初于历山,往于田,日号泣于旻天,于父母,负罪引慝。祗载见瞽叟,夔夔斋栗,瞽亦允若。至诚感神,矧兹有苗。"禹拜昌言曰:"俞!"班师振旅。帝乃诞敷文德,舞干羽于两阶,七旬有苗格。

21　At the end of three decades, the people of Meaou continued rebellious against *the emperor's* commands, when Yih came to the help of Yu, saying, "It is virtue which moves Heaven; there is no distance to which it does not reach. Pride brings loss, and humility receives increase;—this is the way of Heaven. In the early time of the emperor, when he was living by mount Leih, he went into the fields, and daily cried with tears to compassionate Heaven, and to his parents, taking to himself and bearing all guilt and evil. *At the same time*, with respectful service, he appeared before Koo-sow, looking grave and awe-struck, till Koo also became truly transformed by his example. Entire sincerity moves spiritual beings;—how much more will it move this prince of Meaou!" Yu did homage to the excellent words and said, "Yes." *Thereupon* he led back his array, having drawn off the troops. The emperor *also* set about diffusing his accomplishments and virtue more widely. They danced with shields and feathers between the two staircases *of the court*. In seventy days the prince of Meaou came to make his submission.

周 书①
THE BOOKS OF SHANG[CHOW]②

旅 獒
THE HOUNDS OF LEU

一节　惟克商,遂通道于九夷八蛮。西旅厎贡厥獒,太保乃作《旅獒》,用训于王。

1　After the conquest of Shang, the way being open to the nine wild and the eight savage tribes, the people of the western tribe of Leu sent in as tribute some of their hounds, on which the Great-guardian made "The Hounds of Leu" by way of instruction to the king.

二节　曰:"呜呼! 明王慎德,西夷咸宾。无有远迩,毕献方物,惟服食器用。

2　He said, "Oh! the intelligent kings have paid careful attention to their virtue, and the wild tribes on every side have willingly acknowledged subjection to them. The nearer and the more remote

---

①　Legge,J. *The Chinese Classics*,*Vol*. *3*. Hong Kong:The London Missionary Society's Printing Office,1865:345-350.
②　"旅獒"一节载于《周书》,应为"THE BOOK OF CHOW"。

have all made offerings of the productions of their countries; —
clothes, food, and vessels for use.

三节　王乃昭德之致于异姓之邦,无替厥服;分宝玉于伯叔之国,时
庸展亲。人不易物,惟德其物!

3　The kings have then displayed the things thus produced by their
virtue, and *distributed them* to *the princes of* the States of different
surnames, *to encourage them* not to neglect their duties. The precious
things and gems they have distributed among their uncles in charge of
States, thereby increasing their attachment *to the throne*. The
recipients have *thus* not despised the things, but have seen in them the
power of virtue.

四节　德盛不狎侮。狎侮君子,罔以尽人心;狎侮小人,罔以尽其力。

4　Complete virtue allows no contemptuous familiarity. When a
prince treats superior men with such familiarity, he cannot get them to
give him all their hearts; when he so treats inferior men, he cannot get
them to put forth for him all their strength.

五节　不役耳目,百度惟贞。

5　If he be not in bondage to his ears and eyes, all his conduct will
be ruled by correctness.

六节　玩人丧德,玩物丧志。

6　By trifling with men he ruins his virtue; by finding his
amusement in things he ruins his aims.

七节　志以道宁,言以道接。

7 The aims should repose in what is right; words should be listened to according to their relation to right.

八节　不作无益害有益,功乃成;不贵异物贱用物,民乃足。犬马非其土性不畜,珍禽奇兽不育于国,不宝远物,则远人格;所宝惟贤,则迩人安。

8 *A prince* should not do what is unprofitable to the injury of what is profitable, and then his merit maybe completed. He should not value strange things to the contemning things that are useful, and then his people will be able to supply *all his needs*. *Even* dogs and horses which are not native to his country he will not keep; fine birds and strange animals he will not nourish in his kingdom. When he does not look on foreign things as precious, foreigners will come to him; when it is worth which is precious to him, *his own* people near at hand will enjoy repose.

九节　呜呼!夙夜罔或不勤,不矜细行,终累大德。为山九仞,功亏一篑。

9 Oh! early and late never be but earnest. If you do not attend jealousy to your small actions, the result will be to affect your virtue in great matters; —as when, in raising a mound of nine fathoms the work is unfinished for want of one basket *of earth*.

十节　允迪兹,生民保厥居,惟乃世王。

10 If you really follow this course, the people will preserve their possessions, and the throne will descend from generation to generation.

PREFACE TO THE SHOO KING,

ATTRIBUTED TO CONFUCIUS.

堯 虞 位 將 宅 文 堯 昔 一節 書
典 舜 讓 遜 天 思 聰 在 序
○ 作 于 于 下 光 明 帝

1   I. Anciently there was the emperor Yaou, all-informed, intelligent, accomplished, and thoughtful. His glory filled the empire. He wished to retire from the throne, and resign it to Shun of Yu. *Descriptive of all this*, there was made THE CANON OF YAOU.

PREFACE TO THE SHOO KING. This is often called 'The small Preface' (小序), to distinguish it from the larger one (大序 and 尙書序), prefixed by K'ung Gan-kwǒ to his commentary on the Classic. It was among the other monuments recovered from the wall of Confucius' house, which were given to Gan-kwǒ to be deciphered and edited. He incorporated it with the Work itself, breaking it up into its several parts, and prefixing to each Book the portion belonging to it. Other scholars of the Han dynasty edited it in its complete form at the end of the classic. It seems to me better, and to afford more facility of reference to it hereafter, to prefix it here as a whole.

If it were indeed the work of Confucius himself, its value would be inestimable; but its many peculiarities of style, as well as many inanities, forbid us to believe that it is the composition of the Sage. Ch'ing K'ang-shing (鄭康成), Ma Yung (馬融), and Wang Suh (王肅), those great scholars of the Han dynasty, all attribute it to him; and to justify them for doing so, Keang Shing (江聲) appeals to the words of Sze-ma Ts'een (in the 史記孔子世家):—'He prefaced the Records of the Shoo, from the times of T'ang and Yu, down to Muh of Ts'in, arranging their subjects in order (see 江微君尙書集注音疏, on the 序). This, however, would only be evidence at the most that Confucius had made a preface to the Shoo King; but Ts'een's statement, in which he has been followed by many subsequent chroniclers, was grounded merely on the existence of this document itself, many parts of which he has introduced into his histories (本記), though not all in the order in which they are given by Gan-kwǒ. It is enough to admit with Choo He, that this preface was the production of some writer in the end of the Chow or the beginning of the Ts'in dynasty.—I shall discuss here but sparingly its various statements. That will be done, where necessary, in the introductions to the several Books.

理雅各著《中国经典》(第三卷)内页(J. Legge，*The Chinese Classics*，*Vol*. 3. Hong Kong：London Missionary Society's Printing Office，1865：1.)

二

《诗经》(节选)
(1971 年)

理雅各　译

王韬　佐译

编者按语：

在理雅各(James Legge，1815—1897)前，欧洲耶稣会士已经开始对中国典籍进行外译。一般认为，利玛窦(Matteo Ricci，1552—1610)1593年用拉丁文翻译的四书，是西人对于四书翻译的最早尝试。也有学者提出，在利玛窦前，罗明坚(Michele Ruggieri，1543—1607)也翻译过四书。只是以上译作均未公开出版。此后，金尼阁(Nicolas Trigault，1577—1628)在1626年用拉丁文翻译五经，可惜，也未公开出版。① 以上是中国典籍四书五经西传的最早尝试。

法国耶稣会士孙璋(Alexander de Lacharme，1695—1765)于1733年翻译了拉丁文本《诗经》；1735年，马若瑟(Joseph de Prémare，1666—1736)曾以法文译出《诗经》八首。孙璋的手稿后经汉学家莫尔(M. Jules Mohl，1800—1876)整理出版，是为欧洲第一个《诗经》全译本。

最早由中文译成英文的著作，概为1719年译成，但直至1761年才出版的《好逑传》(*Hau kiou choaan, or the pleasing history*)的英译本，该

---

① 张万民.《诗经》在17—18世纪英国的流传. 上海：华东师范大学出版社，2015：53-72.

书由詹姆斯·威尔金森（James Wilkinson）翻译,并经托马斯·帕西（Thomas Percy）编辑,伦敦多利兹出版社出版。《好逑传》是明末清初的一部才子佳人小说,作者是名教中人,该书的书名即来自《诗经》开篇《关雎》中的"窈窕淑女,君子好逑"一句。此后,德庇时（Sir John Davis, 1795—1890）也翻译过《好逑传》（*The Fortunate Union：A Romance*）,但理雅各认为,德氏将书名翻译得并不恰切。①

理雅各很早就立志将中国《十三经》译为英文。1861—1872 年,相继出版《中国经典》（*The Chinese Classics：With a Translation，Critical and Exegetical Notes*）五卷八本,包括《论语》《大学》《中庸》《孟子》《书经》《诗经》及《春秋左传》。1879—1891 年相继出版《中国圣典》（*The Sacred Books of China*）六卷,包括《书经》《诗经（与宗教有关的部分）》《孝经》《易经》《礼记》《道德经》《庄子》等。②

在《中国经典》第四卷共两本约 1000 页的篇幅里,理雅各约提到王韬（Wang Taou）约 17 次。从中大概可以看出,王韬之于理雅各翻译《诗经》的协助,或者说王韬同理雅各就《诗经》翻译的切磋,几乎与英文选词无涉,其贡献主要在中文词义的研读与辨判之上。

这里节选的译本源自《中国经典》第 4 卷（1871 年香港出版）。限于篇幅,仅节选其中《关雎》《桃夭》《兔罝》《芣苢》《汉广》《静女》《氓》《木瓜》《黍离》《兔爰》《采葛》《女曰鸡鸣》《有女同车》《山有扶苏》《狡童》《风雨》《子衿》《野有蔓草》《蒹葭》《鹿鸣》《皇皇者华》《采薇》《菁菁者莪》《隰桑》《文王》等 25 首,且未包括原译文下方的长篇注解。

---

① Legge，J. *The Chinese Classics*，*Vol*.4.Hong Kong：The London Missionary Society's Printing Office，1871：3.

② 张万民.欧美《诗经》论著提要.诗经研究丛刊,2010(1)：20-56.

国风·周南
LESSONS FROM THE STATES
THE ODES OF CHOW AND THE SOUTH

关　雎①

Kwan ts'eu

一　章

关关雎鸠,在河之洲。窈窕淑女,君子好逑。

1　*Kwan-kwan* go the ospreys,

On the islet in the river.

The modest, retiring, virtuous, young lady:—

For our prince a good mate she.

二　章

参差荇菜,左右流之。窈窕淑女,寤寐求之。

求之不得,寤寐思服。悠哉悠哉,辗转反侧。

2　Here long, there short, is the duckweed,

---

① Legge, J. *The Chinese Classics*, *Vol*. 4. Hong Kong: The London Missionary
Society's Printing Office, 1871: 1-4.

To the left, to the right, borne about by the current.

The modest, retiring, virtuous, young lady: —

Waking and sleeping, he sought her.

He sought her and found her not,

And waking and sleeping he thought about her.

Long he thought; oh! long and anxiously;

On his side, on his back, he turned, and back again.

三　章

参差荇菜,左右采之。窈窕淑女,琴瑟友之。

参差荇菜,左右芼之。窈窕淑女,钟鼓乐之。

3　Here long, there short, is the duckweed;

On the left, on the right, we gather it.

The modest, retiring, virtuous, young lady: —

With lutes, small and large, let us give her friendly welcome.

Here long, there short, is the duckweed;

On the left, on the right, we cook and present it.

The modest, retiring, virtuous young lady: ——

With bells and drums let us show our delight in her.

桃　夭[①]

T'aou yaou

一　章

桃之夭夭,灼灼其华。之子于归,宜其室家。

---

① Legge, J. *The Chinese Classics*, *Vol*. 4. Hong Kong: The London Missionary Society's Printing Office, 1871: 12-13.

1　The peach tree is young and elegant;

Brilliant are its flowers.

This young lady is going to her future home,

And will order well her chamber and house.

二　章

桃之夭夭,有蕡其实。之子于归,宜其家室。

2　The peach tree is young and elegant;

Abundant will be its fruit.

This young lady is going to her future home,

And will order well her house and chamber.

三　章

桃之夭夭,其叶蓁蓁。之子于归,宜其家人。

3　The peach tree is young and elegant;

Luxuriant are its leaves.

This young lady is going to her future home,

And will order well her family.

兔　罝[①]

T'oo tseu

一　章

肃肃兔罝,椓之丁丁。赳赳武夫,公侯干城。

1　Carefully adjusted are the rabbit nets;

---

① Legge, J. *The Chinese Classics*, *Vol.* 4. Hong Kong: The London Missionary Society's Printing Office, 1871: 13-14.

Clang clang go the blows on the pegs.

That stalwart, martial man

Might be shield and wall to his prince.

二　章

肃肃兔罝,施于中逵。赳赳武夫,公侯好仇。

2 Carefully adjusted are the rabbit nets,

And placed where many ways meet.

That stalwart, martial man

Would be a good companion for his prince.

三　章

肃肃兔罝,施于中林。赳赳武夫,公侯腹心。

3 Carefully adjusted are the rabbit nets,

And placed in the midst of the forest.

That stalwart, martial man

Might be head and heart to his prince.

芣　苢①

Fow-e

一　章

采采芣苢,薄言采之。采采芣苢,薄言有之。

1 We gather and gather the plantains;

Now we may gather them.

---

① Legge, J. *The Chinese Classics*, *Vol*. 4. Hong Kong: The London Missionary Society's Printing Office, 1871: 14-15.

We gather and gather the plantains;

Now we have got them.

二　章

采采芣苢,薄言掇之。采采芣苢,薄言捋之。

2　We gather and gather the plantains;

Now we pluck the ears.

We gather and gather the plantains;

Now we rub out the seeds.

三　章

采采芣苢,薄言袺之。采采芣苢,薄言襭之。

3　We gather and gather the plantains;

Now we place the seeds in our skirts.

We gather and gather the plantains;

Now we tuck our skirts under our girdles.

汉　广①

Han kwang

一　章

南有乔木,不可休思。汉有游女,不可求思。

汉之广矣,不可泳思。江之永矣,不可方思。

1　In the south rise the trees without branches,

Affording no shelter.

① Legge，J. *The Chinese Classics*，Vol．4．Hong Kong：The London Missionary Society's Printing Office，1871：15-16.

By the Han are girls rambling about,

But it is vain to solicit them.

The breadth of the Han

Cannot be dived across;

The length of the Këang

Cannot be navigated with a raft.

二　章

翘翘错薪,言刈其楚。之子于归,言秣其马。

汉之广矣,不可泳思。江之永矣,不可方思。

2　Many are the bundles of firewood;

I would cut down the thorns [to form more].

Those girls that are going to their future home,

I would feed their horses.

The breadth of the Han

Cannot be dived across;

The length of the Këang

Cannot be navigated with a raft.

三　章

翘翘错薪,言刈其蒌。之子于归,言秣其驹。

汉之广矣,不可泳思。江之永矣,不可方思。

3　Many are the bundles of firewood;

I would cut down the southernwood [to form more].

Those girls that are going to their future home,

I would feed their colts.

The breadth of the Han

Cannot be dived across;

The length of the Këang

Cannot be navigated with a raft.

国风·邶风
THE ODES OP PEL

静 女 [①]

Tsing neu

一 章

静女其姝,俟我于城隅。爱而不见,搔首踟蹰。

1　How lovely is the retiring girl!

　　She was to await me at a corner of the wall.

　　Loving and not seeing her,

　　I scratch my head, and am in perplexity.

二 章

静女其娈,贻我彤管。彤管有炜,说怿女美。

2　How handsome is the retiring girl!

　　She presented to me a ted tube.

　　Bright is the red tube;——

① Legge, J. *The Chinese Classics*, *Vol*. 4. Hong Kong: The London Missionary Society's Printing Office, 1871: 68-69.

Idelight in the Beauty of the girl.

三　章

自牧归荑，洵美且异。匪女以为美，美人之贻。

3　From the pasture lands she gave me a shoot of the white grass,

Truly elegant and rare.

It is not you, O grass, that are elegant;——

You are the gift of an elegant girl.

国风 · 卫风
THEODES OF WEI

氓 ①

Mǎng

一 章

氓之蚩蚩，抱布贸丝。匪来贸丝，来即我谋。

送子涉淇，至于顿丘。匪我愆期，子无良媒。

将子无怒，秋以为期。

1　A simple-looking lad you were,

Carrying cloth to exchange it for silk.

[But] you came not so to purchase silk；—

You came to make proposals to me.

I convoyed you through the K'e,

As far as Tun-k'ew.

'It is not I,' [I said], 'who would protract the time；

But you have had no good go-between.

---

①　Legge，J. *The Chinese Classics*，*Vol*. 4. Hong Kong：The London Missionary
Society's Printing Office，1871：97-101.

I pray you be not angry,

And let autumn be the time. '

二　章

乘彼垝垣，以望复关。不见复关，泣涕涟涟。
既见复关，载笑载言。尔卜尔筮，体无咎言。
以尔车来，以我贿迁。

2　I ascended that ruinous wall,

To look towards Fuh-kwan;

And when I saw [you] not [coming from] it;

My tears flowed in streams.

When I did see [you coming from] Fuh-kwan,

I laughed and I spoke.

You had consulted, [you said], the tortoise-shell and the reeds,

And there was nothing unfavourable in their response.

'Then come,' [I did], 'with your carriage,

And I will remove with my goods. '

三　章

桑之未落，其叶沃若。于嗟鸠兮，无食桑葚；
于嗟女兮，无与士耽。士之耽兮，犹可说也；
女之耽兮，不可说也。

3　Before the mulberry tree has shed its leaves,

How rich and glossy are they!

Ah! thou dove,

Eat not its fruit [to excess].

Ah! thou young lady,

Seek no licentious pleasure with a gentleman.

When a gentleman indulges in such pleasure,

Something may still be said for him;

When a lady does so,

Nothing can be said for her.

四　章

桑之落矣，其黄而陨。自我徂尔，三岁食贫。

淇水汤汤，渐车帷裳。女也不爽，士贰其行。

士也罔极，二三其德。

4　When the mulberry tree sheds its leaves,

They fall yellow on the ground.

Since I went with you,

Three years have I eaten of your poverty;

And [now] the lull waters of the K'e

Wet the curtains of my carriage.

There has been no difference in me,

But you have been double in your ways.

It is you, Sir, who transgress the right,

Thus changeable in your conduct.

五　章

三岁为妇，靡室劳矣；夙兴夜寐，靡有朝矣。

言既遂矣，至于暴矣。兄弟不知，咥其笑矣。

静言思之，躬自悼矣。

5　For three years I was your wife,

And thought nothing of my toil in your house.

I rose early and went to sleep late,

Not intermitting my labours for a morning.

Thus [on my part] our contract was fulfilled,

But you have behaved thus cruelly.

My brothers will not know [all this],

And will only laugh at me.

Silently I think of it,

And bemoan myself.

六　章

及尔偕老，老使我怨。淇则有岸，隰则有泮。

总角之宴，言笑晏晏。信誓旦旦，不思其反。

反是不思，亦已焉哉！

6　I was to grow old with you;—

Old, you give me cause for sad repining.

The K'e has its banks,

And the marsh has its shores.

In the pleasant time of my girlhood, with my hair simply

gathered in a knot,

Harmoniously we talked and laughed.

Clearly were we sworn to good faith,

And I did not think the engagement would be broken.

That it would be broken I did not think,

And now it must be all over!

木 瓜①

Muh kwa

一 章

投我以木瓜，报之以琼琚。

匪报也，永以为好也！

1　There was presented to me a papaya,

　And I returned for it a beautiful *keu*-gem;

　Not as a return for it,

　But that our friendship might be lasting.

二 章

投我以木桃，报之以琼瑶。

匪报也，永以为好也！

2　There was presented to me a peach,

　And I returned for it a beautiful *yaou*-gem;

　Not as a return for it,

　But that our friendship might be lasting.

三 章

投我以木李，报之以琼玖。

匪报也，永以为好也！

3　There was presented to me a plum,

　And I returned for it a beautiful *këw*-stone;

① Legge，J. *The Chinese Classics*，*Vol*. 4. Hong Kong：The London Missionary Society's Printing Office，1871：107-108.

Not as a return for it,

But that our friendship might be lasting.

国风·王风
THE ODES OF THE ROYAL DOMAIN

黍 离[①]

Shoo li

一　章

彼黍离离,彼稷之苗。

行迈靡靡,中心摇摇。

知我者,谓我心忧;

不知我者,谓我何求。

悠悠苍天,此何人哉?

1　There was the millet with its drooping heads;

There was the sacrificial millet coming into blade.

Slowly I moved about,

In my heart all-agitated.

Those who knew me

Said I was sad at heart.

① Legge,J. *The Chinese Classics*,*Vol*. 4. Hong Kong:The London Missionary Society's Printing Office,1871:110-113.

Those who did not know me

Said I was seeking for something.

O distant and azure Heaven!

By what man was this [brought about]?

二　章

彼黍离离,彼稷之穗。

行迈靡靡,中心如醉。

知我者,谓我心忧;

不知我者,谓我何求。

悠悠苍天,此何人哉?

2　There was millet with its drooping heads;

There was the sacrificial millet in the ear.

Slowly I moved about,

My heart intoxicated, as it were, [with grief].

Those who knew me

Said I was sad at heart.

Those who did not know me

Said I was seeking for something.

O thou distant and azure Heaven!

By what man was this [brought about]?

三　章

彼黍离离,彼稷之实。

行迈靡靡,中心如噎。

知我者,谓我心忧;

不知我者,谓我何求。

悠悠苍天,此何人哉?

3　There was the millet with its drooping heads;

There was the sacrificial millet in grain.

Slowly I moved about,

As if there were a stoppage at my heart.

Those who knew me

Said I was sad at heart.

Those who did not know me

Said I was seeking for something.

O thou distant and azure Heaven!

By what man was this [brought about]?

兔　爰①

T'oo yuen

一　章

有兔爰爰,雉离于罗。

我生之初,尚无为;

我生之后,逢此百罹。

尚寐,无吪!

1　The hare is slow and cautious;

The pheasant plumps into the net.

In the early part of my life,

Time still passed without commotion.

In the subsequent part of it,

We are meeting with all these evils.

---

① Legge, J. *The Chinese Classics*, *Vol. 4*. Hong Kong: The London Missionary Society's Printing Office, 1871: 117-118.

I wish I might sleep and never move more.

二　章

有兔爰爰,雉离于罦。

我生之初,尚无造;

我生之后,逢此百忧。

尚寐,无觉!

2　The hare is slow and cautious;

The pheasant plumps into the snare.

In the early part of my life,

Time still passed without anything stirring.

In the subsequent part of it,

We are meeting with all these sorrows.

I wish I might sleep, and never wake more.

三　章

有兔爰爰,雉离于罿。

我生之初,尚无庸;

我生之后,逢此百凶。

尚寐,无聪!

3　The hare is slow and cautious;

The pheasant plumps into the trap.

In the early part of my life,

Time still passed without any call for our services.

In the subsequent part of it

We are meeting with all these miseries.

I would that I might sleep, and hear of nothing more.

采 葛①

Ts'ae koh

一 章

彼采葛兮,一日不见,如三月兮!

1　There he is gathering the dolichos!

A day without seeing him

Is like three months!

二 章

彼采萧兮,一日不见,如三秋兮!

2　There he is gathering the oxtail-southernwood!

A day without seeing him

Is like three seasons!

三 章

彼采艾兮,一日不见,如三岁兮!

3　There he is gathering the mugwort!

A day without seeing him

Is like three years!

① Legge, J. *The Chinese Classics*, *Vol*. 4. Hong Kong: The London Missionary Society's Printing Office, 1871: 120.

国风·郑风
THE ODES OF CH'ING

女曰鸡鸣①

Neu yueh ke ming

一　章

女曰鸡鸣,士曰昧旦。

子兴视夜,明星有烂。

将翱将翔,弋凫与雁。

1　Says the wife, 'It is cock-crow;'
　　Says the husband, 'It is grey dawn.'
　　'Rise, Sir, and look at the night,—
　　If the morning star be not shining.
　　Bestir yourself, and move about,
　　To shoot the wild ducks and geese.

①　Legge, J. *The Chinese Classics*, *Vol*. 4. Hong Kong：The London Missionary Society's Printing Office，1871：134-135.

二　章

弋言加之,与子宜之。

宜言饮酒,与子偕老。

琴瑟在御,莫不静好。

2　'When your arrows and line have found them,

I will dress them fitly for you.

When they are dressed, we will drink [together over them],

And I will hope to grow old with you.

Your lute in your hands

Will emit its quiet pleasant tones.

三　章

知子之来之,杂佩以赠之。

知子之顺之,杂佩以问之。

知子之好之,杂佩以报之。

3　'When I know those whose acquaintance you wish,

I will give them of the ornaments of my girdle.

When I know those with whom you are cordial,

I will send to them of the ornaments of my girdle.

When I know those whom you love,

I will repay their friendship from the ornaments of my girdle. '

有女同车①

Yew neu t'ung keu

一　章

有女同车,颜如舜华;

将翱将翔,佩玉琼琚。

彼美孟姜,洵美且都。

1　There is the lady in the carriage [with him]

With a countenance like the flower of the ephemeral hedge-tree.

As they move about,

The beautiful *keu*-gems of her girdle-pendant appear.

That beautiful eldest Këang

Is truly admirable and elegant.

二　章

有女同行,颜如舜英;

将翱将翔,佩玉将将。

彼美孟姜,德音不忘。

2　There is the young lady walking [with him],

With a countenance like the ephemeral blossoms of the hedge-tree.

As they move about,

The gems of her girdle-pendant tinkle.

Of that beautiful eldest Këang

The virtuous fame is not to be forgotten.

---

① Legge, J. *The Chinese Classics*, *Vol*. 4. Hong Kong: The London Missionary Society's Printing Office, 1871: 136-137.

山有扶苏①

Shan yew foo-soo

一　章

山有扶苏,隰有荷华。

不见子都,乃见狂且。

1　On the mountains is the mulberry tree;

In the marshes is the lotus flower.

I do not see Tsze-too,

But I see this mad fellow.

二　章

山有乔松,隰有游龙。

不见子充,乃见狡童。

2　On the mountains is the lofty pine;

In the marshes is the spreading water-polygonum.

I do not see Tsze-ch'ung,

But I see this artful boy.

---

① Legge, J. *The Chinese Classics*, *Vol. 4*. Hong Kong: The London Missionary Society's Printing Office, 1871: 137-138.

狡 童①

Këaou t'ung

一 章

彼狡童兮，不与我言兮。

维子之故，使我不能餐兮。

1   That artful boy!

He will not speak with me!

But for the sake of you，Sir，

Shall I make myself unable to eat?

二 章

彼狡童兮，不与我食兮。

维子之故，使我不能息兮。

2   That artful boy!

He will not eat with me!

But for the sake of you，Sir，

Shall I make myself unable to rest?

---

① Legge，J. *The Chinese Classics*，*Vol*. 4. Hong Kong：The London Missionary Society's Printing Office，1871：139.

风 雨①

Fung yu

一 章

风雨凄凄,鸡鸣喈喈。既见君子,云胡不夷?

1　Cold are the wind and the rain,

　　And shrilly crows the cock.

　　But I have seen my husband,

　　And should I but feel at rest?

二 章

风雨潇潇,鸡鸣胶胶。既见君子,云胡不瘳?

2　The wind whistles and the rain patters,

　　While loudly crows the cock.

　　But I have seen my husband,

　　And could my ailment but be cured?

三 章

风雨如晦,鸡鸣不已。既见君子,云胡不喜?

3　Through the wind and rain all looks dark,

　　And the cock crows without ceasing.

　　But I have seen my husband,

　　And how should I not rejoice?

---

① Legge, J. *The Chinese Classics*, *Vol*. 4. Hong Kong: The London Missionary Society's Printing Office, 1871: 143.

子 衿①

Tsz' K'en

一 章

青青子衿,悠悠我心。纵我不往,子宁不嗣音?

1　O you, with the blue collar,

Prolonged is the anxiety of my heart.

Although I do not go [to you],

Why do you not continue your messages [to me]?

二 章

青青子佩,悠悠我思。纵我不往,子宁不来?

2　You with the blue [strings to your] girdle-gems,

Long, long do I think of you.

Although I do not go [to you],

Why do you not come [to me]?

三 章

挑兮达兮,在城阙兮。一日不见,如三月兮。

3　How volatile are you and dissipated,

By the look-out tower on the wall!

One day without the sight of you

Is like three months.

---

① Legge, J. *The Chinese Classics*, *Vol*. 4. Hong Kong: The London Missionary Society's Printing Office, 1871: 144.

野有蔓草①

Yay yew man ts'aou

一　章

野有蔓草,零露溥兮。

有美一人,清扬婉兮。

邂逅相遇,适我愿兮。

1　On the moor is the creeping grass,

　　And how heavily is it loaded with dew!

　　There was a beautiful man,

　　Lovely, with clear eyes and fine forehead!

　　We met together accidentally,

　　And so my desire was satisfied.

二　章

野有蔓草,零露瀼瀼。

有美一人,婉如清扬。

邂逅相遇,与子偕臧。

2　On the moor is the creeping grass,

　　Heavily covered with dew.

　　There was a beautiful man,

　　Lovely, with clear eyes and fine forehead!

　　We met together accidentally,

　　And he and I were happy together.

---

① Legge, J. *The Chinese Classics*, *Vol*. 4. Hong Kong: The London Missionary Society's Printing Office, 1871: 147.

国风·秦风
THE ODES OF TS'IN

蒹　葭①

Këen këa

一　章

蒹葭苍苍,白露为霜。

所谓伊人,在水一方。

溯洄从之,道阻且长;

溯游从之,宛在水中央。

1　The reeds and rushes are deeply green,

And the white dew is turned into hoarfrost.

The man of whom I think

Is somewhere about the water.

I go up the stream in quest of him,

But the way is difficult and long.

I go down the stream in quest of him,

And lo! he is right in the midst of the water.

---

① Legge，J. *The Chinese Classics*，*Vol*．4．Hong Kong：The London Missionary Society's Printing Office，1871：195.

二　章

蒹葭凄凄,白露未晞。

所谓伊人,在水之湄。

溯洄从之,道阻且跻;

溯游从之,宛在水中坻。

2　The reeds and rushes are luxuriant,

And the white dew is not yet dry.

The man of whom I think

Is on the margin of the water.

I go up the stream in quest of him,

But the way is difficult and steep.

I go down the stream in quest of him,

And lo! he is on the islet in the midst of the water.

三　章

蒹葭采采,白露未已。

所谓伊人,在水之涘。

溯洄从之,道阻且右;

溯游从之,宛在水中沚。

3　The reeds and rushes are abundant,

And the white dew has not yet ceased.

The man of whom I think

Is on the bank of the river.

I go up the stream in quest of him,

But the way is difficult and turns to the right.

I go down the stream in quest of him,

And lo! he is on the island in the midst of the water.

小雅二
MINOR ODES OF THE KINGDOM

鹿鸣之什二之一①

DECADE OF LUH MING

鹿　鸣

Luh Ming

一　章

呦呦鹿鸣,食野之蘋。

我有嘉宾,鼓瑟吹笙。

吹笙鼓簧,承筐是将。

人之好我,示我周行。

1　With pleased sounds the deer call to one another,

　　Eating the celery of the fields.

---

① Legge，J. *The Chinese Classics*，*Vol.* 4. Hong Kong：The London Missionary Society's Printing Office，1871：245-247.

I have here admirable guests;

The lutes are struck, and the organ is blown [for them];—

The organ is blown till its tongues are all moving.

The baskets of offerings [also] are presented to them.

The men love me,

And will show me the perfect path.

二　章

呦呦鹿鸣,食野之蒿。

我有嘉宾,德音孔昭。

视民不恌,君子是则是效。

我有旨酒,嘉宾式燕以敖。

2　With pleased sounds the deer call to one another,

Eating the southernwood of the fields.

I have here admirable guests,

Whose virtuous fame is grandly brilliant.

They show the people not to be mean;

The officers have in them a pattern and model.

I have good wine,

Which my admirable guests drink, enjoying themselves.

三　章

呦呦鹿鸣,食野之芩。

我有嘉宾,鼓瑟鼓琴。

鼓瑟鼓琴,和乐且湛。

我有旨酒,以燕乐嘉宾之心。

3　With pleased sounds the deer call to one another,

Eating the salsola of the fields.

I have here admirable guests,

For whom are struck the lutes, large and small.

The lutes, large and small, are struck,

And our harmonious joy is long-continued.

I have good wine,

To feast and make glad the hearts of my admirable guests.

皇皇者华[①]

Hwang-hwang chay hwa

一 章

皇皇者华,于彼原隰。

駪駪征夫,每怀靡及。

1 Brilliant are the flowers,

On those level heights and the low grounds.

Complete and alert is the messenger, with his suite,

Ever anxious lest he should not succeed.

二 章

我马维驹,六辔如濡。

载驰载驱,周爰咨诹。

2 My horses are young;

The six reins look as if they were moistened.

I gallop them, and urge them on,

Everywhere pushing my inquiries.

---

① Legge, J. *The Chinese Classics*, *Vol*. 4. Hong Kong: The London Missionary Society's Printing Office, 1871: 249-250.

三　章

我马维骐,六辔如丝。

载驰载驱,周爰咨谋。

3　My horses are piebald;

The six reins are like silk.

I gallop them, and urge them on,

Everywhere seeking information and counsel.

四　章

我马维骆,六辔沃若。

载驰载驱,周爰咨度。

4　My horses are white and black-maned;

The six reins look glossy.

I gallop them and urge them on,

Everywhere seeking information and advice,

五　章

我马维駰,六辔既均。

载驰载驱,周爰咨询。

5　My horses are grey;

The six reins are well in hand.

I gallop them and urge them on,

Everywhere seeking information and suggestions.

采 薇①

Ts'ae we

一 章

采薇采薇,薇亦作止。

曰归曰归,岁亦莫止。

靡室靡家,玁狁之故。

不遑启居,玁狁之故。

1　Let us gather the thorn-ferns, let us gather the thorn-ferns;

The thorn-ferns are now springing up.

When shall we return? When shall we return?

It will be late in the [next] year.

Wife and husband will be separated,

Because of the Hëen-yun.

We shall have no leisure to rest,

Because of the Hëen-yun.

二 章

采薇采薇,薇亦柔止。

曰归曰归,心亦忧止。

忧心烈烈,载饥载渴。

我戍未定,靡使归聘。

2　Let us gather the thorn-ferns, let us gather the thorn-ferns;、

The thorn-ferns are now tender.

---

① Legge, J. *The Chinese Classics*, *Vol*. *4*. Hong Kong: The London Missionary Society's Printing Office, 1871: 258-261.

When shall we return? When shall we return?

Our hearts are sorrowful.

Our hearts are sad and sorrowful;

We shall hunger, we shall thirst.

While our service on guard is not finished,

We can send no one home to enquire about our families.

三　章

采薇采薇,薇亦刚止。

曰归曰归,岁亦阳止。

王事靡盬,不遑启处。

忧心孔疚,我行不来!

3　Let us gather the thorn-ferns, let us gather the thorn-ferns;

The thorn-ferns are now hard.

When shall we return? When shall we return?

The year will be in the tenth month.

But the king's business must not be slackly performed;

We shall have no leisure to rest.

Our sorrowing hearts are in great distress;

But we shall not return from our expedition.

四　章

彼尔维何? 维常之华。

彼路斯何? 君子之车。

戎车既驾,四牡业业。

岂敢定居? 一月三捷。

4　What is that so gorgeous?

It is the flowers of the cherry tree.

What carriage is that?

It is the carriage of our general.

His war carriage is yoked;

The four steeds are strong.

Dare we remain inactive?

In one month we shall have three victories.

五　章

驾彼四牡，四牡骙骙。

君子所依，小人所腓。

四牡翼翼，象弭鱼服。

岂不日戒？猃狁孔棘！

5　The four steeds are yoked,

The four steeds, eager and strong;—

The confidence of the general,

The protection of the men.

The four steeds move regularly, like wings;—

There are the bow with its ivory ends, and the seal-skin quiver.

Shall we not daily warn one another?

The business of the Hëen-yun is very urgent.

六　章

昔我往矣，杨柳依依。

今我来思，雨雪霏霏。

行道迟迟，载渴载饥。

我心伤悲，莫知我哀！

6　At first, when we set out,

The willows were fresh and green;

Now, when we shall be returning,

The snow will be falling in clouds.

Long and tedious will be our marching;

We shall hunger; we shall thirst.

Our hearts are wounded with grief,

And no one knows our sadness.

彤弓之什二之三

THE DECADE OF TOTG KUKG

菁菁者莪[①]

Ts'ing-ts'ing chay ngo

一　章

菁菁者莪,在彼中阿。

既见君子,乐且有仪。

1　Luxuriantly grows the aster-southernwood,

In the midst of that large mound.

Since we see our noble lord,

We rejoice, and he shows us all courtesy.

二　章

菁菁者莪,在彼中沚。

① Legge, J. *The Chinese Classics*, *Vol*. 4. Hong Kong: The London Missionary Society's Printing Office, 1871: 279-280.

既见君子,我心则喜。

2　Luxuriantly grows the aster-southernwood.

In the midst of that islet.

Since we see our noble lord,

Our hearts are full of joy.

三　章

菁菁者莪,在彼中陵。

既见君子,锡我百朋。

3　Luxuriantly grows the aster-southernwood,

In the midst of that great height.

We see our noble lord,

And he gives us a hundred sets of cowries.

四　章

汎汎杨舟,载沉载浮。

既见君子,我心则休。

4　It floats about,—the willow boat,

Now sinking, now rising again.

Since we see our noble lord,

Our hearts are at rest.

都人士之什二之八

THE DECADE OF TOO JIN SZE

隰　桑①

Sih sang

一　章

隰桑有阿,其叶有难。

既见君子,其乐如何。

1　In the low, wet grounds, the mulberry trees are beautiful,

And their leaves are luxuriant.

When I see the princely men,

How great is the pleasure!

二　章

隰桑有阿,其叶有沃。

既见君子,云何不乐。

2　In the low, wet grounds, the mulberry trees are beautiful,

And their leaves are glossy.

When I see the princely men,

How can I be other than glad?

① Legge, J. *The Chinese Classics*, *Vol*. 4. Hong Kong: The London Missionary Society's Printing Office, 1871: 414-415.

三　章

隰桑有阿,其叶有幽。

既见君子,德音孔胶。

3　In the low, wet grounds, the mulberry trees are beautiful,

And their leaves are dark.

When I see the princely men,

Their virtuous fame draws them close [to my heart].

四　章

心乎爱矣,遐不谓矣?

中心藏之,何日忘之!

4　In my heart I love them,

And why should I not say so?

In the core of my heart I keep them,

And never will forget them.

大雅三
GREATER ODES OF THE KINGDOM

文王之什三之一

DECADE OF KING WAN

文　王 [①]

Wǎn wang

一　章

文王在上,于昭于天。

周虽旧邦,其命维新。

有周不显,帝命不时。

文王陟降,在帝左右。

1　King Wǎn is on high;

　　Oh! bright is he in heaven.

① Legge,J. *The Chinese Classics*,*Vol.4*. Hong Kong:The London Missionary Society's Printing Office,1871:427-431.

Although Chow was an old country,

The [favouring] appointment lighted on it recently.

Illustrious was the House of Chow,

And the appointment of God came at the proper season.

King Wǎn ascends and descends,

On the left and the right of God.

二　章

亹亹文王,令闻不已。

陈锡哉周,侯文王孙子。

文王孙子,本支百世。

凡周之士,不显亦世。

2　Full of earnest activity was king Wǎn,

And his fame is without end.

The gifts [of God] to Chow

Extend to the descendants of king Wǎn;—

To the descendants of king Wǎn,

In the direct line and the collateral branches for a hundred generations.

All the officers of Chow

Shall [also] be illustrious from age to age.

三　章

世之不显,厥犹翼翼。

思皇多士,生此王国。

王国克生,维周之桢。

济济多士,文王以宁。

3　They shall be illustrious from age to age,

Zealously and reverently pursuing their plans.

Admirable are the many officers

Born in this royal kingdom.

The royal kingdom is able to produce them,—

The supporters of [the House of] Chow.

Numerous is the array of officers,

And by them king Wǎn enjoys his repose.

四 章

穆穆文王,于缉熙敬止。

假哉天命,有商孙子。

商之孙子,其丽不亿。

上帝既命,侯于周服。

4 Profound was king Wǎn;

Oh! continuous and bright was his feeling of reverence.

Great is the appointment of Heaven!

There were the descendants of [the sovereigns] of Shang;—

The descendants of the sovereigns of Shang,

Were in number more than hundreds of thousands;

But when God gave the command,

They became subject to Chow.

五 章

侯服于周,天命靡常。

殷士肤敏,裸将于京。

厥作裸将,常服黼冔。

王之荩臣,无念尔祖。

5 They became subject to Chow.

The appointment of Heaven is not constant.

The officers of Yin, admirable and alert,

Assist at the libations in [our] capital;——

They assist at those libations,

Always wearing the hatchets on their lower garment and their peculiar cap.

O ye loyal ministers of the king,

Ever think of your ancestor!

六　章

无念尔祖,聿修厥德。

永言配命,自求多福。

殷之未丧师,克配上帝。

宜鉴于殷,骏命不易。

6　Ever think of your ancestor,

Cultivating your virtue,

Always striving to accord with the will [of Heaven].

So shall you be seeking for much happiness.

Before Yin lost the multitudes,

[Its kings] were the assessors of God.

Look to Yin as a beacon;

The great appointment is not easily [preserved].

七　章

命之不易,无遏尔躬。

宣昭义问,有虞殷自天。

上天之载,无声无臭。

仪刑文王,万邦作孚。

7   The appointment is not easily [preserved]

Do not cause your own extinction.

Display and make bright your righteousness and name,

And look at [the fate of] Yin in the light of Heaven.

The doings of High Heaven,

Have neither sound nor smell.

Take your pattern from king Wǎn,

And the myriad regions will repose confidence in you.

THE SHE KING.

PART I.
LESSONS FROM THE STATES.

BOOK I. THE ODES OF CHOW AND THE SOUTH.

I. *Kwan ts'eu.*

詩經
國風一
周南一之一
關雎

關雎

一章 關關雎鳩。在河之洲。窈窕淑女。君子好逑。

二章 參差荇菜。左右流之。窈窕淑女。寤寐求之。求之

1 *Kwan-kwan* go the ospreys,
   On the islet in the river.
   The modest, retiring, virtuous, young lady:—
   For our prince a good mate she.

2 Here long, there short, is the duckweed,
   To the left, to the right, borne about by the current.
   The modest, retiring, virtuous, young lady:—
   Waking and sleeping, he sought her.

TITLE OF THE WHOLE WORK.—詩經, 'The Book of Poems,' or simply 詩, 'The Poems.' By poetry, according to the Great Preface and the views generally of Chinese scholars, is denoted the expression, in rhymed words, of thought impregnated with feeling; which, so far as it goes, is a good account of this species of composition. In the collection before us, there were originally 311 pieces; but of six of them there are only the titles remaining. They are generally short: not one of them, indeed, is a long poem. Father Lacharme calls the Book—'*Liber Carminum*,' and with most English writers the ordinary designation of it has been 'The Book of Odes.' I can think of no better name for the several pieces than *Ode*, understanding by that term a short lyric poem. Confucius himself is said to have 'fitted them to the string.'

VOL. IV.   1

理雅各著《中国经典》（第四卷）内页（J. Legge, *The Chinese Classics*, Vol. 4. Hong Kong: London Missionary Society's Printing Office, 1871: 1.）

《春秋》(附《左传》)(节选)①
(1872 年)

理雅格　译

王韬　佐译

编者按语:

限于篇幅,点校者选择《郑伯克段于鄢》和《曹刿论战》两篇。本节收录的,既包括中文原文、英文译文,也包括译者理雅各在原译文下方所做的长篇注解,其中括号内的中文注释,照录自原书,非编者所附加。

在第五卷正文之中,理雅各多次提到王韬的名字。总的来说,王韬在《中国经典》的翻译中,确切说,所扮演的并非译者的角色。

隐公元年
DUKE YIN
First year

一　章

元年,春,王正月。

1　[It was his] first year, the spring, the king's first month.

---

① Legge, J. *The Chinese Classics*, *Vol*. 5. Hong Kong: The London Missionary Society's Printing Office, 1872:1-8.

二　章

三月,公及邾仪父盟于蔑。

2　In the third month, the duke and E foo of Choo made acovenant in Mëeh.

三　章

夏,五月,郑伯克段于鄢。

3　In summer, in the fifth month, the earl of Ch'ing overcame Twan in Yen.

四　章

秋,七月,天王使宰咺来归惠公、仲子之赗。

4　In autumn, in the seventh month, the king [by] Heaven's [grace] sent the [sub-] administrator Heuen with a present of [two] carriages and their horses for the funerals of duke Hwuy and [his wife] Chung Tsze.

五　章

九月,及宋人盟于宿。

5　In the ninth month, [the duke] and an officer of Sung made a covenant in Suh.

六　章

冬,十有二月,祭伯来。

6　In winter, in the twelfth month, the earl of Chae came [to Loo].

七 章

公子益师卒。

7 Kung-tsze Yih-sze died.

左传曰:惠公元妃孟子。孟子卒,继室以声子,生隐公。宋武公生仲子。仲子生而有文在其手,曰为鲁夫人,故仲子归于我。生桓公而惠公薨,是以隐公立而奉之。

元年春,王周正月,不书即位,摄也。

三月,公及邾仪父盟于蔑,邾子克也。未王命,故不书爵。曰"仪父",贵之也。公摄位而欲求好于邾,故为蔑之盟。

夏四月,费伯帅师城郎。不书,非公命也。

初,郑武公娶于申,曰武姜,生庄公及共叔段。庄公寤生,惊姜氏,故名曰"寤生",遂恶之。爱共叔段,欲立之。亟请于武公,公弗许。及庄公即位,为之请制。公曰:"制,岩邑也,虢叔死焉,他邑唯命。"请京,使居之,谓之京城大叔。祭仲曰:"都,城过百雉,国之害也。先王之制:大都,不过参国之一;中,五之一;小,九之一。今京不度,非制也,君将不堪。"公曰:"姜氏欲之,焉辟害?"对曰:"姜氏何厌之有? 不如早为之所,无使滋蔓!蔓,难图也。蔓草犹不可除,况君之宠弟乎?"公曰:"多行不义,必自毙,子姑待之。"

既而大叔命西鄙、北鄙贰于己。公子吕曰:"国不堪贰,君将若之何?欲与大叔,臣请事之;若弗与,则请除之。无生民心。"公曰:"无庸,将自及。"大叔又收贰以为己邑,至于廪延。子封曰:"可矣,厚将得众。"公曰:"不义不昵,厚将崩。"

大叔完、聚,缮甲、兵,具卒,乘,将袭郑,夫人将启之。公闻其期,曰:"可矣!"命子封帅车二百乘以伐京。京叛大叔段,段入于鄢,公伐诸鄢。五月辛丑,大叔出奔共。

书曰:"郑伯克段于鄢。"段不弟,故不言弟;如二君,故曰克;称郑伯,讥失教也:谓之郑志。不言出奔,难之也。

遂置姜氏于城颍,而誓之曰:"不及黄泉,无相见也。"既而悔之。颍考叔为颍谷封人,闻之,有献于公,公赐之食,食舍肉。公问之,对曰:"小人有母,皆尝小人之食矣,未尝君之羹,请以遗之。"公曰:"尔有母遗,繄我独无!"颍考叔曰:"敢问何谓也?"公语之故,且告之悔。对曰:"君何患焉?若阙地及泉,隧而相见,其谁曰不然?"公从之。公入而赋:"大隧之中,其乐也融融!"姜出而赋:"大隧之外,其乐也泄泄!"遂为母子如初。

君子曰:"颍考叔,纯孝也,爱其母,施及庄公。《诗》曰:'孝子不匮,永锡尔类'。其是之谓乎!"

秋七月,天王使宰咺来归惠公、仲子之赗。缓,且子氏未薨,故名。天子七月而葬,同轨毕至;诸侯五月,同盟至;大夫三月,同位至;士逾月,外姻至。赠死不及尸,吊生不及哀,豫凶事,非礼也。

八月,纪人伐夷。夷不告,故不书。

有蜚。不为灾,亦不书。

惠公之季年,败宋师于黄。公立而求成焉。九月,及宋人盟于宿,始通也。

冬十月庚申,改葬惠公。公弗临,故不书。惠公之薨也,有宋师,太子少,葬故有阙,是以改葬。卫侯来会葬,不见公,亦不书。郑共叔之乱,公孙滑出奔卫。卫人为之伐郑,取廪延。郑人以王师、虢师伐卫南鄙。请师于邾。邾子使私于公子豫,豫请往,公弗许,遂行。及邾人、郑人盟于翼。不书,非公命也。

新作南门。不书,亦非公命也。

十二月,祭伯来,非王命也。

众父卒。公不与小敛,故不书日。

TITLE OF THE WORK.—春秋,附左传. ' The Spring and Autumn; with the Tso Chuen. ' 'Spring and Autumn' is equivalent to 'Annals, digested under the four seasons of every year,' only two seasons being given for the sake of brevity. The subject of the name is fully discussed in the Prolegomena, ch. I. I have printed all the text of Tso K'ëw-ming, immediately after the year of the Classic to which it belongs. Where his remarks are simply comments on the text, I have embodied them with my own notes. His narratives, however, are all translated entire, and the additional narratives which he gives, not belonging to events referred to in the text, and indicated by a are included in the notes, within brackets.

Title of the Book.—隐公, 'Duke Yin.' Of the 12 dukes of Loo, whose years are chronicled in the Chun Ts'ëw, Yin is the first, his rule extending from B. C. 721—711. From the establishment of Pih-k'in, son of the famous duke of Chow, as marquis of Loo, in B. C. 1114, there had been 13 chiefs. Yin's father and predecessor, duke Hwuy (惠公) married first a daughter of the House of Sung (孟子); and on her death he supplied her place with Shing Tsze(声子), one of her relatives who had followed her from Sung to the harem of Loo. This lady was the mother of Yin; but duke Hwuy by and by took as a *second wife* the daughter of the duke Woo(武) of Sung, called 仲子. Acc. to Tso-she, she had been born with some remarkable lines on one of her hands, which were read as meaning that she would become marchioness of Loo. By her Hwuy had a son of higher dignity than Yin, in consequence of the superior position of his mother, and who afterwards made himself duke Hwan. This child being too young to take charge of the State on his father's death, was set aside in favour of Yin, who, however, only considered himself as occupying in room of his younger brother till the latter should come of age.

Yin's name was Seih-koo (息姑), Yin being the honorary or sacrificial title conferred after his death, and meaning,—'Sorrowfully swept away unsuccessful (隐拂不成).'

Loo was only a marquisate. Its chiefs were not dukes. Throughout the Ch'un Ts'ëw, however, we find the chiefs even of the smaller States all dignified with the title of 'duke' after their death. Maou K 'e-ling ingeniously explains this as an instance of the style of the 'historl[i]ographer,' referring to the commenting words in 'The Speech at Pe' (Shoo V. xxix.)—公曰, whereas, in the Preface to the Shoo, par. 66, instead of 公 we read 鲁侯, 'the marquis of Loo.' The confusion which is caused, however, by the practice, in the narratives of Tso K'ëw-ming is very great, as he uses now the name with the title of rank, and now the honorary name and title of duke, with the most entire indifference.

Yin's 1st year synchronized with the 49th of king Ping (平王); the 9th year of He of Ts'e (齐僖公); the 2d of Goh of Tsin(晋鄂侯); the 11th of Chwang of K'ëuh-yuh(曲沃庄伯); the 13th of Hwan of Wei (卫桓公); the 28th of Seuen of Ts'ae(蔡宣公); the 22d of Chwang of Ch'ing (郑庄公); the 35th of Hwan of Ts'aou (曹桓公); the 23d of Hwan of Ch'in (陈桓公); the 29th of Woo of Ke (杞武公); the 7th of Muh of Sung (宋穆公); the 44th of Wan ofTs'in (秦文公); and the 19th of Woo of Ts'oo (楚武公).

Par. 1. This paragraph, it will be seen, is incomplete, the adjunct merely of a 公即位, which is found at the beginning of nearly every other book. The reason of the incompleteness will be considered below.

元年,—'the 1st year.' The Urh-ya① explains 元 by 始 'the

---

① 指《尔雅》。

beginning,' 'first,' and Kung-yang[①] makes the phrase simply = 君之始年, 'the prince's 1st year.' Too Yu tries to find a deeper meaning in the phrase, saying that the 1st year of a rule stands to all the following years in the relation of the original *chaos* to the subsequent *kosmos*, and is therefore called *yuen*, to intimate to rulers that from the first moment of their sway they are to advance in the path of order and right. This consideration explains also, he thinks, the use of 正月, 'the right month,' for 'the 1st month(凡人君即位,欲其体元以居正,故不言一年一月也).' The Urh-ya, however, gives 正 as = 长 'the most elevated,' 'the senior.' But in the denomination of the 1st month as 'the right or correct month,' we must acknowledge a recognition of what are called 'the three *ching*(三正),'—the three different months, with which the dynasties of Hëa, Shang, and Chow commenced the year. Hëa began the year with the 1st month of spring; Shang, a month, and Chow, 2 months earlier. It became so much a rule for the beginning of the year to be changed by every new dynasty, that Ts'in made its first month commence a lunation before that of Chow. To a remark of Confucius, Ana. XV. x., we are indebted for the disuse of this foolish custom, so that all dynasties have since used 'the seasons of Hëa.'—After all, there remains the question why the first month of the year should be called *ching*(正).

王正月,—'the king's first month.' The 'king' here can hardly be any other than P'ing, the king of Chow for the time then being, as Too Yu says;—and in this style does the account of very many of the years of the Ch'un Ts'ëw begin, as if to do homage to the supremacy of the reigning House. Kung-yang makes the king to be Wăn; but though he

---

① 指《公羊传》。

was the founder of the Chow dynasty, the commencement of the year was not yet changed in his time.

The remaining character in this par. occasions the foreign student considerable perplexity. The commencement of the year was really in the 2d month of winter, and yet it is here said to have been in the spring.—春王正月. We have spring when it really was not spring. It must be kept in mind that the usual names for the seasons—春,夏,秋, 冬, only denote in the Ch'un Ts'ëw the four quarters of the Chow year, beginning with the 2d month of winter. It was, no doubt, a perception of the inconvenience of such a calendar which made Confucius, loyal as he was to the dynasty of Chow, say that he preferred that of Hëa to it. Strange as it is to read of spring, when the time is really winter, and of winter when the season is still autumn, it will appear, as we go on, that such is really the style of the Ch'un Ts'ëw. Maou, fully admitting all this, yet contends for a strange interpretation of the text, in which he joins 春 and 王 together, making the phrase to stand for the kings of Chow,—'Spring kings,' who reigned by the virtue of wood, the first of the five elements(五行之首). He presses, in support of this view, the words of Tso-she on this paragraph,—元年春王周正月, which show, he says, that Tso-she joined 春 with 王, as he himself would do; but Tso-she's language need not be so construed, and 春 evidently stands by itself, just as the names of the other seasons do.

We come now to the incompleteness of the par., already pointed out. According to the analogy of the style in the first years of other dukes, it should be stated that in his 1st year and the 1st month of it, the duke took the place (即位) of his predecessor. According to the rule of Chow, on the death of a sovereign—and all the princes were little kings in their several States—his successor, acknowledged to be such as the chief mourner on the occasion and taking the direction of the proper ceremonies for the departed, 'ascended the throne by the bier.' There is an interesting account of such an accession in the Shoo, V. xxii. The thing was done so hurriedly because 'the State could not be a single day without a sovereign(国家不可一日无君),' or because, as we phrase it, 'the king never dies.' What remained of the year, however, was held to belong to the reign of the deceased king, and the new reign began with the beginning of the next year, when there was a more public 'taking of the place,' though I do not know that we have any account of the ceremonies which were then performed. The first 'place-taking' was equivalent to our 'accession;' the second, to our ' coronation.' The proper explanation, therefore, of the incompleteness of the paragraph is that Yin omitted the ordinary 'place-taking' ceremonies, and of course there could be no record of them. Perhaps he made the omission, having it iu[n] mind to resign erelong in favour of his younger brother (so, Tso-she); but to say that the usual 公即位 was here omitted by Confucius, either to show his approval or disapproval of Yin, as Kuh-lëang does, followed by Hoo Gan-kwoh (胡安国, A. D. 1074—1138) and a hundred other commentators,is not to explain the text, but to perplex the reader with vain fancies.

Par. 2. There was nothing proper for record in the 1st and 2d months of the year, and we come here to the third month. Choo (we have Choo-low, 邾娄 in Kung-yang) was a small State, nearly all surrounded by Loo, the pres. dis. of Tsow (邹), dep. Yen-chow. At this time it was only a Foo-yung (附庸) attached to Loo (see Mencius,

V. 下, ii. 4.）; but in a few years after this its chief was raised to the dignity of viscount（子）. The House had the surname of Ts'aou（曹）, and had been invested with the territory by king Woo, as being descended from the ancient emperor Chuen-hëuh. The chief's name, as we learn afterwards from the Ch'un Ts'ëw, was K'ih（克）; E-foo （父, read in the 2d tone, found appended to many designations, by way of honour）is his designation（字）, given to him here, says Tso-she, ['] byway of honour,' for which remark there seems to be no ground. Mëeh（Kuh and Kung both have 眛, with the same sound）was a place belonging to Loo,—in the pres. dis. of Sze-shwuy（泗水）, dep. Yen-chow. We know nothing of any special object sought by the 'covenanting' here. Tso-she merely says that the duke arranged for it to cultivate friendly relations with his neighbour, at the commencement of his temporary administration. 公 heads the record, here and in most other accounts of meetings and covenants on the part of the marquises of Loo with other princes;—an order proper in the historiographers of that State. I can think of no better word for 盟 than 'covenant,' 'to covenant.' On all occasions there was the death of a victim, over which the contracting parties appealed to superior Powers, wishing that, if they violated the terms of their covenant, they might meet with a fate like that of the slain animal. One definition of the term is 誓約 'an agreement with an oath.' Compare the account of Jacob and Laban's covenant, Genesis, xxxi.

The 及 after 公 is to be taken as simply ＝ 与 'with;' 'and.' Kung, Kuh, and others find recondite meanings in it, which will not bear examination.

[Tso-she, after this paragraph, gives an incident of the 4th month, in summer, that 'the earl of Pe led a force, and walled Lang,' adding that no record of it was made, because it was not done with the duke's order. See the 1st note on 'The speech at Pe' in the Shoo. I have translated the notice according to the view of Ch'in Sze-k'ae given there; but Tso-she could not have intended 费伯 to be taken as meaning 'Earl of Pe,' but merely 'Pih (some scion of the House of Loo) of Pe.']

Par. 3. Ch'ing was an earldom which had not been of long duration. In B. C. 805, king Seuen had invested his brother Yëw (友) with the lands of Ch'ing, in the pres. Hwa Chow (华州), dep. Tung-chow, Shen-se. Yëw's son, Keueh-tuh(掘突) known as duke Woo (武公), conquered a territory more to the east, the country of Kwoh and Kwei(虢郐之地)—and settled in it, calling it 'New Ch'ing;'—the name of which is still retained in the district of Sin ch'ing (新郑), dep. K'ae-fung, Ho-nan. Woo's son, Woo-shang (寤生), known as duke [e]Chwang (庄) au[n]d born in B. C. 756, is the earl of this par. Twan was his younger brother. Yen has left its name in the dis. of Yen-ling(鄢陵). Tso-she's account of the event in the text is the following:—

'Duke Woo of Ch'ing had married a daughter of the House of Shin, called Woo Këaug, who bore duke Chwang and his brother Twan of Kung. Duke Chwang was born as she was waking from sleep [the meaning of the text here is uncertain], which frightened the lady so that she named him Woo-shang (= born in waking), and hated him, while she loved Twan, and wished him to be declared his father's heir. Often did she ask this of duko[e] Woo, but he refused it. When duke Chwang came to the earldom, she begged him to confer on Twan the city of Che. "It is *too* dangerous a place, was the reply. "The Younger of Kwoh died there; but in regard to any other place, you may command me." She then requested King; and there Twan took up his residence, and came to be styled T'ae-shuh (= the Great Younger) of King city. Chung of Chae said to the duke, "Any metropolitan city, whose wall is more than 3,000 cubits round, is dangerous to the State. According to the regulations of the former kings, such a city of the 1st order can have its wall only a third as long as that of the capital; one of the 2d order, only a fifth as long; and one of the least order, only a ninth. Now King is not in accordance with these measures and regulations. As ruler, you will not be able to endure *Twan in such a place*." The duke replied, "It was our mother's wish;—how could I avoid the danger?" "The lady Këang" returned the officer, "is not to be satisfied. You had better take the necessary precautions, and not allow the danger to grow so great that it will be difficult to deal with it. Even grass, when it has grown and spread all about, cannot be removed;—how much less the brother of yourself, and the favoured brother as well!"The duke said, "By his many deeds of unrighteousness he will bring destruction on himself. Do you only wait a while."

'After this, T'ae-shuh ordered the places on the western and northern borders *of the State* to render to himself the same allegiance as they did to the earl. Then Kung-tsze Lea said to the duke, "A State cannot sustain the burden of two services;—what will you do now? If you wish to give *Ch'ing* to T'ae-shuh, allow me to serve him as a subject. If you do not mean to give it to him, allow me to put him out of the way, that the minds of the people be not perplexed.""There is no need," the duke replied, "*for such a step. His calamity* will come of itself."

'T'ae-shuh went on to take as his own the places from which he had required their divided contributions, as far as Lin-yen. Tsze-fung [the designation of Kung-tsze Leu above] said, "Now is the time. With these enlarged resources, he will draw all the people to himself."The duke replied, "They will not cleave to him, so unrighteous as he is. Through his prosperity he will fall *the more*."

'T'ae-shuh wrought at his defene[c]es, gathered the people about him, put in order buff-e[c]oats and weapons, prepared footmen, and chariots, intending to surprise Ch'ing, while his mother was to open to him *from within*. The duke heard the time agreed on between them, and said, "Now we can act." So he ordered Tsze-fung, with two hundred chariots, to attack King. King revolted from T'ae-shuh, who then entered Yen, which the duke himself proceeded to attack;and in the 5th month, on the day Sin-ch'ow, T'ae-shuh fled from it to Kung.

'In the words of the text,—"The earl of Ch'ing overcame Twan in Yen," Twan is not called the *earl's* younger brother, because he did not show himself to be such. They were *as* two *hostile* princes, and therefore we have the word"overcame." The duke is styled the earl of Ch'ing *simply*, to condemn him for his failure to instruct *his brother properly*, Twan's flight is not mentioned, *in the text*, because it was difficult to do so, having in mind Ch'ing's wish that *Twan might be killed*.

'Immediately after these events, duke Chwang placed *his mother* Këang in Shing-ying, and swore an oath, saying, "I will not see you again, till I have reached the yellow spring [*i.e.*, till I am dead, and under the yellow earth]."But he repented of this. *By and by*, Ying K'aou-shuh, the border-warden of the vale of Ying, heard of it, and presented an offering to the duke, who caused food to be placed beforc him. K'aou-shuh put a piece of meat on one side; and when the duke asked the reason, he said, "I have a mother who always shares in what I eat. But she has not eaten of this meat which you, my ruler, have given, and I beg to be allowed to leave this piece for her." The duke said, "You have a mother to give it to. Alas! I alone have none." K'aou-shuh asked what the duke meant, who then told him all the circumstances, and how he repented of his oath. "Why should you be distressed about that?" said the officer. "If you dig into the earth to the yellow springs, and then make a subterranean passage, where you can meet each other, who can say that your oath is not fulfilled?' The duke followed this suggestion; and as he entered the passage sang,

> "This great tunnel, within,
>
> With joy doth run."

When his mother came out, she sang,

> "This great tunnel, without,
>
> The joy flies about."

[After this, they were mother and son as before.]

'A superior man may say, "Ying K'aou-shuh was filial indeed. His love for his mother passed over to and affected duke Chwang. Was there not here an illustration of what is said in the Book of Poetry,

> "A filial son of piety unfailing,
>
> There shall for ever be conferred blessing on you?"'

Spae[c]e would fail me were I to make any repairs on the criticisms interspersed by Tso-shein this and other narratives, or vindicate the translation of his narratives which I give. The reader will perceive that without the history in the Chuen, the Confucian text would give very little idea of the event which it professes to record and there are numberless instances, more flagrant still, in the Book. The 君子, who moralizes, is understood to be Tso-she himself. We have no other instance in the Ch'un Ts'ëw of 克 used as in this paragraph.

Par. 4. 天王, 'Heaven's king, or 'king by Heaven's grace,' is of course king P'ing. The sovereign of China, as Heaven's vice-gereut over the empire, is styled 天子 'Heaven's son;' in his relation to the feudal princes as their ruler, he was called 天王, 'Heaven's king.' 仲子 is 'the second Tsze," i. e., the daughter of the duke of Sung, who became the 2d wife of duke Hwuy as mentioned in the note on the title of this book; not Hwuy's mother, as Kuh-lëang absurdly says. 賵 is explained in the diet, as 赠死者, 'presents to the dead,' and 所以助主人送葬者, 'aids to the presiding mourner to bury his dead.' But such presents were of various kinds, and 賵 denotes the gift specially of one or more carriages and their horses. So both Kung and Kuh. The king sent such presents on the death of any of the princes or their wives; and here we have an instance in point. But there is much contention among the critics as to who the messenger was;—whether the king's chief Minister 冢宰, or some inferior officer of his department. The former view is taken by Kuh-lëang, and affirmed by the editors of the K'ang-he Ch'un Ts'ëw;—but, as I must think, erroneously. Under the 冢宰 or 太宰, were two 小宰, and four 宰夫, called by Biot *Grand-administrateur general,*' '*Sous-administrateurs generaux,*' and *aides-administrateurs generaux.*' It belonged to the department of the last, on all occasions of condolence, to superintend the arrangements, with every thing that was supplied by way of presents or offerings,—the silks, the n[u]tensils, the money, (see the Chow Le. I., iii. 56—73). The officer in the text was, no doubt, one of those aid-administrators;

and this removes all difficulty which the critics find in the mention of an officer of higher rank by his name.

The rule was that princes should be buried five months after their death, and Tso-she says that the king's message and gift arrived too late, so far as duke Hwuy was concerned. This criticism may be correct; but he goes on to say that Chung Tsze was not yet dead, and the message and gift were too early, so far as she was concerned. The king could never have been guilty of such an impropriety as to anticipate the lady's death in this way, and the view of Tso-she can only provoke a smile. He adds:—'The king's burial took place 7 months after his death, when all the feudal princes were expected to be present. The prince of a State was buried 5 months after his death, when all the princes, with whom he had covenanted, attended. The funeral of a great officer took place 3 months after his death, and was attended by all of the same rank; that of an officer, at the end of a month, and was attended by his relatives by affinity. Presents on account of a death were made before the burial, and visits of condolence were paid before the grief had assumed its greatest demonstrations. It was not proper to anticipate such occurrences.'

On first translating the Ch'un Ts'ëw, I e[c]onstrued the par. as if these were a 之 between 公 and 仲, and supposed that only one carriage and its horses were sent for the funeral of Chung Tsze, who had been the wife of Hwuy. I gave up the construction in deferene[c]e to the prevailing opinion of the commentators; but it had been adopted by no less a se[c]holer than Ch'ing E (程颐; A. D. 1033—1107).

[Tso-she has here two other entries under this season:—'In the 8th month an officer of Ke attacked E;' and 'There were loe[c]usts.' He adds that E sent no official announcement of the attack to Loo, and that therefore it was not recorded and that no notice was entered of the locusts, because they did not amount to a plague.]

Par. 5. Sung was a dukedom,—having its chief city in the pres. dis. of Shang-k'ëw (商邱), dep. Kwei-tih, Ho-nan. The charge given to the viscount of Wei on his being appointed to the State is still preserved in the Shoo, V. viii. The dukes of Sung were descended from the kings of Yin or Shang; and of course their surname was Tsze (子). Suh was a small State, in the present Tung-p'ing (东平) Chow, dep. T'ae-gan, Shan-tung. It was thus near Loo, but a good way from Sung. Its chiefs were barons with the surname Fung (风).

Tso-she tells us that in the last year of duke Hwuy, he defeated an army of Sung in Hwang, but that now duke Yin sought for peace. It was with this object that the covenant in the text was made.

I translate as if 公 preceded 及, for so the want must generally be supplied throughout the classic. Rung and Kuh both understand some inferior officer of Loo (微者), but in other places they themselves supply 公. By 宋人, however, we must understand an officer of Sung. It is better to translate so than to say simply—'a man of Sung.'

[Between this par. and the next Tso-she has the three following narratives:—

'In winter, in the 10th month, on the day Kăng-shin, the body of duke Hwuy was removed and buried a second time.' As the duke was not present, the event was not recorded. When duke Hwuy died, there was war with Sung, and the heir-prince was young, so that there was some omission in the burial. He was therefore now buried again, and in another grave. The marquis of Wei came to be present at the burial. He did not have an interview with the duke, and so his visit was not recorded. '

'After the e[c]onfusion occasioned by Kung-shuh of Ch'ing, Kung-sun Hwah [Twan or Kung shuh's son] fled to Wei and the people of Wei attacked Ch'ing in his behalf, and requested Lin-yen for him. Ching then attacked the southern border of Wei, supported by a king's army and an army of Kwoh, and also requested the aid of troops from Choo. The viscount of Choo sent a private message to Kung-tsze Yu*of Loo*, who asked leave from the duke to go. It was refused; but he went and made a covenant with an officer of Choo and an officer of Ch'ing in Yih. No record was made of this, because *Yu's going* was against the duke's order. '

'The southern gate of the city was made new. ' It was done without the duke's order, and so was not recorded.]

Par. 6. Chae [so 祭 is here read] was an earldom, in the present Ch'ing Chow (郑州), dep. K'ae-fung, held by the descendants of one of the duke of Chow's sons. Acc. to Tso-she the earl here was a minister at court., and came to Loo, for what purpose we know not, without the orders of the king. Kung-yang, indeed, thinks he came as a refugee, and that 伯 is the designation of the individual merely (字), and not his title; while Kuh-lëang makes the coming to have been to do a sort of homage to duke Yin. Bat this is simply guess work.

Par. 7. Of Yih-sze we know nothing but what this brief par. tells. He was 'a duke's son,' but whether the son of Hwuy, or of Hwuy's father, we cannot tell. It is best in such a case to take 公子 as if it were surname. So Ho Hëw (何休) says here, 公子者氏也. Kuh-lëang finds a condemnation of Yih-sze in the omission of the day of his death; but the old method of interpretation which found praise or blame in the mention of or silence as to days, in the use of the name, the designation, the title, and such matters, is now discarded. 卒 is the proper term to use for the death of an officer.

Tso-she gives the designation of Yih-sze as Chung-foo, and says that the clay of his death is not recorded, because the duke did not attend at the ceremony of dressing the corpse, to it into the coffin.

庄公十年①

DUKE CHWANG

Tenth year

一　章

十年,春,王正月,公败齐师于长勺。

1　In his tenth year, in spring, in the king's first month, the duke defeated the army of Ts'e at Ch'ang-choh.

二　章

二月,公侵宋。

2　In the second month, the duke made an incursion into Sung.

三　章

三月,宋人迁宿。

3　In the third month, the people of Sung removed [the State of] Suh.

---

① Legge, J. *The Chinese Classics*, *Vol*. 5. Hong Kong: The London Missionary Society's Printing Office, 1872:84-87.

四 章

夏,六月,齐师、宋师次于郎。公败宋师于乘丘。

4　In summer, in the sixth month, an army of Ts'e and an army of Sung halted at Lang. The duke defeated the army of Sung at Shing-k'ëw.

五 章

秋,九月,荆败蔡师于莘,以蔡侯献舞归。

5　In autumn, in the ninth month, King defeated the army of Ts'ae at Sin, and carried Hëen-woo, marquis of Ts'ae, back [to King].

六 章

冬,十月,齐师灭谭,谭子奔莒。

6　In winter, in the tenth, month, an army of Ts'e extinguished T'an. The viscount of T'an fled to Keu.

左传曰:十年,春,齐师伐我。公将战,曹刿请见。其乡人曰:"肉食者谋之,又何间焉。"刿曰:"肉食者鄙,未能远谋。"乃入见。问何以战。公曰:"衣食所安,弗敢专也,必以分人。"对曰:"小惠未徧[遍],民弗从也。"公曰:"牺牲玉帛,弗敢加也,必以信。"对曰:"小信未孚,神弗福也。"公曰:"小大之狱,虽不能察,必以情。"对曰:"忠之属也,可以一战,战则请从。"公与之乘。战于长勺。公将鼓之。刿曰;"未可。"齐人三鼓,刿曰:"可矣。"齐师败绩。公将驰之。刿曰:"未可。"下,视其辙,登,轼而望之,曰:"可矣。"遂逐齐师。既克,公问其故。对曰:"夫战,勇气也。一鼓作气,再而衰,三而竭。彼竭我盈,故克之。夫大国难测也,惧有伏焉。吾视其辙乱,望其旗靡,故逐之。"

夏,六月,齐师、宋师次于郎。公子偃曰:"宋师不整,可败也。宋败,齐必还,请击之。"公弗许。自雩门窃出,蒙皋比而先犯之。公从之。大败宋师于乘丘。齐师乃还。

蔡哀侯娶于陈,息侯亦娶焉。息妫将归,过蔡。蔡侯曰:"吾姨也。"止而见之,弗宾。息侯闻之,怒,使谓楚文王曰:"伐我,吾求救于蔡而伐之。"楚子从之。

秋,九月,楚败蔡师于莘,以蔡侯献舞归。

齐侯之出也,过谭,谭不礼焉。及其入也,诸侯皆贺,谭又不至。冬,齐师灭谭,谭无礼也。谭子奔莒,同盟故也。

Par. 1. Ch'ang-choh was in Loo, but its position has not been identified. Lo Pe (罗泌), clans of Shang removed by king Ch'ing to Loo, one was called the Ch'ang-choh, as having been located in Ch'ang-choh. The Chuen here is:—'The army of Ts'e invaded our *State*, and the duke was about to fight, when *one* Ts'aou Kwei requested to be introduced to him. One of Kwei's fellow-villagers said him, "The flesh-eaters [comp. Ps. xxii. 29], are planning for the occasion; what have you to do to intermeddle?" He replied, "The flesh-eaters are poor creatures, and cannot form any far-reaching plans." So he entered and was introduced, when he asked the duke what encouragement he had to fight. The duke said, "Clothes and food minister to my repose, but I do not dare to monopolise them:—I make it a point to share them with others." "That," replied Kwei, "is but small kindness, and does not reach to all. The people will not follow you *for that*." The duke said, "In the victims, the gems, and the silks, *used in sacrifice*, I do not dare to go beyond *the appointed rules*:—I make it a point to be sincere." "That is but small sincerity; it is not perfect:—the Spirits will not bless you for that." The duke said *again*, "In all matters of legal process, whether small or great, although I may not be able to search them out *thoroughly*, I make it a point to decide according to the real circumstances." " That," answered Kwei, " bespeaks a leal-heartedness;—you may venture one battle on that. When you fight, I beg to be allowed to attend you." The duke took him with him in his chariot. The battle was fought in Ch'ang-choh. The duke was about to order the drums to beat an advance, when Kwei said, "Not yet;" and after the men of Ts'e had advanced three times with their drums beating, he said, "Now is the time." The army of Ts'e received a severe defeat; but when the duke was about to dash after them, Kwei *again* said, "Not yet." He then got down, and examined the tracks left by their chariot-wheels, remounted, got on the front-bar, and looked after *the flying enemy*. After this he said "Pursue;" which the duke did. When the victory had been secured, the duke asked Kwei the reasons of what he had done. "In fighting," was the reply, all depends on the courageous spirit. When the drums first beat, that excites the spirit. A second advance occasions a diminution of the spirit; and with a third, it is exhausted. With our spirit at the highest pitch we fell on them with their spirit exhausted and so we conquered them. But it is difficult to fathom a great State;—I was afraid there might be an ambuscade. I looked *therefore* at the traces of their wheels, and found them all-confused; I looked after their flags, and they were drooping:—then *I gave the order to* pursue them."

Par. 2. This is the first record in the text of the military expedition called 侵. As the word denotes (侵＝渐进), it was a stealthy incursion. Kung-yang says：觕者曰侵，精者曰伐，'an ill-ordered advance is called *ts'in*; one in good array is called *fah*.' Tso-she, better:—有钟鼓曰伐；无钟鼓曰侵，'an advance with bells and drums is called *fah*; without them, *ts'in*.' So far as the text goes, this would

324 / 中華譯學館·中华翻译家代表性译文库

appear to have been a wanton attack on Sung. Maou supposes that Sung may have been confederate with Ts'e in the previous month.

Par. 3. Suh,—see on I. i. 5; where it has been observed that Suh was a long way from Sung. But the word 迁, 'to remove' does not signify that Sung continued to hold possession of the old territory;—it carried the people away and all the valuables of the State into its own territories. The affair would seem to be commemorated in the name of Suh-ts'ëen (宿迁), a dis. of Seu-chow dep., in Këang-soo, which was within the limits of Sung. We shall find hereafter as a neuter verb, where the signification is different.

Par. 4. Lang,—see VIII. 1. Shing-k'ëw is referred to the dis. of Tsze-yang (滋阳), dep. Yen-chow. If this identification be correct, then the allied forces had moved from Lang; or perhaps they had separated, and the army of Sung gone north to Shing-këw. The Chuen says:—'The armies of Ts'e and Sung were halting at Lang, when Yen, a son of duke *Hwan*, said, "The army of Sung is ill drawn up, and maybe defeated. If Sung be defeated, Ts'e will be obliged to retire. I beg leave to attack *the troops of Sung*." The duke refused, but he stole out at the Yu gate, and having covered *his horses* with tigers' skins, fell upon the enemy. The duke followed to support him, when they inflicted a great defeat on the army of Sung at Shing-k'ëw and the army of Ts'e withdrew *from Loo*.'

Part. 5. Here for the first time, Ts'oo, a great Power, appears on the stage of the Ch'un T'sëw, though we have met with it already more than once in the Chuen. King was the original name of Ts'oo, and in the Ch'un T'sëw it is thus named down to the 1st year of duke He. The chiefs of Ts'oo were at first viscounts, with the surname Me (芈; the bleating of a sheep), who traced their lineage up to the prehistoric times, pretending to be descended from Chuen-hëuh. The representative of the line in the times of Wǎn and Woo was Yuh-heung (鬻熊); and his great-grandson, Hëung-yih (熊绎) was invested by king Ch'ing with the lands of King Man (荆蛮), or 'King of the wild south,' and the title of viscount. His capital was Tan-yang (丹阳), referred to a place, 7 *le* south-east from the pres. dis. city of Kwei-chow (归州), dep. E-ch'ang (宜昌), Hoo-pih. In B. C. 886, Hëung-k'eu (熊渠) usurped the title of king, which was afterwards dropped for a time, but permanently resumed by Hëung T'ung (熊通), known as king Woo, in B. C. 703, who also moved the capital to Ying (郢) north of the pres. dep. city of King-chow (荆州). The viscount of Ts'oo at this first appearance of the House in the text was king Wǎn (文王), son of Woo, by name Hëung-tsze(熊赀).

Sin belonged to Ts'ae, and was in the borders of pres. dis. of Joo-yang (汝阳), dep. Joo-ning, Ho-nan. Hëen-woo (Kuh has 武) was the 蔡季 of H. xvii. 5. The style of the par. is unusual, the name of the State King being mentioned, and no 'viscount of King' or 'officer.' Too finds in this an evidence of the still barbarous condition of King or Ts'oo unacquainted with the forms of the States of 'the Middle country.'

The Chuen says:—'The marquis Gae of Ts'ae had married a daughter of the House of Chin, and the marquis of Seih had married another. When die latter lady [媳妇 'Kwei of Seih.' Kwei was the surname of Chin]*on one occasion* was going back to Seih, she passed by Ts'ae, and the marquis said, 'She is my sister-in-law.' He detained her, therefore, and saw her, not treating her as a guest should be treated. When the marquis of Seih heard of it, he was enraged, and sent a messenger to king Wǎn of Tsʻoo, saying, "Attack me, and I will ask assistance from Tsʻae, when you can attack it." The viscount of Ts ʻoo did so; and in autumn, in the 9th month, Tsʻoo defeated the army of Tsʻae at Sin, and carried off the marquis, Hëen-woo.'

Par. 6. Tʻan was a small State, whose lords were viscounts, within the circle of Tsʻe. Its chief town was 70 *le* to the south-east of the dis. City of Leih-shing, dep. Tse-nan. This is the first instance in the text of the 'extinction' of a State. The term implies the destruction of its ruling House, the abolition of its sacrifices, and the absorption of the people and territory by the prevailing Power. The Chuen says:— 'When the marquis of Tsʻe [*i. e.*, the present marquis] fled from the State [see the Chuen on VIII. 5], and was passing by Tan, the viscount showed him no courtesy. When he entered it again, and the other princes were all congratulating him, the viscount did not make his appearance. In winter, therefore, an army of Tsʻe extinguished Tan, which had behaved so improperly. The viscount fled to Keu. having formerly made a covenant with *the lord of* it.

THE CH'UN TS'EW;

WITH THE TSO CHUEN.

BOOK I. DUKE YIN.

First year.

春秋

隱公　附左傳

一章　元年春王正月。

二章　三月、公及邾儀父盟于蔑。

三章　夏五月、鄭伯克段于鄢。

四章　秋七月、天王使宰咺來歸惠公仲子之賵。

五章　九月、及宋人盟于宿。

六章　冬十有二月、祭伯來。

七章　公子益師卒。

左傳曰惠公元妃孟子孟子卒繼室以聲子生隱公宋武公生仲子仲子生而有文在其手曰為魯夫人故仲子歸于我生桓公而惠公薨是以隱公立而奉之

元年春王周正月不書即位攝也

三月公及邾儀父盟于蔑邾子克也未王命故不書爵曰儀父貴之也公攝位而欲求好於邾故為蔑之盟

〇夏四月費伯帥師城郎不書非公命也

初鄭武公娶于申曰武姜生莊公及共叔段莊公寤生驚姜氏故名曰寤生遂惡之愛

VOL. V.　　　　　I

理雅各著《中国经典》(第五卷)内页(J. Legge，*The Chinese Classics*，Vol. 5．Hong Kong：London Missionary Society's Printing Office，1872：1．)

王韬译事年表^①

1828—1848:道咸之际初长成

1828 年(道光八年)　1 岁

　　11 月 10 日(十月初四),王韬,初名王利宾,生于江苏省苏州城外长洲县甫里村。其在早期西文文献中的名字拼作 Wang T'aou。

　　【王韬先祖系昆山王氏,明代巨族。祖父王科进,字敬斋,乡里称善人。

　　父亲王昌桂,字肯堂,一字云亭,一度在松江墨海书馆(The London Missionary Society Mission Press)协助麦都思(Walter Henry Medhurst,1796—1857)等人翻译《圣经》。

　　上有三兄,十日间,皆染痘殇而殁。其弟王利贞,字叔亨,一字咨卿,读书未成名而卒,年仅二十七岁。其姐王媖,字伯芬,嫁吴村周氏,1873 年去世。其妻杨梦蘅,名保艾,字台芳,结婚四年后在上海去世。后续娶林琳为妻,字怀蘅,一字泠泠。王韬无子,生有两个女儿,长女曰王婉,字苕仙,归吴兴茂才钱征,早殇;次女曰王娴,字樨仙,生不能言。】

---

① 王韬译事年表简编和译事年谱提纲的编写,参考了王韬自传《弢园老民自传》(参见李天纲编校《弢园文新编》,中西书局 2012 年版)、《王韬日记》(方行、汤志钧整理,中华书局 1987 年版)、《王韬年谱》(张志春编著,河北教育出版社 1994 年版)和《王韬卷》(海青编,中国人民大学出版社 2013 年版)。

1845 年（道光二十五年） 18 岁

春，赴昆山科考，王韬以一等第三名被新阳县学录取。督学使者为秦中张筱坡侍郎，称其"文有奇气"。

1846 年（道光二十六年） 19 岁

秋，王韬赴金陵应乡试。这次乡试王韬落第，始在锦溪古镇走上同其父一样的设馆授徒谋生道路。

冬，娶同村孝廉（举人）杨野舲第三女杨保艾为妻，为其取字梦蘅。妻兄杨引传，字延绪，号醒逋、苏补、淞浔外史、老圃等，斋名独悟庵，曾著有《独悟庵集》《野烟录》等，是《浮生六记》最早发现者和刊印者，是王韬最亲近的朋友之一。

1847 年（道光二十七年） 20 岁

春初仍至锦溪书馆授徒。王韬一边教书，一边研读先贤典籍、域外丛书、稗史说部，立志著书立说。王韬家境艰难，常遭偷盗，身处"接得申江一纸书，故乡米贵信难居"的境地。在此期间写成《锁窗笔记》《丁未诗集二卷》。

1848 年（道光二十八年） 21 岁

正月，赴上海探望开馆授徒的父亲，参观了松江墨海书馆。时麦都思邀请其参观活字版机器印书。后结识伟烈亚力（Alexander Wylie，1815—1887）、理雅各（James Legge，1815—1897）、艾约瑟（Joseph Edkins，1823—1905）、慕维廉（William Muirhead，1822—1900）、美魏茶（William Charles Milne，1815—1863）等英国传教士。

是年，王韬回昆山再次参加科考，惜名落孙山。

1849—1862：躬逢乱世传西学

1849 年（道光二十九年）　22 岁

夏六月，父亲王昌桂在上海病逝，麦都思遣人邀请王韬再赴上海，遂于农历九月入墨海书馆。初到上海，王韬最早只是希望了解西人的"象纬、舆图诸学"。

后与麦都思、艾约瑟、伟烈亚力、理雅各等人合作翻译书籍长达十三年之久。但王韬称此十三年"非其志也"。

【此十三年间，与同一时期在墨海书馆协助西人翻译书籍的李善兰（1811—1882，浙江海宁人，号壬叔，曾与伟烈亚力等人翻译《几何原本》《谈天》《代数学》《代微积拾级》，与艾约瑟合译《重学》，与威廉臣合译《植物学》等）、蒋敦复（1808—1867，江苏宝山人，原名尔锷，字纯甫，号剑人，曾协助慕维廉译《大英国志》）、管嗣复（？—1860，江苏江宁人，字小异，曾协助裨治文翻译《大美联邦志略》等），以及华亭郭友松（1820—1887，松江府娄县人，名福衡，著有《玄空经》等，自署娄县老福）等人，结为莫逆之交。

此外，他还与姚梅伯、张啸山、周弢甫、龚孝拱等人交往甚密。】

1850 年（道光三十年）　23 岁

王韬在墨海书馆的工作是协助麦都思译《新约全书》，以替代原来中文译文有所欠缺的旧译本。由王韬用典雅的古文参与润色的《圣经》译本被称为"委办译本"，于 7 月 25 日出版，得到麦都思等高度赞赏。

1851 年（咸丰元年）　24 岁

英国领事馆通事浙人应雨耕［其在早期西文文献中的名字拼作 Ying Lung T'ien，名龙田，直隶人，籍浙江兰溪，曾协助英人威妥玛（Thomas Francis Wade，1818—1895）编写出版《语言自迩集》］在随威妥玛游历英国后，口述其经历，王韬笔受作《瀛海笔记》。

1852 年(咸丰二年)　25 岁

初夏,介绍李善兰至墨海书馆协助西人伟烈亚力翻译西方数学典籍。初冬,结识蒋敦复,蒋氏号称江南才子,王韬遂与李善兰、蒋敦复成莫逆之交,人称"三异民"。

与艾约瑟合作编译《中西通书》,年出一册。《中西通书》乃介绍西方政治、社会、文化、科技知识的历书小册子。先后由艾约瑟和伟烈亚力担任主编,王韬主要负责中西日历部分的编辑工作。

续娶福建泉漳会馆董事林益扶的小女儿林琳为妻。

1853 年(咸丰三年)　26 岁

介绍蒋敦复入墨海书馆工作,协助慕维廉译编《大英国志》等书。与艾约瑟合译《格致新学提纲(上)》《光学图说》。前者随《中西通书》出版,内容修订后收入 1890 年版《西学原始考》。

5 月,英国驻华公使文翰(Sir George Bonham,1803—1863)从天京(金陵)回到上海,带回太平天国送给王韬的《天条书》《幼学诗》《三字经》等十二本书。王韬交予麦都思翻译,并从旁协助。

6 月,写成《瀛堧杂志》初稿,蒋敦复为之作序。

1854 年(咸丰四年)　27 岁

与洪仁玕同在上海伦敦会首席牧师麦都思门下一起研习。是年,正式接受洗礼,加入伦敦会,成为基督徒。

是年,协助麦都思等翻译出版《旧约全书》。

【管小异此年在苏州遇艾约瑟,到墨海书馆后协助翻译《西医略论》等医书三种,风行海内,并与王韬昕夕聚首。】

1857 年(咸丰七年)　30 岁

1 月,协助伟烈亚力在上海创办第一个中文月刊《六合丛谈》。由伟烈亚力口译王韬笔述的《重学浅说》一卷,后冠于艾约瑟所译《重学》一书之首。

与伟烈亚力还合作译编了《华英通商事略》一卷和《西国天学源流》一卷。

上述三部著述均首先连载于《六合丛谈》。

同年农历四月陪同江苏巡抚徐有壬至墨海书馆参观印书车,并拜会慕维廉、韦廉臣(Alexander Williamson,1829—1890)等人。

【郭嵩焘对于墨海书馆这一时期的工作表示赞赏,并谓"麦君著书甚勤,其间相与校定者,一为海盐李壬叔,一为苏州王兰卿。李君淹博,习勾股之学。王君语言豪迈,亦方雅士也"。】

1858 年(咸丰八年) 31 岁

是年和艾约瑟合作编译《格致新学提纲(下)》出版,分门别类地介绍西方的科技知识,分附于《中西通书》之后。

【《中西通书》以每年的中西日历为主,同时附有介绍中西社会、政治、经济、科学、文化知识的历书小册子,每年一本。伟烈力亚听王韬讲中国旧时历法与西方犹太古历有相似之处,便请王韬撰写 1859 年《中西通书序》,置于卷首。】

1861 年(咸丰十一年) 34 岁

3 月,随艾约瑟等人赴太平天国首都天京访同,受到太平天国赞王蒙得恩长子蒙时雍(其官职为赞嗣君)的接待,会见了黄文安、李文炳等太平天国官员。艾约瑟通过蒙时雍转交给天王洪秀全一篇题为《上帝有形为喻无形乃实论》的文章,洪秀全以诏书形式作答,王韬参与了艾约瑟文章的润饰。

1862 年(同治元年) 35 岁

2 月 2 日,化名黄畹上书大平天国苏福省民务官刘肇钧,为太平天国围攻上海出谋献策,并托刘肇钧把上书转呈李秀成。

4月4日,英法军队和清军攻破上海七宝镇附近的刘肇钧营垒,王韬上书被副将熊兆周缴获,转交江苏巡抚薛焕,薛焕立即上奏朝廷。

4月25日,同治帝降旨缉拿黄畹。王韬在上海虽改名叫王瀚,但原名曾称王畹,上书中因避太平天国讳,故写成黄畹(吴语黄王不分)。王韬曾短暂避祸乡下,后秘密潜回上海躲进英国驻上海领事馆,受到麦华佗(Sir Walter Henry Medhurst 1823—1885,麦都思之子)领事和英国驻华公使卜鲁斯(Sir Frederick William Adolphus Wright-Bruce,1814—1867)的庇护。

10月4日,王韬只身一人登上英国"鲁纳"号邮轮逃抵香港,进入英华书院,协助院长理雅各翻译中国儒家经典,从此开始了长达23年的流亡生活。

王韬遁往香港后,改名王韬,字子潜(紫诠),号仲弢,又号天南遁叟。

1863—1883:遁逃香港译和著

1864年(同治三年)　37岁

理雅各主持的《尚书》英译工作基本完成,开始准备翻译《诗经》。王韬纂集各类《诗经》注释,辑成《毛诗集释》30卷,供理雅各翻译《诗经》时参考。

丁日昌将出任苏松太道,王韬便以黄平甫的名义,向其建言,指出西人翻译之书,如"伟烈氏之历算,艾氏之重学,合信氏(Benjamin Hobson,1816—1873)之医学","慕氏之地理,裨氏(Elijah Coleman Bridgman,1801—1861)之国志",以及徐继畲之《瀛寰志略》、魏默深(即魏源)之《海国图志》等书的得失,提出"窃不自量,欲以一生精力,辑成《续海国图志》一书,以备国史、四裔志之采录"。

1865年(同治四年)　38岁

王韬协助理雅各翻译的《书经》(《尚书》)完成。此书翻译在1861年曾得到香港英商渣甸(Joseph Jardine，1822—1861)资助,是为《中国经典》第 3 卷。

1867 年(同治六年)　40 岁

理雅各以事返英,邀王韬同游欧洲。12 月 15 日(十一月二十)启程西行,年底抵达新加坡和锡兰访问。

蒋敦复经王韬推荐入苏松太道丁日昌衙署中供职,后入江苏按察使应宝时幕府中。

1868 年(同治七年)　41 岁

访问法国、英国。在法国参观汉学家茹理安,亦称儒莲(Stanislas Aignan Julien,1797—1873)的汉文书库,并盛赞儒氏翻译中国典籍之多精,并望其"采择西国各书,哀集元事,巨细弗遗,邮简寄示,俾韬得成《元代疆域考》","为《元史》拾遗、匡谬、纠讹"。

在苏格兰协助理雅各翻译《春秋左传》,纂辑《春秋左氏传集释》。并参观苏格兰爱丁堡大学考试,在理雅各、慕维廉陪同下游览了爱丁堡博物馆、医院、印刷厂、浴池等处。

1870 年(同治九年)　43 岁

回国后,在江苏巡抚丁日昌的推动下编纂《法国志略》。

在《香港近事编录》《中外新闻七日报》《香港华字日报》连载《普法战纪》。

继续协助理雅各翻译儒家经典。

1871 年(同治十年)　44 岁

秋九月末,《普法战纪》完稿。王韬协助理雅各所译《诗经》在香港出版,称为《中国经典》第 4 卷。

1872 年（同治十一年）　45 岁

是年，王韬协助理雅各所译《春秋左传》出版，即《中国经典》第 5 卷。

曾国藩曾欲招王韬至上海制造局译书，因曾薨，未果。后李鸿章有意招揽王韬译书，但终未能成事。李鸿章大为惋惜："昆山王君，不世英才，胸罗万有，沦落香港，殊为可惜。执事能为我招致，不惜千金买骏骨"。

1873 年（同治十二年）　46 岁

王韬结束"佣书"工作，与同人集资购买英华书院设备，在香港中环创办中华印务总局，首先以活字大版排印《普法战纪》一书。该书为王韬学术生涯的巅峰之作。

1874 年（同治十三年）　47 岁

1 月 5 日，在香港创办《循环日报》，自任主笔，仿西报体例，每日于首栏发表一篇政论文章，评议时政。

王韬在该报发表的政论，显示出其过去译著的功用，使其以中外共时的视角观察、分析世事时情，比如其在《上冯子立都转书》中运用了《华英通商事略》中的中外贸易历史，强调变通学习西法的重要性。

1875 年（光绪元年）　48 岁

短篇小说集《遁窟谰言》和笔记小说《瓮牖余谈》在上海《申报》馆刊印出版。上海风物志《瀛壖杂志》在广州出版。

丁日昌就任船政大臣后，王韬建议设立翻译西书馆，翻译西国各种图书，并认为"翻译一端，人或视为不急之务，而不知收效之远、著功之广，足以转移人心，实有不可少缓者也"。

此时，王韬与李善兰已无联系十四年，听说李氏患病，便致信问候。

1876 年（光绪二年）　49 岁

王韬以活字版在中华印务总局首次排印《弢园尺牍》一书。《弢园尺牍》第一版仅 8 卷,收入 1846 年至 1875 年王韬与友人的往来书信。

此时,王韬对变法有了更深入的认识,指出先治民后治,凡事必当实
事求是。"从未有尚虚文而收实效者。翻然一变,宜在今日。"

1878 年(光绪四年)　51 岁

2 月,王韬在《循环日报》上发表了《论各省会城宜设新报馆》的社论,
系统阐释其新闻思想,同《论日报渐行于中土》《论中国设西文日报之利》
共同奠定中国近代新闻事业的发展和形成的基础。

专门记述上海妓院情形及王韬本人绮游访艳经历的《海耶冶游录》和
《花国剧谈》二书,在香港中华印务总局首次出版。

1879 年(光绪五年)　52 岁

1873 年《普法战纪》出版后,在日本引起强烈反响,1875 年《瓮牖余
谈》《遁窟谰言》等也传入日本,王韬受到日文文化界的钦慕。

4 月 30 日(闰三月初十)启程赴日本访同,先与驻日公使何如璋、副使
张斯桂(曾为丁韪良译《万国公法》作序)、黄遵宪(1848—1905)等会面。
在日期间与各界人士有广泛交往,与各类幕府华族、硕儒名士,以及维新
名流、医官武士、艺妓烟花均有接触。

1880 年(光绪六年)　53 岁

5 月,中华印务总局出版《蘅华馆诗录》5 卷,共收入 1846 年至 1879
年诗作 542 首。

是年,《扶桑游记》在日本东京报知社刻印出版。王韬还为在中华印
务总局出版的郑观应时论著作《易言》作跋。

1881 年(光绪七年)　54 岁

与黄胜合作译编的《火器略说》由中华印务总局刊行。王韬与丁日昌
再论中俄和约事宜。

夏,王韬请求马建忠上书李鸿章,为其"从容委曲言之",以实现他"久病思归,以正丘首"之愿。

1882 年(光绪八年) 55 岁

与马建忠书,陈越南问题方略。

搜集故友蒋敦复的诗文作品,以为其刊刻。

1883 年(光绪九年) 56 岁

是年,王韬时论文选《弢园文录外编》在香港出版发行。《弢园文录外编》共 8 卷 110 篇文章,绝大部分为王韬发表于《循环日报》的时评政论。

1884—1897:千帆返沪归著述

1884 年(光绪十年) 57 岁

王韬对天下大势有了更清晰的认识,他指出:"今昔异情,世局大变,五洲交通,地球合一",不应画疆自守,而要师西之长技,夺其所恃。甫归上海,王韬即被英人美查聘为《申报》总编辑。从下半年起,王韬开始在《申报》所属系列杂志《点石斋画报》上发表短篇小说集《淞隐漫录》,每期一篇,并随文配图。

1885 年(光绪十一年) 58 岁

春正月,创办弢园书局。

是年秋,上海格致书院聘请王韬为掌院,延请中西教读训以西国语言文字,并开设格致、机器、象纬、舆图、制造、建筑、电气、化学等课程。

1886 年(光绪十二年) 59 年

弢园书局因缺乏资金暂时歇业,为出版重订《普法战纪》,受到盛宣怀、伍廷芳等加以资助。

王韬邀请傅兰雅(John Fryer,1839—1928)在格致书院讲习,撰写《格致汇编》。

1887 年(光绪十三年)　60 岁

十月首次编辑刊行《格致书院课艺》,将从 1886 年以来论文考试中的优胜试卷及评语一并刊出。《淞隐漫录》120 篇在《点石斋画报》连载完毕,由点石斋印局汇集单行本出版。

1889 年(光绪十五年)　62 岁

《春秋朔闰至日考》《春秋日食辨正》《春秋朔闰表》汇集成一册,以《春秋经学三种》为名由美华书局出版。

是年《弢园尺牍续钞》《重订法国志略》(24 卷)、《漫游随录》等著作相继出版。

修订《西国天学源流》《重学浅说》《西学图说》《西学原始考》《泰西著述考》《华英通商事略》,合编为《西学辑存六种》。

1890 年(光绪十六年)　63 岁

王韬《西学辑存六种》全部刻印出版。是年农历四月初八,王韬又将《蘅华馆诗录》重新编订出版。这版补充收入 1880 年以后的诗作,共收诗作 629 首,比初版增加 87 首。

1893 年(光绪十九年)　66 岁

秋九月,《淞滨琐话》12 卷在沪北淞隐庐排印,包括 68 篇小说。

是年,王韬审订的《格致书院课艺》丙戌(1886)至癸巳(1893)年分类汇编刻印出版。

1894 年(光绪二十年)　67 岁

为孙中山《上李鸿章书》润色修正,并托李鸿章幕府文案罗逢禄代为引见,事未成。

1895 年(光绪二十一年)　68 岁

经郑观应介绍与康有为相识,并陪同参观格致书院,介绍办学经验。

1897 年(光绪二十三年)　70 岁

5 月 24 日(农历四月二十三),王韬在上海寓所病故。其传奇人生就此终结。

后　记

　　如果不是恩师浙江大学许钧教授的召集，我可能不会专注于王韬及王韬参与的译作长达一年的时间。2019年9月5日，恩师许钧先生来电话，问我是否有意参加他主持的重大学术工程"中华译学馆·中华翻译家代表性译文库"，我一口就应承了下来。自2012年我正式拜入许门，恩师在多个场合鼓励我做好翻译史学术研究，我感到很受鼓舞。点校重要译家的代表性译作，对于学问的精进和学术志趣的培养十分重要，我感到特别高兴。

　　起先，许老师有意安排我整理徐光启和王韬两卷，这实际上是一个完美的学术规划。众所周知，两次西学翻译、佛经翻译、文学翻译和民族翻译，是中国翻译史上四大经典课题，而徐光启和王韬恰是两次西学翻译浪潮中的两位符号性人物。照理说，将他们的代表性译文整理、研究好了，不光可以丰富我对于17世纪和19世纪中西交流史的学术积累，更有助于我今后在两次西学翻译研究领域作出更具创新性的翻译史研究成果。我向许老师表达了这一认识，但同时也提到，由于我刚刚启动了一项国家社科基金重大项目，预期要用五年的时间才能完成，可能在时间上无法兼顾，故不得不放弃其中的徐光启卷。后来，当我从许老师那里听说，徐光启卷由我素未谋面但十分敬佩的黎难秋教授主持后，感到这是最好的安排。黎老师对于中国近代科技翻译史料的占有，鲜有人能望其项背。

　　王韬是中国近代史上的符号性人物，作为西学东渐与中学西传的桥梁，但其与伟烈亚力、艾约瑟、麦都思及理雅各等诸多西人，以及诸如张宗良等中国人合作完成的译作,在此之前还未得到全面点校。译著的点校,在点,在校,也在注。不同于其他著述,点校的价值在于这项工作不仅在于让经典著述重新面世,还在于点校者提供的按语或注释,有可能解决读者阅读中可能遇到的难题。本着这样的理解,我和我的学生万立博士,开始查找王韬的代表性译文,编辑王韬译事年表,并着手撰写作为非典型译者王韬的研究论文。期间,万立展现出的学术韧性和求真精神,使得这段合作变得十分难忘。

点校 19 世纪的作品,特别是其中有些我们不太熟悉的科技史作品,是一件十分磨人的工作。为了弄清楚原文中充斥的陌生译词(很多译名经过 100 多年后,已经发生了重大变化),我们尽力去寻找这些作品可能的出处与原文。功夫不负有心人,我们真的找到并还原了其中绝大部分人名、地名、作品名及术语名所对应的外文,并附上了其今天的通用译名。回想这个过程,每解决一个问题,都是一次令人欣喜的经历。这些或大或小的发现,我们最终选择以夹注附表等形式注明与分享,并为王韬 11 篇代表性译文中的绝大多数,或制作了"译名对照表",或提供了对照原文。比如我们在点到"噶罗巴"这个地名时,会注明其原是 Kelapa,即今印尼雅加达的译名,而非有的书中认为其是"古巴/Cuba"的译名。我在想,除了翻译史研究本身外,这项工作对于相关学科的学科发达史研究,对于致力于术语译名统一和规范化研究,也许均会起到某些帮助。

本卷点校的译文主要包括原载于《中西通书》《六合丛谈》中的《格致新学提纲》《华英通商事略》《西国天学源流》《重学浅说》等西学著述,也包括《尚书》《诗经》《春秋》等重要作品。由于条件所限,本卷未收录王韬辅译的《圣经》委办本,或于今后点校出版。目力所及,除《格致新学提纲》外,其他译著皆为首次点校,其中载有丰富的历史信息,并带哲学意味。当我们点到《重学浅说》结尾处那句"凡器质增多,能力亦大,但比例渐小,故繁器之助力有限"时,会想到可能一切学问,最终都归于哲学,自然科学也不例外。所谓哲学者,研究人类认识发展规律之自然科学也。当我们点到《格致新学提纲》中培根的那句"实事求是,必考物以合理,不造理以

合物"时,想到的是,不仅 19 世纪的译者和今天的读者是共情的,就是 17
世纪的英国科学家培根的思想,也与今天是相联通的。再者,由我这样常
年在松江生活工作的学人,带领我的博士生万立点校 150 多年前同样生
活工作在松江(当时属于江苏)墨海书馆的王韬的作品,是一件在情感的
距离上感到比较亲近的事。

此次点校工作所以能够顺利完成,要感谢 5G 时代。这些资料本身和
相关文献本存于哈佛大学图书馆、哥伦比亚大学图书馆、奥地利国家图书
馆、澳大利亚国家图书馆等处,但互联网为各种方式查询、搜索提供了可
能。前人所提供的这些数字化的史料,为我们节省了许多时间和精力,在
此对使这些珍贵史料数字化的无名人士致以由衷的谢意。我也要感谢我
的学生鲁鸣,她在美国留学这一年,正好赶上这次新冠疫情,她为我提供
了很难找到的《西学辑存六种》等资料。

最后,感谢浙江大学卢巧丹老师的协助,感谢浙江大学出版社陆雅娟
编辑的辛勤工作、包灵灵老师的指导。尤其感谢我指导的博士后王春荣
和硕士生孙雅文为《普法战纪》一文的点校所做的完善和大量核对工作。
尽管我们尽可能准确完整地点好王韬卷,但一定会有这样或那样的不足
之处,因此恳请方家多批评、指正。

屈文生

2020 年 8 月 15 日子时

于上海松江

中華譯學館·中华翻译家代表性译文库

许 钧 郭国良 / 总主编

第一辑

鸠摩罗什卷

玄 奘卷

林 纾卷

严 复卷

鲁 迅卷

胡 适卷

林语堂卷

梁宗岱卷

冯 至卷

傅 雷卷

卞之琳卷

朱生豪卷

叶君健卷

杨宪益 戴乃迭卷

第二辑

徐光启卷

李之藻卷

王 韬卷

伍光建卷

梁启超卷

王国维卷

马君武卷

冯承钧卷

刘半农卷

傅东华卷

郑振铎卷

瞿秋白卷

董秋斯卷

图书在版编目(CIP)数据

中华翻译家代表性译文库. 王韬卷 / 屈文生,万立
编. —杭州 : 浙江大学出版社,2022.1
ISBN 978-7-308-21887-0

Ⅰ.①中… Ⅱ.①屈… ②万… Ⅲ.①社会科学—文
集②王韬(1828—1897)—译文—文集 Ⅳ.①C53

中国版本图书馆 CIP 数据核字(2021)第 215537 号

中華譯學館

中华翻译家代表性译文库·王韬卷
屈文生　万　立 编

出 品 人	褚超孚
丛书策划	张　琛　包灵灵
责任编辑	陆雅娟
责任校对	田　慧
封面设计	闰江文化
出版发行	浙江大学出版社
	(杭州市天目山路 148 号　邮政编码 310007)
	(网址:http://www.zjupress.com)
排　　版	浙江时代出版服务有限公司
印　　刷	浙江省邮电印刷股份有限公司
开　　本	710mm×1000mm　1/16
印　　张	22
字　　数	300 千
版 印 次	2022 年 1 月第 1 版　2022 年 1 月第 1 次印刷
书　　号	ISBN 978-7-308-21887-0
定　　价	88.00 元

版权所有　翻印必究　　印装差错　负责调换
浙江大学出版社市场运营中心联系方式　　(0571)88925591;http://zjdxcbs.tmall.com